East Asian Americans and Political Participation

Political Participation in America
Raymond A. Smith, Series Editor

African Americans and Political Participation,
Minion K. C. Morrison, Editor

Gay and Lesbian Americans and Political Participation,
Raymond A. Smith and Donald P. Haider-Markel

Jewish Americans and Political Participation,
Jerry D. Stubben and Gary A. Sokolow

Latino Americans and Political Participation,
Sharon A. Navarro and Armando X. Mejia, Editors

Women and Political Participation,
Barbara Burrell

East Asian Americans and Political Participation

A Reference Handbook

Tsung Chi

A B C 🟦 C L I O

Santa Barbara, California • Denver, Colorado • Oxford, England

Library of Congress Cataloging-in-Publication Data

Chi, Tsung, 1959-
  East Asian Americans and political participation : a reference handbook / Tsung Chi.
      p. cm. — (Political participation in America)
  Includes bibliographical references and index.
  ISBN 1-57607-290-8 (acid-free paper) — ISBN 1-85109-507-1 (e-book) 1. Asian Americans—Politics and government. 2. Political participation—United States. 3. United States—Ethnic relations—Political aspects. 4. Chinese Americans—Politics and government. 5. Japanese Americans—Politics and government. 6. Korean Americans—Politics and government. I. Title. II. Series.

  E184.A75C49 2005
  324'.089'95073—dc22

2005003335

07 06 05   10 9 8 7 6 5 4 3 2 1

This book is also available on the World Wide Web as an e-book.
Visit abc-clio.com for details.

ABC-CLIO, Inc.
130 Cremona Drive, P.O. Box 1911
Santa Barbara, California 93116-1911

This book is printed on acid-free paper.
Manufactured in the United States of America

To my son, Martin

Contents

Series Foreword

Participation in the political process is a cornerstone of both the theory and the practice of democracy; indeed, the word "democracy" itself means rule by the people. Since the formation of the New Deal coalition in 1932, the study of U.S. politics has largely been organized around the concept that there exist distinct "blocs" of citizens, such as African Americans, women, Catholics, and Latinos. This trend was reinforced during the 1960s when the expansion of the media and the decline of traditional sources of authority promoted direct citizen mobilization. And more recently, the emphasis on "identity politics" has reinforced the notion of distinct groups organized along lines of shared personal characteristics rather than common economic interests.

Although political participation is a mainstream, even canonical, subject in the study of U.S. politics, there are few midrange reference materials available on this subject. Indeed, the available reference materials do not include works that provide both a systematic empirical base *and* explanatory and contextualizing material. Likewise, because of the fragmentation of the reference material on this subject, it is difficult for readers to draw comparisons across groups, even though this is one of the most meaningful ways of understanding the phenomenon of political participation. The Political Participation in America series is designed to fill this gap in the reference literature on this subject by providing key points of background (e.g., demographics, political history, major contemporary issues) and then systematically addressing different types of political participation, providing both substance and context for readers. In addition, each chapter includes case studies that either illuminate larger issues or highlight some particular subpopulation within the larger group.

Each volume of the ABC-CLIO Political Participation in America series focuses on one of the major subgroups that make up the electorate in the United States. Each volume includes the following components:

- Introduction to the group, comprising a demographic, historical, and political portrait of the group, including political opinions and issues of key importance to members of the group
- Participation in protest politics, including marches, rallies, demonstrations, and direct actions
- Participation in social movements and interest groups, including involvement of members of the group in and through a wide variety of organizations and associations
- Participation in electoral politics, including a profile of involvement with political parties and voting patterns
- Participation in political office-holding, including elected, appointed, and "unofficial" offices from the local to national levels

The end of each book also includes an A–Z glossary featuring brief entries on important individuals and events; a chronology of political events salient to the group; a resource guide of organizations, newsletters, Web sites, and other important contact information, all briefly annotated; an annotated bibliography of key primary and secondary documents, including books and journal articles; excerpts from major primary documents, with introductions; and a comprehensive index to the volume.

Raymond A. Smith
Series Editor

Preface

East Asian Americans encompass Chinese Americans, including people with roots in mainland China, Taiwan, and Hong Kong; Japanese Americans; and Korean Americans. Many of them and their ancestors arrived in America long before many immigrants from Europe. However, mainly because of its small population size and heterogeneous composition, this minority group of so-called quiet Americans or the model minority had not been viewed as a significant political force in American society until the 1970s when more immigrants from the other side of the Pacific Ocean began to arrive in the United States in large numbers. With a rapidly growing population concentrated in principal electoral states on the East and West Coasts, this minority group has ever since become an increasingly important political actor, whose emerging power can no longer be ignored in the American political arena and the literature on American minority politics.

In comparison to other Asian groups, such as Asian Indians, Filipinos, and Vietnamese, who arrived mostly in recent decades, the East Asians came to the United States much earlier in the nineteenth century. Understandably, they are larger in number and also have a longer history of political activism than other Asians in America. Together, they represented 100 percent, 57.2 percent, 45.2 percent, and 42.2 percent of all Asian Americans in 1910, 1950, 1990, and 2000, respectively. As for their levels of political activism, East Asian Americans, especially Chinese and Japanese Americans, have been politically more organized, skillful, and thus more influential than other Asian groups. Moreover, given the geographical proximity and cultural similarities of their homelands, Chinese, Japanese, and Korean Americans together constitute a relatively homogenous group in comparison with other Asian American groups. However, the three groups historically tended to place almost exclusive emphasis on their respective ethnic interests. Intragroup communication and coordination were largely absent until the 1960s, when more panethnic organizations were built on an emerging pan-Asian consciousness and identification so as to serve the collective interests of East Asian Americans in general.

This book explores a variety of participatory activities of East Asian Americans in four key spheres of American politics, including protest politics and social movements, interest-group politics, electoral politics, and political officeholding. In addition to providing background information, its main purpose is to investigate the patterns of political participation of an emerging minority group to fill the gap that has long existed in the literature of American minority politics.

Chapter 1 provides an overview of East Asian Americans' historical experiences of immigration to America, demographic characteristics, and political attitudes with respect to their implications for each group's participation in the American political process. These issues are addressed separately for Chinese, Japanese, and Korean Americans for the purpose of making both intragroup comparisons among East Asian Americans, as well as intergroup comparisons between them and other ethnic groups in the United States.

Contrary to popular perception, East Asian Americans have a long tradition of participation in protest politics and social movements, the most high-profile form of political participation outside the electoral system. Chapter 2 begins with an overview of their early protests, dating back to the mid-nineteenth century, followed by a systematic introduction to the Asian American movement, a historical watershed in Asian American protest politics in terms of its origin, participants, goals, signature events, and problems. More specifically, this chapter studies how East Asian Americans got involved in mass protests and social movements to pursue their common interests.

Chapter 3 examines the organizational bases of East Asian American politics. Because East Asian Americans also have a long history of participation in interest-group politics, this chapter first reviews the history of their early ethnic interest groups. As for contemporary interest groups, they are classified into ethnic-specific interest groups and panethnic interest groups, and then both types of groups are studied at the national as well as regional levels to demonstrate how these groups function in the American political arena in pursuit of their ethnic interests.

As the most direct and powerful method of political participation, electoral politics, including party politics, is no stranger to East Asian Americans in the recent decades. However, it has been a long and winding road for many East Asian Americans to become citizens and voters. Given the importance of this issue, Chapter 4 first explores the history of the group's participation or lack of participation in the American electoral process, followed by an investigation of how rapid growth in the East Asian American population since the 1960s has been translated into more electoral power for the group. More specifically, election-related issues such as naturalization and citizenship, registration, voting turnout, voting preferences, and political party affiliation are all introduced and discussed in this chapter. Lastly, the chapter details the issues of campaign contributions by East Asian Americans at the federal, state, and local levels, along with a study of the campaign finance controversies in 1996–1997 and their profound impacts on East Asian American political participation.

Years of hard work by East Asian Americans in the areas of protest politics, interest-group politics, and electoral politics culminated in their success in the area of participation in political officeholding, the most recently adopted form of political participation for the group. Chapter 5 analyzes the patterns of East Asian American involvement in the areas of elected and politically appointed officials from Hawaii to the mainland at the federal, state, and local levels. This chapter also studies another group of East Asian American elites, the community and organizational leaders who are, by any measure, as important as those public officials in terms of their contributions to the community.

In addition to systematic discussion of specific types of political participation in the chapters, detailed case studies are included throughout chapter sections to support the general discussion.

The above five chapters are followed by several reference materials, including primary documents related to East Asian Americans, an A–Z glossary, a resource guide to East Asian American organizations, a chronology of major events, and an annotated bibliography. These materials altogether will help interested readers better understand the subject.

Throughout the book, the terms "Asians," "East Asians," "Chinese," "Japanese," and "Koreans" refer to those who lived in the United States before the 1940s and 1950s, because most of them were immigrants deprived of citizenship. For the years after 1950, the terms "Asian Americans," "East Asian Americans," "Chinese Americans," "Japanese Americans," and "Korean Americans" are used because most are now citizens, regardless of where they were born.

I am indebted to Professors Xiao-huang Yin and Pei-te Lien for their help with this project. I also wish to thank the ABC-CLIO editors who carefully read the manuscript and provided invaluable suggestions. Special thanks go to the John Randolph Haynes and Dora Haynes Foundation for providing funds to support this project.

List of Abbreviations

80–20 PAC	80–20 Political Action Committee, Incorporated
AAFCFR	Asian Americans for Campaign Finance Reform
AAI	Asian American Institute
AALDEF	Asian American Legal Defense and Education Fund
AAPA	Asian American Political Alliance
AAPCHO	Association of Asian/Pacific Community Health Organizations
ACC	Asian Community Center
ACJ	American Citizens for Justice
AFL	American Federation of Labor
AFL-CIO	American Federation of Labor-Congress of Industrial Organizations
AIPAC	American Israel Public Affairs Committee
ALC	Asian Law Caucus
APAICS	Asian Pacific American Institute for Congressional Studies
APALA	Asian Pacific American Labor Alliance
APALC	Asian Pacific American Legal Center
A/PA Unit	Asian/Pacific American Unit
APC	Asian Pacific Caucus
APEX	Asian Professional Exchange
APIAHF	Asian & Pacific Islander American Health Forum
APIAVote	Asian and Pacific Islander American Vote
APPCON	Asian Pacific Planning Council
APPEAL	Asian Pacific Partners for Empowerment and Leadership
APSU	Asian Pacific Student Union
AWIU	Agricultural Workers Industrial Union
CAAAV	Committee against Anti-Asian Violence
CACA	Chinese American Citizens Alliance
CAPAL	Conference on Asian Pacific American Leadership

CAUSE	Center for Asian Americans United for Self Empowerment (2003–) Chinese Americans United for Self Empowerment (1993–2003)
CAWU	Cannery and Agricultural Workers Union
CCBA	Chinese Consolidated Benevolent Association
CERL	Chinese Equal Rights League
CPC	Chinese American Planning Council
CTIR	Center for Taiwan International Relations
CWRIC	Commission on Wartime Relocation and Internment of Civilians
DNC	Democratic National Committee
FAA	Federal Aviation Administration
FAPA	Formosan Association for Public Affairs
FAPR	Formosan Association for Public Relations
FEC	Federal Election Commission
ICSA	Intercollegiate Chinese for Social Actions
IHTA	International Hotel Tenants Association
ILGWU	International Ladies Garment Workers Union
ISTEA	Intermodal Surface Transportation Efficiency Act
JAA	Japanese Association of America
JACL	Japanese American Citizens League
JMLA	Japanese-Mexican Labor Association
KAA	Korean American Association
KAC	Korean American Coalition
KACLA	Korean American Coalition in Los Angeles
KADC	Korean American Democratic Committee
KAGW	Korean American Garment Workers
KARA	Korean American Republican Association
KNA	Korean National Association
LEAP	Leadership Education for Asian Pacifics
LLDEF	Lambda Legal Defense and Education Fund
MAASU	Midwest Asian American Students Union
MANAA	Media Action Network for Asian Americans
NAACP	National Association for the Advancement of Colored People
NAKA	National Association of Korean Americans
NAPABA	National Asian Pacific American Bar Association
NAPALC	National Asian Pacific American Legal Consortium
NAPAWF	National Asian Pacific American Women's Forum
NAPCA	National Asian Pacific Center on Aging
NCAPA	National Council of Asian Pacific America

NDCAPA	National Democratic Council of Asian and Pacific Americans
NMU	National Maritime Union
NNAAV	National Network against Anti-Asian Violence
OCA	Organization of Chinese Americans, Inc.
PAC	Political Action Committee
PACE	Philippine-American College Endeavor
PNAAPS	Pilot Study of the National Asian American Political Survey
TACL	Taiwanese American Citizens League
TCCNA	Taiwanese Chamber of Commerce of North America
TMD	Theatrical Missile Defense
TSA	Transportation Security Administration
TSEA	Taiwan Security Enhancement Act
TWLF	Third World Liberation Front
WHO	World Health Organization
WUFI	World United Formosans for Independence

1
Overview

Patterns of political participation of East Asian Americans are closely related to their historical experiences of immigration to America, demographic characteristics, and political attitudes. This chapter first provides a historical overview for each of the three East Asian subgroups from the time of their arrival in the New World. Second, their demographic, social, and economic characteristics are thoroughly identified and compared to give both a quantitative and qualitative portrait of them. Third, because political participation of East Asian Americans can be attributed not only to many of their demographic characteristics but also to their political attitudes, the chapter also examines their perceptions, orientations, and evaluations of politics in general and of political institutions, government officials, and public policies in particular. Last, a number of key issues facing the East Asian American community as a whole are identified and discussed.

Historic Overview

Although Chinese, Japanese, and Korean immigrants arrived in the United States at different points in time, they all shared similar historical experiences in the new land, which were characterized by racism and, thus, exclusionism.

Chinese

The Chinese were the first Asian group to immigrate to the United States. Even though 1820 marked the first reported arrival of Chinese people in America, and Chinese sailors and peddlers began to show up in New York in the 1830s, they did not come in large numbers until 1848 when many Chinese were attracted by the gold rush in California and the Pacific Northwest. In 1851 the Chinese population in California alone reached 25,000 (Schultz, et al. 2000; Chan 1991).

Along with this first wave of Chinese immigration came anti-Chinese sentiment on the West Coast that precluded many Chinese laborers from becoming permanent settlers. In 1858 California passed a law to bar entry to Chinese. One decade later, in 1868, the Burlingame Treaty was signed between China and the United States to legalize the importation of Chinese cheap laborers, who would be under the protection of the American government. However, with rising anti-Chinese agitation in the subsequent years, this first wave of immigration was abruptly ended in 1882. Over China's protest, the Chinese Exclusion Act was passed, which forbade Chinese immigration into the United States. The act, which was the first piece of legislation to specifically exclude a particular group of immigrants, also denied those Chinese laborers already on American soil the right to become naturalized citizens. The act was renewed in 1892 under a new name: the Geary Law. This law was made a permanent U.S. immigration policy in 1904 and resulted in China's boycott of American imports in 1905.

During this period of exclusionism, discriminatory laws were promulgated at both the federal and local levels to systematically expel Chinese from jobs and prevent them from owning land or businesses. Consequently, quite a few Chinese returned home, as evident in a decline of the Chinese population in the next two decades: from 118,746 in 1900 to 85,202 in 1920 (Table 1.1). In addition to the Chinese Exclusion Act, the Johnson-Reed Act, also called the Immigration Act of 1924, reduced each country's annual quota to 2 percent of its immigrants already in the United States in 1890. Because China, Japan, and Korea received no quota at all, this harsh act virtually denied entry to all East Asians. However, a small number of Chinese merchants, students, tourists, and diplomats with their spouses and children arrived in the United States during the 1920s as "exempt classes" under special provisions of the exclusion acts, contributing to a mild increase in the Chinese population from 85,202 in 1920 to 106,334 in 1940 (Table 1.1). It was not until 1943 that the Chinese exclusion laws were repealed by Congress as a gesture of goodwill toward China, a wartime ally of the United States fighting against Japan. Entry was granted to 105 Chinese every year—still a negligible sum—but the right of naturalization to eligible Chinese was also included.

World War II and the following cold war had profound impacts on all East Asian immigrants in many aspects. As for the Chinese specifically, in addition to the abolishment of the Chinese Exclusion Act during the war, several events that occurred in the following years changed the demographic features of Chinese Americans. First, about 15,000 Chinese who served in the U.S. armed forces during World War II became eligible for citizenship. Second, a 1947 amendment to the War Brides Act of 1945, which had initially excluded veterans of Asian ancestry, allowed U.S. servicemen who married Asian women to bring them to the United States as citizens. Totally, about 10,000 Chinese wives of mainly Chinese American servicemen arrived, marking a sharp increase in the female and juvenile Chinese American populations. Third, the triumph of the Chinese communist revolution in 1949 and the subsequent cold war confrontation between the United States and China left many Chinese Americans no choice but permanently to stay in the United States. Fourth, many educated Chinese were granted entry to the United States under a variety of refugee acts. In 1948 the Displaced Persons Act gave permanent resident status to 3,500 Chinese caught in the United States because of the Chinese civil war between the nationalists and communists. After the communist victory in China in 1949, the United States granted refugee status to 5,000 Chinese, most of whom were graduate students at American universities. In 1953 the Refugee Relief Act allowed Chinese political refugees to come to the United States. Finally, many of the Chinese students from Taiwan, Hong Kong, and Southeast Asia who came to the United States to study in colleges and universities in the 1950s and 1960s managed to stay after receiving graduate degrees. Although the immigration quota of 105 per year assigned in 1943 was insignificant, not only did the above historical events contribute to another surge in the Chinese American population but also transformed its originally homogeneous composition into a more diverse group in terms of gender, age, class, and educational background (Wang 1998; Schultz, et al. 2000).

Japanese

Japanese immigrants first arrived in the United States a few decades after the Chinese. During most of the Tokugawa period (1600–1868), Japan had isolated itself from the outside world. This policy of seclusion was abruptly ended in 1853 when the U.S. Commodore Matthew Perry sailed into Edo Bay with his "black ships." The next year a treaty was signed between the two countries to grant trade privileges to the United States. In 1860 Japan sent a diplomatic mission to the United States, which was the first documented arrival of Japanese people in the United States. In 1869 J. H. Schnell took several dozen Japanese to Gold Hill, California, to establish the Wakamatsu Tea and Silk Colony. They were the first Japanese immigrants to the mainland United States, about two decades later than the Chinese immigrants who arrived after the gold rush.

Also in 1868 and 1869, 149 Japanese laborers were imported to work in Hawaii. Hawaiian sugar plantation owners formed the Planters' Society and the Bureau of Immigration in 1864. Then they began to send agents to recruit workers by the thousands, mainly from East Asia. As a result of their efforts, as well as the Japanese government's decision to lift the ban on all emigration in 1885, tens of thousands of Japanese contract laborers entered Hawaii legally before it was annexed by the United States in 1899. Between 1894 and 1908, about 142,000 Japanese, mostly males, arrived in Hawaii (Chan 1991). This early, large-scale migration of Japanese workers to Hawaii planted the seed of later success for this Asian group in electoral politics in this small island state.

On the mainland it was ironic that after the passage of the Chinese Exclusion Act that forbade Chinese immigration in 1882, Japanese immigration was encouraged by West Coast businesses to replace the Chinese as a source of cheap labor. As of 1900 the Japanese population in the United States reached 85,716 (Table 1.1). However, the Japanese, like the Chinese before them, did not escape from being the target of the general anti-Asian sentiment of the time. As a result, the Japanese government agreed in the 1907 Gentlemen's Agreement to limit its immigration to the United States to nonlaborers. However, this agreement allowed the wives of Japanese residents, so-called picture brides who were selected in Japan through the exchange of pictures, to come to the United States. Consequently, the Japanese population continued to grow, reaching 152,745 in 1910—surpassing the Chinese population for the first time in the American history of immigration—and 220,596 in 1920 (Table 1.1). However, this steady increase was ended by the passage of the Immigration Act in 1924. In 1930 there were 278,743 Japanese in the United States, and there was virtually no increase in the next decade (Table 1.1).

In contrast to the Chinese who received better treatment during World War II, the Japanese experienced their worse nightmare in 1942 when President Franklin D. Roosevelt signed Executive Order 9066, by which more than 40,000 Japanese on the West Coast, along with their 70,000 American-born children, were removed from their homes and imprisoned in internment camps (Chan 1991). This represented about 40 percent of the total Japanese population at the time.

After the war, the Japanese received neither immigration quotas nor the right of naturalization until 1952 when the McCarran-Walter Act was passed that allowed 185 Japanese per year to enter into the United States. However, many Japanese wives of mostly non–Asian American servicemen who married Japanese women during the U.S. occupation period and the Korean and Vietnam wars entered not as war brides but as nonquota immigrants or spouses of U.S. citizens under the act of 1952. In the 1950s the immigration of Japanese women every year ranged from 2,000 to 5,000, and this number averaged 2,500 per year in the 1960s (Chan 1991). This aspect of Japanese immigration contributed a significant increase in the Japanese population from 285,115 in 1940 to 326,379 in the 1950 to 464,332 in 1960 (Table 1.1).

Koreans

The last group from East Asia to immigrate to the United States was from Korea. The first Korean immigrant arrived in Hawaii in 1901, two years after Hawaii became a U.S. territory (Schultz, et al. 2000). Between 1902 and 1905, about 7,000 predominantly male Korean laborers immigrated to Hawaii to work in the sugarcane and pineapple plantations. Of them, about 1,000 eventually proceeded to the mainland. However, this first wave of Korean immigration was ended in 1905 when the Korean government terminated emigration to Hawaii and Mexico after some 1,000 Koreans were maltreated in Mexico (Chan 1991). As subjects of Japanese imperialism, Koreans were further prohibited from emigrating to the United States by the same 1907 Gentlemen's Agreement signed by the Japanese government to limit its immigration to the United States to nonlaborers. This was why there were only 5,008 Koreans in the United States in 1910. Between 1907 and 1924, most of the Korean immigrants were women, coming to the United States as picture brides. The 1924 Immigration Act finally put an end to this small wave of Korean immigration (Wong 1986).

The Korean population did not pass the 10,000 mark for the first half of the twentieth century until after the Korean War broke out in 1950 (Table 1.1). The McCarran-Walter Act of 1952 allowed 100 Koreans per year to enter into the United States, and the passage of the Refugee Act in 1953 also contributed a small increase in Korean immigration. However, most Koreans came to the United States after the war ended in 1953 as war brides of American servicemen. In the remaining years of the 1950s, almost 500 Korean women arrived every year, but a statistical figure for 1960 is not available to reflect the increase in the Korean population during the 1950s. The influx averaged about 1,500 per year in the 1960s and about 2,300 in the 1970s (Chan 1991).

Just like World War II and its aftermath, the year 1965 marked another watershed in America's history of immigration. The 1965 Immigration Act, signed by President Lyndon Johnson, abolished the discriminatory, racially based national-origin quota system that had favored European immigrants. This act has greatly changed the pattern of immigration to the United States. Emphasizing family reunions and attracting those with professional skills, this reform of U.S. immigration law offered great opportunities for tens of thousands of East Asians to enter, leading to a dramatic rise of the Asian American population in the United States in the following decades. Between 1960 and 2000, it increased from less than 1 million to about 10 million. As for East Asian Americans, the combined population of Chinese, Japanese, and Korean Americans went from 1.1 million in 1970 to 1.9 million, 3.3 million, and 4.3 million in 1980, 1990, and 2000, respectively. The most impressive increase occurred in the Korean American population; it increased more than fivefold from 1970 to 1980 and tripled from 1980 to 2000 (Table 1.1). Compared to the 4.2-percent growth rate of the non-Hispanic Caucasian American population between 1980 and 1990 (Shinagawa 1998), the overall Asian American population increased 95.2 percent, and the East Asian American population went up 74 percent during the same period of time. Between 1990 and 2000, as their population bases were getting larger and larger, the growth rates were 39.8 percent and 30.3 percent for Asian Americans and East Asian Americans, respectively.

In the 1990s, the Chinese American population was increased slightly by President George H. W. Bush's decision to grant permanent resident status to about 30,000 Chinese students who were studying in U.S. colleges and universities at the time of the Tiananmen Square massacre in China on June 4, 1989. Although small in number, the addition of this new Chinese group has had a significant impact on the demographic features of Chinese Americans, especially in terms of educational level and sense of homeland (because previously the Chinese who acquired permanent resident status were mainly from Taiwan and Hong Kong, not from the mainland). Overall, the Chinese American population totaled 2.4 million in 2000, still the largest one among the three East Asian American groups. However, for the first time in history, the fast-growing Korean American population surpassed the Japanese American population in 2000. The latter actually suffered a population loss between 1990 and 2000, primarily because of a decrease in native-born Japanese Americans.

The abolishment of the previously discriminatory immigration laws in 1965 did not coincide with the end of racial antipathy against Asian Americans, which always intensified during times of economic recession. For instance, trade frictions between the United States and Japan gave rise to "Japan-bashing" sentiment in the 1970s and 1980s,

Table 1.1
East Asian American Population of the United States, 1900–2000

Year	U.S. Population	Asian Americans*	Chinese	Japanese	Korean
1900	76,212,168	204,462	118,746	85,716	0
1910	92,228,531	249,926	94,414	152,745	5,008
1920	106,021,568	332,432	85,202	220,596	6,181
1930	123,202,660	489,326	102,159	278,743	8,332
1940	132,212,168	489,984	106,334	285,115	8,568
1950	151,325,798	599,091	150,005	326,379	7,030
1960	179,323,175	877,932	237,292	464,332	n.a.
1970	203,211,926	1,429,562	436,062	591,290	69,150
1980	226,545,805	3,455,421	812,178	716,331	357,393
1990	248,709,873	7,273,662	1,645,472	847,562	798,849
2000	281,421,906	10,171,820	2,422,970	795,051	1,072,682

Sources: The 1900–1990 data are compiled from Deborah G. Baron and Susan B. Gall, eds. 1996. *Asian American Chronology.* New York: UXL. The 2000 data are from the U.S. Census Bureau, *Census 2000,* Summary File 4 (SF4)-sample data.

*In addition to Chinese, Japanese, and Korean Americans, the term "Asian Americans" also includes Filipino, Asian Indian, Vietnamese, Cambodian, Laotian, and Hmong Americans.

deepening the already existent anti-Asian agitation. It led to a series of violent incidents directed at Asians, including the killings of Vincent Chin in Detroit in 1982; five Southeast Asian children in Stockton, California, in January 1989; and Jim Loo in North Carolina in July 1989. The combined events of more than 3,000 Korean American businesses damaged or destroyed in the riots in Los Angeles in 1992, and the case of Wen Ho Lee, a Taiwanese American nuclear scientist who was charged with downloading classified data to a personal computer and accused of being a spy for China and later spent nine months in jail in 2000, also served as wake-up calls for the entire East Asian American community, thus giving rise to more participation of these minority groups in American politics.

Demographic Profiles

Not only did the passage of the Immigration Act of 1965 dramatically alter the racial and ethnic composition of the nation as a whole, but it also had a significant impact on the demographic, social, and economic characteristics of East Asian Americans. In this section, the following characteristics are introduced and discussed: immigration status, region of residence, gender, age, marital status, education, English proficiency, occupational patterns, and household income. For political scientists, many of these factors are key correlates of political participation.

Immigration Status

Table 1.2 shows that a majority of East Asian Americans were immigrants in 2000, which was totally different from the situation before the passage of the 1965 Immigration Act. Before 1965, because all the Asian exclusion acts severely limited the number of newcomers, East Asian American communities became mostly native born. However, the native born still constituted the backbone of the Japanese American group in 2000, while new arrivals contributed to 70.4 percent and 82.2 percent of Chinese and Korean American groups, respectively. It is not surprising that the percentage of immigrants was relatively low among Japanese Americans, because post–World War II Japan was politically stable and economically well developed. Therefore, there was not much incentive for Japanese to emigrate, whereas many Chinese (including mainland Chinese, Taiwanese, and Hong

Table 1.2
Immigration Status of East Asian Americans, 2000 (in thousands)

Immigration Status	Chinese	Japanese	Korean
Native Born	706	481	240
Immigrants*	1,716	314	833
Total	2,422	795	1,073

Source: U.S. Census Bureau, *Census 2000,* Summary File 4 (SF4)-sample data.

*Because the Census Bureau counts everyone who is willing to respond at the time of the survey, regardless of his/her legal status, the category "immigrants" could include naturalized citizens, resident aliens, and illegal immigrants.

Kong residents) and Koreans left their homelands mainly for political reasons. This lower percentage of immigrants for the Japanese American community clearly has something to do their higher degree of assimilation in American society.

Region of Residence

As statistical figures in Table 1.3 indicate, East Asian Americans are overwhelmingly concentrated in the bicoastal areas of the United States and the state of Hawaii. California, New York, and Hawaii were home to about 2.5 million East Asian Americans, or 57.8 percent of the total population of these groups. Among them, California, having 37.7 percent of the total East Asian population, was obviously the first choice for all three groups.

Except for Japanese Americans, New York was the second choice. Due to an early, large-scale migration of Japanese workers to Hawaii in the 1890s and 1900s, this island state had the second largest Japanese American population in the United States. This high concentration of East Asian Americans has tremendous implications for the rise of their political participation in these three states, especially given that in those states their populations are further concentrated in metropolitan areas, such as New York City, Los Angeles, Honolulu, San Francisco, San Jose, and San Diego, leading to increasing political influence at the local level.

Table 1.3
Top Three States with Large East Asian American Populations, 2000

States	East Asians	Chinese	Japanese	Korean
California	1,615,378	980,642	288,854	345,882
New York	581,899	424,774	37,279	119,846
Hawaii	281,901	56,600	201,764	23,537
Total	2,479,178	1,462,016	527,897	489,265

Source: U.S. Census Bureau, *Census 2000,* Summary File 2 (SF2), 100-Percent Data.

Gender

Gender is one of the most important demographic characteristics, because its ratio balance is vital for the growth of the group. The fewer women each group has, the fewer families are formed, and thus fewer children are born. In the past, because immigrants from East Asia were mainly laborers, East Asians in the United States were predominantly males. Today, this picture of gender imbalance of more males no longer exists. However, as demonstrated in Table 1.4, a different kind of gender imbalance of more females than males was salient in 2000 among Japanese and Korean Americans. Only Chinese Americans had a near fifty-fifty balance. The large numbers of female Japanese and Korean Americans are perhaps attributable to a sizable immigration of Japanese and Korean women to the United States as war brides or spouses of American servicemen in the post–World War II era.

Age

Age is another primary background variable closely related to some vital social and economic characteristics of the group, such as fertility rate, education, and income. In the case of East Asian Americans, Table 1.4 suggests that while Chinese Americans' media age of 35.5 was almost exactly equal to the national median age of 35.3 in 2000 (U.S. Census Bureau, *Census 2000,* Summary File 1), Japanese Americans were much older and Korean Americans were slightly younger than the national median. Moreover, Chinese Americans had the smallest age gap between males and females among the three groups.

Table 1.4
Gender Percentages and Median Age of East Asian Americans, 2000

	Chinese	Japanese	Korean
Male	48.2%	43.7%	44.3%
Median Age	35.0	41.2	30.3
Female	51.8%	56.3%	55.7%
Median Age	36.0	44.0	34.9
All Persons	100.0%	100.0%	100.0%
Median Age	35.5	42.6	32.7

Source: U.S. Census Bureau, *Census 2000,* Summary File 4 (SF4)-sample data.

Females universally tend to have a longer life expectancy, and this is also true for East Asian Americans in the United States.

In terms of age distribution, 35 percent of Chinese native born and 73 percent of immigrants in 1990 were between the ages of twenty and fifty-nine, persons of working age, while the percentages were 54 percent and 64 percent for Japanese Americans, and 14 percent and 68 percent for Korean Americans. It is worth noting that only 14 percent of Korean native born were persons of working age, and 55 percent of them were nine years or younger, which largely explains why Korean Americans were the youngest among the three groups.

Marital Status

Marriage is related to the creation of family units, which in turn constitute the basis of a community. For heavily family-oriented East Asian Americans, immigrants of these groups were a bit more likely to be married than non-Hispanic Caucasian Americans in 1990. The percentages were 67 percent, 65 percent, 65 percent, and 60.7 percent for Chinese, Japanese, Korean, and non-Hispanic Caucasian Americans, respectively. However, their native born were much less likely to be married than either the immigrants or non-Hispanic Caucasian Americans by sizable margins. The percentages dropped to 44 percent, 57 percent, and 33 percent for Chinese, Japanese, and Korean native born, respectively.

Table 1.5
Marital Status of East Asian Americans in 2000, by Gender
(in percentage)

	Chinese	Japanese	Korean
Male	100.0	100.0	100.0
Never Married	32.1	32.8	35.9
Now Married	63.4	58.9	60.5
Widowed	1.4	2.4	0.8
Divorced	3.1	5.9	2.8
Female	100.0	100.0	100.0
Never Married	25.6	22.8	26.4
Now Married	62.8	59.1	60.9
Widowed	7.1	10.8	6.8
Divorced	4.5	7.3	5.9

Source: U.S. Census Bureau, *Census 2000,* Summary File 4 (SF4)-sample data.

Table 1.6
Marriage Patterns of East Asian Americans in California,
1990, by Gender (in percentage)

	Chinese	Japanese	Korean
Male			
Intraethnic Marriage	75.8	62.1	78.1
Interethnic Marriage	16.7	21.2	18.3
Interracial Marriage	7.5	16.7	3.6
Total	100.0	100.0	100.0
Female			
Intraethnic Marriage	74.3	48.1	68.5
Interethnic Marriage	13.9	20.0	16.1
Interracial Marriage	11.8	31.9	15.4
Total	100.0	100.0	100.0

Source: Based on Larry Hajime Shinagawa. 1998. "The Impact of Immigration on the Demography of Asian Pacific Americans." In *National Asian Pacific American Political Almanac, 1998–99.* Edited by James S. Lai. 8th ed. Los Angeles: UCLA Asian American Studies Center, Table 21.

As demonstrated in Table 1.5, in 2000 the percentages of married Chinese, Japanese, and Korean Americans were 63.1 percent, 59.1 percent, and 60.7 percent, respectively. There were no discernible differences between males and females across the three groups. However, it is evident that more East Asian American females than males were either widowed or divorced.

In terms of marriage patterns, Table 1.6 suggests that a majority of both East Asian American men and women in the state of California were intermarried either to persons with the same ethnic background or to other Asian Americans. This marriage pattern has played a central role in shaping racial and ethnic identities and community cohesion among East Asian Americans.

More specifically, East Asian American males were more likely to be intermarried than females, and Japanese Americans were more likely than Chinese and Korean Americans to have an interracial marriage. The high percentage of interracial marriage among female Japanese Americans is likely attributed to the large number of Japanese wives of non–Asian American servicemen after World War II.

Education

In addition to family orientation and other Confucian values, East Asian culture is also characterized by a heavy emphasis on education. Understandably, East Asian Americans have a remarkable educational profile. In 1990, 37.5 percent of East Asian Americans twenty-five years and older had at least a bachelor's degree. The percentages were 45.7 percent for males and 30.8 percent for females, which were much higher than those of non-Hispanic Caucasian American males and females, whose percentages in 1994 were 28 and 21 percent, respectively. Among East Asian Americans, Chinese Americans had the highest proportion of people who earned at least a bachelor's degree, as well as who earned graduate degrees. As displayed in Table 1.7, the level of educational attainment for East Asian Americans continued to grow into 2000: more than 40 percent of East Asian Americans twenty-five years and older had at least a bachelor's degree. For Chinese Americans, the earlier pattern persisted in 2000. Among the three groups, they had the highest proportion of people who earned degrees in all three postgraduate categories.

Education is not only a ticket to upward social mobility, but also one of the most salient determinants of political activism. The relatively higher level of educational attainment of East Asian Americans demonstrates the potential of their political participation in future years.

Table 1.7
Educational Attainment of East Asian Americans over 25, 2000
(in percentage)

	Chinese	Japanese	Korean
Less Than Bachelor Degree	52.0	58.1	56.2
Bachelor's Degree	24.2	28.8	29.1
Master's Degree	14.9	8.4	9.0
Professional School Degree	3.6	2.8	3.2
Doctorate Degree	5.3	1.9	2.5
Total	100.0	100.0	100.0

Source: U.S. Census Bureau, *Census 2000,* Summary File 4 (SF4)-sample data.

English Proficiency

Ability to speak English is a crucial factor in determining how well an immigrant will be assimilated into mainstream society. Economically, immigrants' proficiency in English is very much related to their income levels. Politically, it enhances their ability and will to participate in American politics.

As indicated in Table 1.8, in 2000 a majority of East Asian Americans, regardless of their immigration status, rated themselves as speaking only English, or speaking English very well or well, and it is not surprising that the native born were more proficient in English than the foreign born. With respect to interethnic comparisons, there was little difference among Chinese, Japanese, and Korean immigrants, while nearly 80 percent of Japanese native born spoke only English—a much higher percentage than their Chinese and Korean counterparts.

Occupational Patterns

When East Asian immigrants first arrived in the United States, they were predominantly laborers and blue-collar workers. Today, a majority of East Asian Americans are not in those traditional occupations. In contrast, as demonstrated in Table 1.9, 52.2 percent, 50.7 percent, and 38.7 percent of Chinese, Japanese, and Korean Americans, respectively, were in management and professional job categories in 2000. As for interethnic comparisons, there was only a slight gap between Chinese and Japanese Americans, but Korean Americans were significantly behind.

Table 1.8
English Proficiency of East Asian Americans, 2000
(in percentage)

	Chinese	Japanese	Korean
Immigration Status			
Native Born			
Very Well	44.7	13.0	51.4
Well	11.7	5.0	10.2
Not Well	3.9	2.2	5.0
Not at All	0.3	0.1	0.2
Speak Only English	39.4	79.7	33.2
Total	100.0	100.0	100.0
Foreign Born			
Very Well	32.7	30.6	26.7
Well	30.1	34.6	29.1
Not Well	21.9	20.9	25.5
Not at All	9.2	1.6	4.2
Speak Only English	6.1	12.3	14.5
Total	100.0	100.0	100.0

Source: U.S. Census Bureau, *Census 2000,* Summary File 4 (SF4)-sample data.

Table 1.9
Occupational Patterns of East Asian Americans, 2000
(in percentage)

	Chinese	Japanese	Korean
Management and Professional	52.2	50.7	38.7
Service	13.9	11.9	14.8
Sales and Office	20.8	26.9	30.2
Farming, Fishing, and Forestry	0.1	0.4	0.2
Construction, Extraction, and Maintenance	2.6	4.2	3.9
Production, Transportation, and Material Moving	10.4	5.9	12.2
Total	100.0	100.0	100.0

Source: U.S. Census Bureau, *Census 2000,* Summary File 4 (SF4)-sample data.

Household Income

In 2000 the median household income of Chinese, Japanese, and Korean Americans was $51,444, $52,060, and $40,037, respectively (U.S. Census Bureau, *Census 2000,* Summary File 4). Largely because of the smaller percentage of Korean Americans who had management and professional jobs than Chinese and Japanese Americans, Korean Americans had the lowest median income among the three groups.

In contrast, the median household income in the same year was $41,994 for the general U.S. population and $45,367 for non-Hispanic white Americans (U.S. Census Bureau, *Census 2000,* Summary File 4). The reasons why East Asian Americans in general had higher median income was not only because of a higher concentration of them in management and professional occupations but also because of a larger number of wage earners in their households.

Political Attitudes

In general, East Asian Americans are less likely to participate in politics than mainstream Americans. This long-existent reality can be attributed not only to many of their demographic characteristics, but also their political attitudes, including their perceptions, orientations, and evaluations of political objects, such as political institutions, public officials, and public policies.

Surveys specifically targeted at Asian Americans are very few. In the decade between 1992 and 2002, there were two monumental surveys conducted to study the political attitudes and activities of this minority group. The first one was a survey of 5,000 Asian American adults in California in August 1992 (Gall and Gall 1993), while the second one, *A Pilot Study of the National Asian American Political Survey (PNAAPS),* was conducted between November 2000 and January 2001 and examined the attitudes of 1,218 Asian American adults who lived in Chicago, Honolulu, Los Angeles, New York, and San Francisco (Lien 2001a; Lien, et al. 2004). Results of these surveys show a broad spectrum of attitudes of East Asian Americans toward politics in general and toward political institutions, public officials, and public policies in particular. Changes in some aspects of their political attitudes over the past decade can be identified from comparisons of the two sets of results.

Attitudes toward Politics in General

Political Ideology

In 1992 Chinese (44.6 percent), Japanese (50.3 percent), and Korean Americans (59.5 percent) were more likely to classify themselves as either very conservative or somewhat conservative. Among the three groups, Korean Americans were the most conservative, while, relatively speaking, Chinese Americans were the most liberal. It is noteworthy that none of the Korean Americans self-identified as very liberal.

According to the two survey results, there was a dramatic shift in East Asian Americans' political ideology in the last decade of the twentieth century. In 2001 Chinese (30 percent), Japanese (34 percent), and Korean Americans (33 percent) were more likely to classify themselves as either very liberal or somewhat liberal. Only 13 percent of Chinese, 24 percent of Japanese, and 31 percent of Korean Americans still considered themselves as either very conservative or somewhat conservative. The most drastic change occurred to the size of conservative Chinese Americans, which dropped from 44.6 percent to 13 percent between 1992 and 2001. Another discernible change was that East Asian Americans as a whole were more likely to describe themselves as middle of the road.

All the above changes in East Asian Americans' political ideology have had tremendous implications for their party affiliations and voting preferences, both of which are discussed later.

Table 1.10
Political Ideology of East Asian Americans, 1992 and 2001
(in percentage)

	Chinese		Japanese		Korean	
	1992	2001	1992	2001	1992	2001
Very Conservative	9.5	2.0	15.3	4.0	36.7	4.0
Somewhat Conservative	35.1	11.0	35.0	20.0	22.8	27.0
Middle of the Road	30.2	42.0	31.1	37.0	22.8	28.0
Somewhat Liberal	19.0	26.0	13.1	25.0	17.7	29.0
Very Liberal	5.8	4.0	3.8	9.0	0.0	4.0
Not Sure		15.0		4.0		8.0

Sources: The 1992 figures are based on Susan B. Gall and Timothy L. Gall, eds. 1993. *Statistical Record of Asian Americans.* Detroit: Gale Research, p. 29, while the 2001 figures are from Pei-te Lien, M. Margaret Conway, and Janelle Wong. 2004. *The Politics of Asian Americans: Diversity and Community.* New York: Routledge, p. 75.

Political Awareness and Interest

In 1992 a majority of Chinese (88.7 percent), Japanese (89.0 percent), and Korean Americans (93.7 percent) responded that they followed "what's going on in government and politics" either most of the time or some of the time (Gall and Gall 1993). In the 2001 survey, participants were asked to answer a similar question as to how interested they were "in politics and what's going on in government in general." Of those interviewed, 64 percent of Chinese, 59 percent of Japanese, and 71 percent of Korean Americans expressed that they were either very interested or somewhat interested (Lien, et al. 2004). In addition to the passage of time between the studies, another reason to account for the discrepancy between 1992 and 2001 might be that people who tend to follow what's going on in government and politics are not necessarily interested in it. In any case, Korean Americans are the most attentive among the three groups.

Fairness and Discrimination in U.S. Society

Over half of Chinese (59.3 percent), Japanese (50.8 percent), and Korean Americans (67.1 percent) surveyed in 1992 either disagreed or strongly disagreed that "generally speaking, Asian-Americans get their fair share in this society" (Gall and Gall 1993). The 2001 survey results echoed this perception of unfairness in U.S. society against East Asian Americans. In 2001, 39 percent of Chinese, 40 percent of Japanese, and 42 percent of Korean Americans indicated that they have personally experienced discrimination in the United States (Lien 2001a). These figures are exceedingly similar across all three groups. Combined with the 1992 results, it seems that Korean Americans have experienced more unfairness and discrimination in the society, and hence, it may not be a coincidence that they are the most attentive to public affairs.

Perception of Political Influence and Activities

Approximately seven to eight out of every ten East Asian Americans (80 percent of Chinese Americans, 68 percent of Japanese Americans, and 71 percent of Korean Americans) who responded to the 2001 survey claimed that they had either very little or no influence at all over local government decisions. Once again, these percentages are similar across the three groups. Among them, only 1 percent of Chinese Americans believed that they had a lot influence over government decisions (Lien, et al. 2004).

Bearing the above figures in mind, one would not be surprised to see that 76.4 percent of Chinese, 61.3 percent of Japanese, and 65.8 percent of Korean Americans responded in the 1992 survey that they either disagreed or strongly disagreed with the statement, "Asian-Americans are politically active in this country." Again, only 0.8 percent of Chinese Americans strongly agreed that Asian Americans are politically active (Gall and Gall 1993). All in all, East Asian Americans uniformly held perceptions that they had a low level of political efficacy, one of the central determinants of political participation, and that the political activism of Asian Americans was of little significance.

Attitudes toward Political Institutions

Attitudes toward the U.S. Judicial System
In the 1992 and 2001 surveys, there were no questions about Asian Americans' attitudes toward any specific levels or branches of the U.S. government. However, coincidentally or not, each survey included one question about a high-profile, race-related judicial case that occurred at the time the survey was conducted. The first was the Rodney King case in 1992 that involved the beating of an African American motorist by Caucasian police officers who were later tried and acquitted, which subsequently ignited rioting in Los Angeles in that year. The other was the aforementioned case of Wen Ho Lee in 2000. Specifically focusing on these two cases, the following survey results displayed to a certain extent East Asian Americans' attitudes toward the U.S. judicial system.

Among the 1992 respondents, 29.6 percent of Chinese Americans, 41.6 percent of Japanese Americans, and 25.3 percent of Korean Americans either disagreed or strongly disagreed that "the verdict of the Rodney King case indicates that minorities, including Asians, cannot get justice in this country." A relative majority of them either strongly agreed or agreed with the above statement (Gall and Gall 1993). In 2001 only 8 percent of Chinese Americans, 20 percent of Japanese Americans, and 30 percent of Korean Americans who heard of the case of Wen Ho Lee either strongly approved or somewhat approved of the government's handling of the case (Lien 2001a). Though a majority of all three ethnic groups had negative views of the judicial system's handling of both cases, it is important to note that their levels of negativity varied, with Chinese Americans holding the most negative views.

Political Party Affiliation

According to the 1992 survey results shown in Table 1.11, both Chinese (37.6 percent vs. 29 percent) and Korean Americans (49.4 percent vs. 30.4 percent) were more likely to identify themselves as Republicans than as Democrats, while Japanese Americans affiliated more with the Democratic Party (42.1 percent) over the GOP (32.8 percent).

As discussed earlier, there was a dramatic shift in East Asian Americans' political ideology from being more conservative to being more liberal during the 1990s. Therefore, not surprisingly, a similar pattern emerged in their party affiliations. In the 2001 survey, as demonstrated in Table 1.11, a majority of Chinese (32 percent vs. 9 percent), Japanese (40 percent vs. 12 percent), and Korean Americans (43 percent vs. 22 percent) favored the Democratic Party over the GOP. As the percentage of conservative Chinese Americans dropped from 44.6 percent to 13 percent between 1992 and 2001, the percentage of Republicans among Chinese Americans decreased from 37.6 percent to 9 percent during the same period. There was also a sizable loss in Republican affiliation among Japanese (from 32.8 percent to 12 percent) and Korean Americans (49.4 percent to 22 percent) in the same decade.

Table 1.11
Political Party Affiliation of East Asian Americans, 1992 and 2001 (in percentage)

	Chinese		Japanese		Korean	
	1992	*2001*	*1992*	*2001*	*1992*	*2001*
Republican	37.6	9.0	32.8	12.0	49.4	22.0
Democrat	29.0	32.0	42.1	40.0	30.4	43.0
Independent	27.7	3.0	24.6	20.0	19.0	12.0

Sources: The 1992 figures are based on Susan B. Gall and Timothy L. Gall, eds. 1993. *Statistical Record of Asian Americans*. Detroit: Gale Research, p. 25; the 2001 figures are from Pei-te Lien, M. Margaret Conway, and Janelle Wong. 2004. *The Politics of Asian Americans: Diversity and Community*. New York: Routledge, p. 109.

One interesting phenomenon in the 2001 survey is that more than half of Chinese Americans (56 percent) and approximately a quarter of Japanese (28 percent) and Korean Americans (23 percent) either did not think in terms of a party affiliation or were unsure about it (Lien, et al. 2004). It seems that when the respondents were not given such choices in the 1992 survey, many of them, rather unmindfully, identified themselves either as Republicans or Independents. This pattern was more salient for Chinese Americans than for Japanese and Korean Americans, indicating that Chinese Americans have the weakest sense of party affiliation among the three ethnic groups.

Attitudes toward Government Officials

In the eyes of East Asian Americans, how much can public officials be trusted and how responsive are they to citizens' complaints? The 2001 survey identified certain patterns of Asian Americans' perception of the job performance of local and state government officials.

Generally speaking, an absolute majority of East Asian Americans indicated that local and state government officials can be trusted at least some of the time. Specifically, 30 percent of Chinese Americans, 32 percent of Japanese Americans, and 43 percent of Korean Americans believed that their government officials could be trusted either just about always or most of the time, and 35 percent, 54 percent, and 44 percent, respectively, indicated that they trusted officials some of the time. However, among the three groups, Chinese Americans had the lowest level of trust with 10 percent of them indicating that public officials cannot be trusted at all. Furthermore, a quarter of Chinese Americans were unsure about their level of trust, also the highest among the three groups (Lien, et al. 2004).

When asked to predict what would happen if they took a complaint about a government activity to a local public official, 38 percent of Chinese Americans, 43 percent of Japanese Americans, and 63 percent of Korean Americans expected that the local official would pay very little or no attention to their complaint, while 31 percent of Chinese Americans, 46 percent of Japanese Americans, and 31 percent of Korean Americans believed that the local official would pay a lot or some attention to it. Apparently, among the three groups, Korean Americans were most pessimistic about public officials' responsiveness to their needs. It is also notable that 31 percent of Chinese Americans were unsure about the level of attention their public officials would pay, which was again the highest among the three groups (Lien, et al. 2004).

Attitudes toward Public Policies

How do East Asian Americans position themselves on key public policy debates that are closely related to their community interest? The answer has enormous implications for their participation in the process of policy formulation. The following survey results concentrated on three domestic policy areas (affirmative action, immigration, and campaign contributions), and one foreign policy issue (U.S. involvement in Asia).

Affirmative Action

The 2001 survey results suggested that 67 percent of Chinese Americans, 44 percent of Japanese Americans, and 74 percent of Korean Americans thought that affirmative action was "a good thing" for Asian Americans, while only 3 percent, 8 percent, and 6 percent, respectively, believed that it was "a bad thing" (Lien 2001a).

In the 1992 survey, no specific questions concerning affirmative action were addressed; instead, it included a more general question about government aid to minority groups. When asked if they agreed with the statement, "Government should not make any special effort to help minorities because they should help themselves," 63.4 percent of Chinese Americans, 57.9 percent of Japanese Americans, and 64.5 percent of Korean Americans either strongly disagreed or disagreed with it (Gall and Gall 1993).

Regardless of whether the question was asked specifically or generally, both survey results indicated that East Asian Americans consistently supported those public policies in favor of minority groups. However, among them, Japanese Americans were the least supportive, while Korean Americans were the most supportive over time.

Immigration

About half of Chinese (49 percent) and Japanese (50 percent) Americans included in the 2001 survey supported the passage of federal laws limiting the number of legal immigrants admitted each year into this country. Korean Americans were very exceptional in their view toward this policy issue, with only 25 percent of them supporting and 37 percent opposing such limits (Lien 2001a).

Campaign Contributions

When asked whether non-U.S. citizens who are legal permanent residents should be permitted to make donations to political campaigns, a key concern in the area of electoral politics, 53 percent of Chinese Americans, 45 percent of Japanese Americans, and 48 percent of Korean Americans agreed that they should, while 14 percent, 31 percent, and 13 percent, respectively, opposed allowing such contributions (Lien 2001a). Again, Japanese Americans were the least supportive among the three groups.

U.S. Involvement in Asia

In the sphere of U.S. foreign policy, participants in the 1992 survey were asked about their opinions on the extent to which the United States should be involved in Asia. The results were consistent across the three groups, with 34.7 percent of Chinese Americans, 29.0 percent of Japanese Americans, and 24.1 percent of Korean Americans supporting more involvement, and 20.9 percent, 23.0 percent, and 21.5 percent, respectively, favoring less involvement (Gall and Gall 1993).

In sum, although there are noticeable variations in political attitudes among East Asian Americans, they share much in common. A typical East Asian American is more likely to be liberal and interested in politics and government, has personally experienced unfairness and discrimination in society, believes that he or she has a low level of political influence, and self-perceives as politically not active. He or she is more likely to be a Democrat, to hold negative views of the U.S. judicial system, and to trust public officials but believe that public officials would pay little or no attention to his or her complaints. Finally, in the areas of public policy, he or she is more likely to support affirmative action, limits to legal immigration, campaign contributions by legal permanent residents, and more U.S. involvement in Asia.

Key Issues Facing East Asian Americans

What are the key issues that have affected the East Asian American community as a whole? What are the most urgent problems they need to solve to protect and advance their collective well-being? The following issues may not be equally weighted by all three ethnic groups, but they are indeed central issues that confront all of them at all times and need to be dealt with as overall concerns.

Language Barriers

When asked about the most important problems facing their respective ethnic groups in the United States today, 46 percent of Chinese Americans and 36 percent of Korean Americans surveyed in 2001 selected "don't speak English well" as the top issue. These results are not surprising, given that only 4 percent of Chinese Americans and 10 percent of Korean Americans indicated in the same survey that they usually speak English at home with family. In contrast, 79 percent of Japanese American respondents speak English at home, and therefore, only 5 percent of them chose language barriers as the most important issue (Lien 2001a). However, Japanese Americans were very exceptional in this regard. For many East Asian immigrants, this problem of language is particularly acute, and the campaign to designate English as the official language is always an issue of great concern.

Anti-Asian Violence and Discrimination

It has been a long and winding road for East Asian Americans, especially Chinese and Japanese Americans, to fight against racial inequality and social injustice in U.S. society. Prejudice, discrimination, and even physical violence against them are never rare. For instance, 15 percent of hate crime victims in Los Angeles County in the 1980s were Asian Americans (Lien 1998), and as indicated earlier, 39 percent of Chinese Americans, 40 percent of Japanese Americans, and 42 percent of Korean Americans in the 2001 survey indicated that they have personally experienced discrimination (Lien 2001a). Depending on the U.S. domestic economy and foreign relations with Asian countries, anti-Asian sentiment has fluctuated over time. When crises came, East Asian Americans were always scapegoats to governments and industries in their homelands. For example, they were blamed for the bombing of Pearl Harbor in 1941, for the trade friction with Japan in the 1970s and 1980s, and for the Chinese government's detention of twenty-four crew members of a U.S. surveillance plane that collided with a Chinese fighter plane on April 1, 2001. As a result, there has been a cry nationwide to unite Asian Americans to defend their civil rights in many spheres of U.S. society, from street corners, schools, and workplaces to the media and movie industries.

Lack of Political Participation and Representation

The next issue facing East Asian Americans is related to the central concern of this book: political participation. To successfully defend their civil rights against inequality and injustice, Asian Americans have to fight in political domains, especially in legislatures and courts. Although their political power has been increasing in recent years, Asian American voters have not yet come to represent a voting group in proportion to their share of the total population. Therefore, Asian Americans as a whole must learn how to convert their relatively higher incomes and educational backgrounds into more votes and then learn how to integrate their votes into a voting bloc and thereby establish a more powerful swing vote.

Lack of Group Identity

Given their status of being the smallest major minority group in American society, East Asian Americans, as well as Asian Americans as a whole, have a desperate need to forge a group identity and unity to be able to act collectively to defend their interests. However, because of the differences in their historical experiences, demographic characteristics, and native languages, and notwithstanding that they share some common cultural heritages such as values and customs, a panethnic identity for Asian Americans is not yet fully formulated.

Lack of Consensus on Issues

Ironically, one of the most compelling issues that faces East Asian Americans today is probably the lack of consensus on what kind of issues should be given top priority and thus need to be first aggregated and articulated. Would it be affirmative action, language barriers, anti-Asian violence, or others? This problem of not being able to speak with one voice is clearly related to the lack of national leaders and a group identity in the East Asian American community.

Conclusion

Patterns of political participation of East Asian Americans have been largely determined by the interplay of the three factors outlined above in this chapter: historical factors, demographic factors, and attitudinal factors.

Historically, East Asian Americans shared similar experiences of immigration to the United States, which were characterized by racism and, thus, exclusionism. This collective memory of dismay is conducive to the advancement of their political participation when the time is right. The right time for East Asian Americans to participate in the U.S. political process came after the end of World War II. Demographically, both the quantity and quality of this minority group have profoundly changed since the war ended, both of which factors are indispensable for political participation. Attitudinally, the political ideology of East Asian Americans and their perceptions toward U.S. political institutions, government officials, and public policies have shaped their levels of political participation in a significant way.

In addition to the three factors discussed above, there are several vital issues facing East Asian Americans as a whole, namely, language barriers, anti-Asian violence and discrimination, lack of political participation and representation, lack of a group identity, and lack of consensus on issues—all of which are related to East Asian Americans' political participation in one way or another. Among them, the issue of anti-Asian violence and discrimination and other related issues about racial equality and social justice are probably of greatest concern to all East Asian Americans. To deal with these problems, East Asian Americans or Asian Americans as a whole, jointly or separately, have participated in forms of protest politics, social movements and interest groups, electoral politics, and political officeholding. These different but related participatory activities are closely examined in light of the three factors in the following chapters.

References

Baron, Deborah G., and Susan B. Gall, eds. 1996. *Asian American Chronology.* New York: UXL.

Chan, Sucheng. 1991. *Asian American: An Interpretive History.* New York: Twayne.

Gall, Susan B., and Timothy L. Gall, eds. 1993. *Statistical Record of Asian Americans.* Detroit: Gale Research.

Lien, Pei-te. 1998. "Sociopolitical Context, Ethnic Identity, and Political Participation: Continuity and Change among Asian Americans in Southern California." In *National Asian Pacific American Political Almanac, 1998–99.* Edited by James S. Lai. 8th ed. Los Angeles: UCLA Asian American Studies Center.

———. 2001a. *A Pilot Study of the National Asian American Political Survey (PNAAPS): Summary Statistical Report for the Entire Sample and by Ethnic Groups.* Unpublished report.

Lien, Pei-te, M. Margaret Conway, and Janelle Wong. 2004. *The Politics of Asian Americans: Diversity and Community.* New York: Routledge.

Schultz, Jeffrey D., Kerry L. Haynie, Anne M. McCulloch, and Andrew L. Aoki, eds. 2000. *Encyclopedia of Minorities in American Politics. Volume 1: African Americans and Asian Americans.* Phoenix: Oryx.

Shinagawa, Larry Hajime. 1998. "The Impact of Immigration on the Demography of Asian Pacific Americans." In *National Asian Pacific American Political Almanac, 1998–99.* Edited by James S. Lai. 8th ed. Los Angeles: UCLA Asian American Studies Center.

U.S. Census Bureau. *Census 2000.* Summary File 1 (SF1), Sample Data.

U.S. Census Bureau. *Census 2000.* Summary File 2 (SF2), 100-Percent Data.

U.S. Census Bureau. *Census 2000.* Summary File 4 (SF4), Sample Data.

Wang, L. Ling-chi. 1998. "Roots and Changing Identity of the Chinese in the United States." In *Adaptation, Acculturation, and Transnational Ties among Asian Americans.* Edited by Franklin Ng. New York: Garland.

Wong, Morrison G. 1986. "Post–1965 Asian Immigrants: Where Do They Come from, Where Are They Now, and Where Are They Going?" *Annals of the American Academy of Political and Social Science* 487: 150–168. Included in *The History and Immigration of Asian Americans.* Edited by Franklin Ng. New York: Garland, 1998.

2

Participation in Protest Politics and Social Movements

ontrary to common perceptions, East Asian Americans—especially Chinese and Japanese Americans—have a long tradition of participating in mainstream politics. Although less significant than that of the mainstream society, their participation can be generally classified into two categories: electoral and nonelectoral activities. Conventionally, the former, including registration and voting, were taken as the main feature of Asian Americans' political participation, and the latter were not widely recognized until recently. Compared with other forms of nonelectoral activities such as lobbying and litigation, East Asian American participation in mass protests, using various tactics like boycotts, strikes, marches, and demonstrations, is their most high-profile, but perhaps not the most effective, form of political participation outside the electoral system. The aim of such action has been mainly to fight for racial equality, as well as economic and social justice, in the spheres of public policy, public opinion, and employment.

Though East Asians were already very active in protest politics in the years before the late 1960s, their activities then were not as visible as those conducted by a new generation of East Asian Americans during and after the late 1960s when the Asian American movement was born in the midst of the mainstream civil rights movement and the anti–Vietnam War movement. The Asian American movement was a watershed that thoroughly enlivened century-old East Asian American protest politics with new members, visions, agendas, and strategies.

Influenced by the Asian American movement, East Asian Americans continued their struggles well into the 1980s and 1990s. Among a plethora of their protests and movements, the following three stand out and deserve more intensive study because of their massive scope, duration, and historical significance: the campaign following the murder of Vincent Chin in 1982, the Redress movement in the 1970s and 1980s, and the reaction of the Korean American community in the wake of the Los Angeles riots in 1992.

History of Early Protests

East Asians began their history of protests as early as the late 1850s, soon after their arrival in the New World. As the latest comer among the three groups and with a very small population in the early years, Koreans left little mark on the history of these early protests. For instance, there were only 5,008 Koreans in 1910, 7,030 in 1950, and fewer than 70,000 in 1970. This is the key reason why they were relatively inactive in protest politics until the late 1970s. It was thus primarily the Chinese and Japanese who were engaged in a variety of protest activities during the one hundred years or so after their arrival. Their protest activities were often simultaneous but were not collaborative.

Chinese

As immigrant workers, both the Chinese and Japanese engaged in strikes mainly for labor justice, demanding better wages and working conditions. Cases that pursued justice in noneconomic spheres were quite rare prior to the 1960s. For instance, a petition was filed in 1859 by thirty Chinese parents whose sons and daughters were excluded from public education addressed to the San Francisco Board of Education to establish a primary school for their children. As a result, the Chinese School in San Francisco opened that fall as the only school in the whole country exclusively for Chinese (Okihiro 1994).

In 1878 the Chinese in San Francisco collected 13,000 signatures to petition the state legislature to grant their children access to the public schools, but this time they failed (Lien 2001b). Another case that also occurred in San Francisco was a protest by the Chinese in 1870 against a "queue ordinance" that required Chinese male prisoners to cut off their braided hair, a symbol of their Chinese identity.

The Chinese also employed other strategies to fight inequality. The 1905 boycott of American goods in China was a direct response to maltreatment of Chinese in the United States under Chinese exclusion laws. Believing that they were about to be expelled from the United States, the Chinese helped organize the boycott. Their spokesman, Ng Poon-Chew, even went to Washington, addressing the House of Representatives and meeting with President Theodore Roosevelt. In San Francisco, Chinese immigrants raised money to help sustain the boycott. However, the monetary assistance stopped after the 1906 earthquake destroyed Chinatown. Even though the boycott did not last long and had minimal impact on America's trade with China, it successfully resulted in better treatment of Chinese people in the United States. The involvement of the Chinese in the United States in this boycott movement was historically notable, not only because they developed different tactics, such as boycotting and lobbying, but also because they used resources in their homeland to their advantage.

In contrast, cases of early protests in the realm of labor justice were so abundant that the history of East Asian protests before the 1960s can be largely subsumed into the general history of labor agitation in the United States. The largest, perhaps also the earliest, strike staged by Chinese in the nineteenth century was a railroad strike in 1867. Due to inequality in wages, working hours, and other working conditions, 2,000 Chinese workers in the High Sierra Mountains of California went on strike, demanding $40 a month ($10 more than what they were receiving), an 8-to-10-hour workday (rather than working from sunrise to sundown), an end to bodily punishment, and the freedom to leave anytime they wanted. No matter how monumental this strike was in history, it was short-lived and fruitless in the end. It lasted just one week after the strikers' food ran out. Similar incidents occurred in the South. In 1870 Chinese railroad workers stopped work and filed suit against their employer, the Houston and Texas Central Railroad, for wages and for a breach of contract. However, the final outcome of this incident is unknown. One year later, when the Alabama and Chattanooga Railroad Company filed for bankruptcy, several hundred Chinese, along with workers of other racial backgrounds, all of whom had not been paid for six months, seized the trains to demand payment, but they failed (Chan 1991).

Although certain elements of interracial antagonism against the white railroad proprietors motivated the Chinese strikers, the workers also protested against owners and labor contractors from their own race. For instance, in 1875 garment workers struck a Chinese sweatshop in San Francisco for better wages (Chan 1991). Also in San Francisco, Chinese shoemakers, unsatisfied with their white bosses, went on strike in 1876 and demanded return of the money they had given to a Chinese trading company and labor contractor. When the contractor refused to meet their demand, 50 shoemakers attacked the trading company of Yee Chung and Company. It was a violent uprising in which many were reportedly injured. Chinese shoemakers continued to strike in the 1880s. In 1887, 300 of them quit work in many Chinese-owned factories and struck for a pay raise, but they, like the railroad workers, failed (Franks 1993). In 1891, 300 plantation workers in Hawaii stopped work and marched to a courthouse, demanding the authority to arrest a Chinese labor contractor for cheating them. The outcome was that 55 of them were imprisoned on charges of assault (Chan 1991).

In the twentieth century, many Chinese workers attempted to join the mainstream labor movement in the United States to have a stronger voice. However, their efforts did not bear any fruit until 1936 when a group of Chinese sailors successfully joined the National Maritime Union (NMU), the largest maritime union in the United States. When the NMU called a strike that year, the Chinese members requested the union to support their desire for equal treatment, a uniform wage scale, and the right of alien Chinese sailors to shore leave. About 3,000 Chinese sailors participated in the strike after the NMU agreed to support their demands (Chan 1991; Lien 2001b).

Japanese

Japanese immigrant workers embarked on their long journey of labor protests during the same period of time as the Chinese. Their initial battlefield was Hawaii. Throughout the 1880s and 1890s, quite a few work stoppages took place to protest mistreatment by lunas (foremen) and poor living and working conditions. In the first two years or so of the twentieth century, there were 39 labor disputes, none of which were organized. The first organized strike did not occur until 1904, when almost 1,200 Japanese workers participated in a week-long strike for higher wages. About 900 protested again later that year. Although some of their demands were met, strikers in both protests did not receive the better wages that they requested. In 1909, 7,000 Japanese workers staged a large-scale strike on Oahu for four months before it died out in August when the strikers ran out of resources. Even though the planters later agreed to terminate the practice of paying unequal wages, their promise was never fully carried out (Chan 1991; Okihiro 1994).

More significantly, Japanese workers were able to form alliances with workers of other nationalities at the turn of the twentieth century in Hawaii, as well as on the mainland. Five labor disputes in the first decade in Hawaii were cases of cooperation between Japanese and others (Franks 1993). In Oxnard, California, in 1903 Japanese and Mexican sugar beet workers jointly formed a historical farm workers' union, the Japanese-Mexican Labor Association (JMLA) with a Japanese president, a Japanese vice president, and a Mexican secretary. In March, 1,200 members of the JMLA went on strike for higher wages. After this historic strike was over, the secretary of the JMLA applied for a charter from the American Federation of Labor (AFL), but the application was denied with the stipulation that a charter would be granted only if no Asians were admitted (Chan 1991; Okihiro 1994; O'Brien and Fugita 1991).

Back in Hawaii, the year of 1920 witnessed the first major case of inter-Asian collaboration in labor protests. About 3,000 Japanese and Filipinos organized the 77 Cents Parade (77 cents being their average daily base wage), marching through the streets of downtown Honolulu. They carried American flags and portraits of President Abraham Lincoln, who for them was the symbol of freedom and equality. Because together Japanese and Filipino workers constituted more than 70 percent of the workforce in Oahu, the 1920 sugar strike suddenly stopped the plantation operations. Even so, the plantation owners refused to meet the workers' demands and the strike was ended after six months. However, after production was resumed, the planters raised wages and made significant improvements in living conditions (Chan 1991; Okihiro 1994; Espiritu 1992).

On the mainland, the collaboration between the Japanese and workers of other racial and ethnic backgrounds continued. In the early 1930s, more than 5,000 Japanese and tens of thousands of Filipino, Mexican, black, and white workers staged over twenty strikes under the auspices of the Japanese section of the Agricultural Workers Industrial Union (AWIU) (Lien 2001b). However, there were also cases in California in which Japanese entrepreneurs were struck by workers from other races. The 1933 El Monte berry strike provides a good example. The Japanese farmers, who belonged to the Central Japanese Association of Southern California, controlled 80 percent of the berry land in the El Monte area outside Los Angeles. In 1933 the Cannery and Agricultural Workers Union (CAWU), a communist-organized union of primarily Mexican workers, went on strike against their Japanese owners (O'Brien and Fugita 1991).

Similar to Chinese workers, the Japanese also went on strike against people from their own race. For instance, more than 1,600 of them in Waipahu, Hawaii, in 1906 demanded that a Japanese luna (foreman) be fired. Even though this request was finally met, they were not able to obtain the higher wages they also sought (Chan 1991). Another example took place on the mainland in 1936: the Venice celery strike. About 200 Japanese celery pickers, in alliance with approximately 800 Mexicans and a small band of Filipinos, struck the Japanese growers who belonged to the Southern California Farm Federation in the Venice area in Los Angeles, demanding higher wages and union recognition. Their demands were rejected and the growers' position was supported by many major Japanese community organizations throughout Southern California (O'Brien and Fugita 1991).

Although the Chinese and Japanese immigrant workers who arrived in the nineteenth century were products of East Asian premodern societies that were characterized by Confucian traditions of paternalistic hierarchy and habitual obedience, they learned quickly from the day they arrived various methods of mass protest in this new, industrial world and were never hesitant to fight tenaciously for racial equality and social and economic justice. Although their demands were largely unmet at the time, especially in the sphere of labor protests, the efforts they made were not all in vain because their children and grandchildren were able to carry the torch of the protesting tradition many years later during the Asian American movement of the 1960s. As for the 1940s and 1950s, both the Chinese and Japanese were very hesitant to get involved in ethnic politics in these decades. They kept very low profiles out of fear of being labeled as disloyal foreigners during the periods of World War II, the communist triumph in China, and the Korean War.

Asian American Movement

Although East Asian Americans have a long tradition of participating in politics, their collective actions were not much visible in the American political arena until the birth of the Asian American movement during the turbulent civil rights era of the 1960s. As a social movement that challenged the status quo of institutionalized powers in American society, the Asian American movement consisted of pan-Asian collective actions that specifically aimed to fight for racial equality and social and economic justice through racial solidarity and political empowerment. Because contemporary mass protests by East Asian Americans have been virtually framed by the movement, any discussion of these protests from the 1960s on would not be truly meaningful if not held within an examination of the large framework of the movement, including its origins, participants and goals, signature events of mass protests, and problems.

Origins

Why did the Asian American movement take place in this particular time of the late 1960s, but not earlier? Generally speaking, it was triggered by a conjunction of several external and internal factors: broader international and domestic developments outside the Asian American community and social and demographic changes within the community.

External Factors: Movements in the 1960s

Internationally, anti-imperialist national liberation movements in Asia, especially China's Great Proletariat Cultural Revolution and Vietnam's resistance to Western powers, prompted the emergence of racial and cultural consciousness in Asian Americans cross the Pacific Ocean. Domestically, the civil rights, Black Power, antiwar, New Left, and women's movements in the 1960s all contributed to the formation of the Asian American movement (Wei 1993; Espiritu 1992). Among them, the strongest influence on the movement was the Black Power movement in terms of goal-achieving tactics and alliance-building methods within the pan-Asian community (Geron 2003). However, it was primarily the antiwar movement that really shaped the racial nature of the movement, making Asian Americans aware of their racial uniqueness and the need for a movement for themselves (Wei 1993).

Asian Americans were as active in the New Left and women's movements as in the antiwar movement, but they separated themselves from these mainstream movements over the issues of racism and racial identity. In the eyes of many Asian Americans, the Vietnam War was not only related to imperialism but also to racism. For many of them, it was a racial war in which the enemy soldiers killed on the battlefields and unarmed civilians devastated throughout the country had faces like their own. In the meantime, Asian American soldiers also experienced racism due to their racial resemblance to the enemy. As a consequence, many Asian American activists replaced the popular antiwar slogans "Give peace a chance" and "Bring the GIs home" with their own "Stop killing our Asian brothers and sisters" and "We don't want your racist war" and declared racial solidarity not only among themselves but with their "Asian brothers and sisters" (cited in Espiritu 1992, 43–44). In sum, their focus on the racist nature of the war really distanced their antiwar protests from the mainstream movement. For example, in 1971 they refused to participate in the main antiwar march in Washington, D.C., because the white-dominated organization in charge did not accept their antiracist appeals. Even when they did join in the marches, they passed out their own antiracist and anti-imperialist materials (Espiritu 1992).

Like many white youths in the late 1960s and early 1970s, many Asian American students joined the New Left movement, seeking to organize people across class lines in pursuit of the goals of proletarian revolution. However, they also differentiated their protest activities from those of the whites by relating racial issues to the movement's emphasis on class struggle. Under the influence of the international socialist models in East Asia and the domestic Black Power movement, Asian American leftists added national liberation to their movement's goals. For instance, an Asian American Marxist organization, East Wind, proclaimed in 1972 that there should be an "Asian nation" for Asian Americans who had been racially oppressed by the mainstream society (Espiritu 1992).

The participation of Asian American women was conspicuous in the Asian American movement as well as the broader women's movement, but they were doubly victimized by sexism and racism. On the one hand, marginalized and even discriminated against by male activists in the Asian American movement and influenced by feminist ideologies in the late 1960s, they began to hold meetings on their own to discuss feminist issues. On the other hand, due to racist attitudes in the general women's movement, Asian American women were reluctant to join white-dominated feminist organizations.

Instead, they began to direct their activities into their own movement in which they added racial flavors to their feminist agenda (Espiritu 1992).

In sum, various social movements in the 1960s, especially the Black Power and the antiwar movements, heavily influenced the Asian American movement. These movements added racial, antiwar, Marxist, and feminist components to the Asian American movement. However, the Asian American movement diverged from these movements because of its unique emphasis on anti-Asian racism and Asian solidarity.

Internal Factors: Sociodemographic Changes
In contrast to developments in the broader societal context, there were also changes within the Asian American community that contributed to the emergence of the Asian American movement in the late 1960s. The most salient change was a significant increase of college students in that decade, resulting from several historical events that occurred in the 1940s and 1950s, including the abolishment of the Chinese Exclusion Act during the war, the promulgation of and amendment to several immigration acts in favor of Asian immigration, and the baby boom of Asian American children after the war (see Chapter 1; Wei 1993). In 1970 there were 107,366 Asian American students in colleges and universities, of which the majority were East Asian Americans: 83 percent of them were of Chinese and Japanese ancestries. It was these Asian American college students, mostly American born with middle-class family backgrounds, who initiated the Asian American movement and became the backbone of it (Wei 1993).

Other related social and demographic changes in the Asian American community as a whole were also conducive to the development of the movement. Along with the significant growth of college-age Asian Americans, due to the same reasons, the Asian American population not only became much larger in size but also transferred from a predominantly immigrant population to a mainly American-born one in the post–World War II era. For example, about two-thirds of California's Asian population was born in the United States (Espiritu 1992). This demographic change had a far-reaching impact on the formation of pan-Asian solidarity. Previously, for lack of a common language, foreign-born Asian Americans from different ethnic backgrounds had difficulties in communicating with one another, which presented perhaps the most serious obstacle to Asian unity. Now, with the native population outnumbering the foreign-born population, more and more Asian Americans from different backgrounds were able to use English to communicate with one another, greatly facilitating the creation of a shared feeling of being "Asians" in the United States (Espiritu 1992).

Another obstacle to Asian American unity was historical hatreds among many Asian immigrants, caused by conflicts between their motherlands in the past. This was mainly about anti-Japanese sentiments among Koreans and Chinese due to Japan's colonization of Korea from 1910 to 1945 and Japan's invasion of China from 1931 to 1945. However, this obstacle gradually lost its significance over time as the Asian American community became increasingly more dominated by second-generation Asian Americans who were in less touch with Asian homelands than their parents (Espiritu 1992).

The last obstacle was composed of economic and residential barriers that previously separated Asian Americans not only from the mainstream society but also from themselves. In the past, because of language barriers, anti-Asian racism in housing situations, and lack of economic opportunities in the larger society, many Asian Americans had no choice but to live in their own ethnic enclaves. These barriers had been severely dismantled in the post–World War II period as racial discrimination in both employment and housing was legally challenged during the civil rights movement (Espiritu 1992). As a result, more and more Asian Americans moved out of their ethnic enclaves into the mainstream of American society. For instance, in New York City, the percentage of Chinese Americans living in Chinatown decreased from 50 percent to less than one-third from 1940 to 1960 (Espiritu 1992). Furthermore, this pattern of declining residential segregation also occurred among different Asian groups, enabling them to interact not only with the mainstream society but also with one another. The latter interaction was undoubtedly essential to the formation of the so-called we-group feeling among Asian Americans.

Participants and Goals

Like any other social movement, the Asian American movement's goals and the volume of momentum gathered toward achieving these goals were largely determined by its participants. As introduced earlier, Asian American college students, primarily native-born students along with recent immigrants and Asian students on student visas (Geron 2003), constituted the backbone of the movement. They shared similar goals with activists involved in the general civil rights,

Black Power, antiwar, New Left, and women's movements to fight against the injustice of the Vietnam War and inequality in race, class, and gender relations in American society, but from Asian American perspectives. More specifically, in alliance with other nonwhite student activists, they protested on their campuses against racism in higher educational institutions. They demanded the establishment of Asian American studies programs to expose students to the cultures and historical experiences of Asian Americans.

The second major group of Asian Americans who participated in the movement consisted of community activists who had strong ties to traditional ethnic enclaves. Frustrated by pervasive poverty and social problems in their communities, in addition to their antiwar and other protest activities, they established many community-based organizations with the specific goals of developing more and better community service programs to improve the quality of life in their communities (Geron 2003). Many of these community-based activists were youths from colleges, high schools, and the streets, but many other members of the community, including the elderly, small business people, workers, and new immigrants were also part of the collective forces (Omatsu 1994).

Labor activists made up the last major group of Asian American activists. Strongly tied to the class-struggle component of the Asian American movement, these working-class activists followed the footsteps of earlier generations of labor protestors, demanding labor justice in workplaces. Their involvement overlapped the earlier protests by the Chinese and Japanese immigrants and the Asian American movement in the 1960s, thus providing a key bridge between the two over time (Geron 2003).

In sum, there were several groups of participants in the Asian American movement with a variety of goals. Be it peace; equality in race, class, and gender in the general society; or justice specifically on their campuses and in their communities and workplaces, these goals were tenaciously pursued by East Asian Americans in a plethora of mass protest activities starting in the late 1960s.

Signature Events of Mass Protests

Among many protests participated in or initiated by Asian American activists, two can be viewed as the "signature" events of the Asian American movement: the San Francisco State College strike and the International Hotel campaign, both of which, especially the former, had profound impacts on East Asian Americans' political actions in the years to come.

San Francisco State College Strike

The Asian American movement marked a watershed in the history of Asian American protests, and the San Francisco State College strike in 1968 was a defining event of the movement. On November 6, 1968, Asian American students of the college, now San Francisco State University, joined a strike with African American, Chicano, Latino, and Native American students under the umbrella of a multiethnic coalition, the Third World Liberation Front (TWLF), calling for ethnic studies and open admissions (Umemoto 1989). This five-month-long strike was the first campus uprising in which Asian American students participated as a collective force (Omatsu 1994).

In spring 1968 the TWLF was formed by African American and Mexican American students and soon joined by several Asian American student organizations, including the Philippine-American College Endeavor (PACE), the Intercollegiate Chinese for Social Actions (ICSA), and the Asian American Political Alliance (AAPA) (Umemoto 1989). On November 6, the TWLF members "entered buildings, dismissed classes, set trash cans on fire and otherwise disrupted campus operations" (Umemoto 1989, 69), marking the beginning of the longest and most violent student strike in American history. The college authorities responded by calling in the police and closing the campus. What followed next was a series of student marches and rallies that were ended violently. Police beat and arrested students. In the first two weeks of the strike, 148 students were arrested (Umemoto 1989). Collectively, the TWLF students emphasized the shared experiences of "people of color," throughout the course of the prolonged strike, they moved from their initial call for ethnic studies and open admissions to demand power and the right to determine their own future (Umemoto 1989). Although their demands were only partially met, after causing a shutdown of the campus for five months, the strike finally bore some important fruit in the end: the establishment of the first school of ethnic studies in the nation, including an Asian American studies program at the college (Fong 2002). Also, the same program was established at the University of California, Berkeley, at the same time.

In the following years, similar programs were founded at other major campuses throughout the nation, as Asian American student organizations mushroomed from California to the Midwest and East Coast (Espiritu 1992; Fong 2002). For instance, the Basement Workshop, composed of mainly working-class Chinese American students from the City College of New York, was founded in 1971. In March of the next year, their members joined one thousand other Asian American students, along with black and Latino supporters, to stage a thirteen-day takeover of the college's administration building, demanding special education for Chinatown youth and ethnic programs for Asian communities. In response, the college later established an Asian American studies program (Lin 1998).

Historically significant as the strike might be, the Asian American movement did not begin at San Francisco State and then spread elsewhere in the nation (Wei 1993). Influenced by the same external and internal factors, many Asian American activists in other locations also began to respond to the critical issues faced by Asian Americans during the same period of time. Their efforts were made spontaneously and quite independently from the strike (Wei 1993). For instance, the foremost pan–Asian American student organization of the strike was the Asian American Political Alliance (AAPA), but it was first founded at the University of California, Berkeley, and then established across the Bay at San Francisco State College a little later (Espiritu 1992). Nonetheless, the strike was the most visible event in the late 1960s that helped define the ethnic identity and collective actions of Asian Americans.

In addition to being the most salient accomplishment in the higher educational curricula that facilitated the movements of later generations of Asian American students, the strike also produced an equally significant outcome: the emergence of a new generation of Asian American activists who continued their struggles from campuses to communities (Umemoto 1989). Many of them formed "serve the people" organizations at the grassroots level, involved in various community-based campaigns for fair housing, tenants' rights, educational rights, union organizing, job creation, and social services (Omatsu 1994).

International Hotel Campaign
Although the San Francisco State College strike was the first student strike on college and university campuses incited by the Asian American movement, the International Hotel anti-eviction campaign between 1969 and 1977, one of the longest urban struggles since the end of the 1960s, was the first struggle that brought a large number of Asian American students into the community (Wei 1993; Geron 2003). Located on Kearny Street just right outside San Francisco's Chinatown and only a few miles from San Francisco State College, the

hotel was a block-long, three-story, low-cost residence mainly for retired Chinese and Filipino workers (Kordziel 2001; Yip 2000). In December 1968 coincidentally just one month after the beginning of the college strike, the hotel owner, Milton Meyers, attempted to evict the tenants and build a more profitable parking lot (Wei 1993; Geron 2003). In response, many Asian American students soon mobilized, starting another chapter of the ongoing saga of the Asian American movement.

Because the location of the hotel was what remained of Manila-town, previously covering ten blocks between Chinatown and the financial district, it was young Filipinos who first took action against the eviction, defending the icon of their ethnic identity and cultural heritage (Wei 1993). Later, Asian American students, mainly Chinese and Japanese from Berkeley, Davis, Stockton, Sacramento, San Jose, and even Fresno, joined the Filipinos to save the hotel (Wei 1993). The lead organization of the campaign was the Asian Community Center (ACC) established by Berkeley AAPA students. In addition, two student-tenant organizations were formed in this rather prolonged struggle: the International Hotel Tenants Association (IHTA) and the International Hotel Collective (Wei 1993; Kordziel 2001). Year after year, working with other organizations, they staged demonstrations and rallies one after another to block eviction attempts. Additionally, the students also cleaned and repaired the hotel to meet the city code and negotiated with the owners and the city (Wei 1993; Kordziel 2001). Meanwhile, the hotel was also used to house numerous other community-service programs and organizations, including the Kearny Street Workshop, Jackson Street Gallery, Chinese Progressive Association, Red Guards, I Wor Kuen (literally, "righteous and harmonious fists"), Chinatown Youth Council, Everybody's Bookstore, and Chinatown Draft Help/Asian Legal Services (Wei 1993; Yip 2000). The hotel thus became a hallmark of the Asian American resistance movement, and the campaign attracted tens of thousands of people from all nationalities in the Bay Area and earned support not only nationally but also internationally (Yip 2000). In addition to various Asian American groups, the broad coalition forces involved in the campaign also included affordable housing advocates, gay and lesbian activists, trade unions, women, and other progressive groups (Geron 2003).

However, all their efforts to save the hotel were in vain. On the night of August 4, 1977, hundreds of protestors formed a human chain to stop the police from carrying out the eviction order, but the hotel was finally emptied of its residents under the glare of international news coverage and later torn down after eight long years (Wei

1993; Yip 2000; Geron 2003). Nothing was built in its space right after the demolition. Following a quarter of a century of negotiations between the community and the city, a plan about how to use the land was finalized and construction on a new fifteen-story hotel began in January 2002, envisioned as a 105-unit affordable housing development for seniors (Delgado 2002).

Were the efforts of hundreds of activists in this campaign really in vain? Physically speaking, their struggle to save the hotel indeed failed. But, symbolically, as years progressed, the International Hotel became a "beacon and magnet" for many Asian Americans to fight the existing power (Yip 2000), as well as an example for many community struggles that followed on the West Coast—from Delano, Seattle, Stockton, Sacramento, San Jose, Los Angeles, to San Diego and other places (Geron 2003). In sum, historical forces in the late 1960s and 1970s had transformed the International Hotel from just an icon of Filipino legacy to a stronghold of the Asian American resistance movement as a whole, as well as a national symbol of urban struggle.

While the San Francisco State College strike and the International Hotel campaign manifested the Asian American struggle on college campuses and in ethnic communities during the Asian American movement, Asian American laborers, like their predecessors, also contributed to a chapter of the movement's history by their defiant activities in workplaces—activities that were both ethnicity and class based. However, the Asian American labor movement was not as noticeable as its counterparts on campuses and in communities, and its lack of signature events was one of the reasons for its lack of visibility.

Asian immigrants in the 1960s were primarily working-class people living in ethnic enclaves. They often held racially segregated jobs in the garment and food industries, as well as in the service sectors of restaurants, laundries, hotels, and maintenance companies (Wong 1994). Influenced by the New Left movement in the 1960s, some activists of the Asian American movement began to establish a number of Marxist-Leninist-Maoist organizations such as the Red Guard Party, Wei Min She (literally, "organization for the people"), I Wor Kuen, and the Asian Study Group. Naturally, from the study of Marxism many of them focused their resources on the well-being of working-class Asian Americans, becoming grassroots organizers in communities or working in factories to build a labor movement for Asian Americans (Wei 1993; Wong 1994). More specifically, they formed worker cooperatives, set up committees, mobilized support from the communities, and, most importantly, led labor protests (Wong 1994).

In the early 1970s, these labor organizers, including members of the Wei Min She and I Wor Kuen, involved themselves in the Lee Mah and Jung Sai strikes for unionization (Wei 1993; Wong 1994). Due to poor working conditions at the Lee Mah electronics and Jung Sai garment factories, efforts were made to unionize workers of both factories. The effort at Lee Mah was ill-fated; both the Teamsters and the owner rejected the workers' vote on unionization, and some workers were fired. In the case of the Jung Sai, 90 out of 135 workers were persuaded to sign pledge cards in order to hold an election on whether or not to join Local 101 of the International Ladies Garment Workers Union (ILGWU). However, one union advocate was fired, and this action led to a strike on July 15, 1974, to protest the firing and demand better working conditions and the right to unionization. The strike continued for half a year before the factory was finally closed. The workers did not give up but brought a suit to the National Labor Relations Board, which, nearly one decade later, ruled in favor of them (Wei 1993).

Also in 1974, Asian American cannery workers in Alaska took legal action to protest the racist policies of the Wards Cove Packing Company. These Asian American labor protests continued in the 1980s. One of the largest demonstrations of Asian American workers in history occurred in 1982 when 20,000 garment workers marched through the streets of New York's Chinatown in support of unionization (Wong 1994).

The Asian American labor movement gradually lost its momentum as the 1980s wore on. Externally, the decline reflected the cooling of social movements in general and the labor movement in particular in American society. Internally, the cause of this loss of momentum could be ascribed to the small number of devoted activists from those Marxist organizations and friction among themselves (Wong 1994). Even so, the movement passed a real milestone in the 1990s. After being opposed by the American labor movement for decades, in 1992 Asian American workers finally established the first Asian American labor organization within the AFL-CIO, the Asian Pacific American Labor Alliance (APALA) (Wong 1994).

Problems

Although the Asian American movement was a significant historical phenomenon that reshaped the old-fashioned Asian American protest politics by infusing it with new members, visions, agendas, and strategies, the movement was not as successful and socially visible as some other social movements, due to certain problems present from its very inception.

First, unlike other minority movements at the time, the Asian American movement had no nationally known leader, such as Dr. Martin Luther King Jr., Malcolm X, Rodolfo "Corky" Gonzales, or Russell Means, some of whom were renowned internationally as well as nationally. This was the key reason why the Asian American movement was largely ignored by the mainstream society and the literature on social movements (Wei 1993).

The second problem associated with the movement was the heterogeneity of the Asian American community, which contributed to mistrust and even friction among the various Asian ethnic groups and thus to the first problem—the lack of a nationally prominent leader. For instance, most Asian American studies programs offered courses only on Chinese and Japanese Americans, not on Korean and other Asian American groups. This ethnic inequality made those smaller groups feel marginalized and frustrated. Furthermore, Asian Americans were divergent not only in ethnicity but also in social class and place of birth. Therefore, there were also cleavages between middle-class and low-income and between native-born and foreign-born Asians. As a result, although there were community activists in the movement who had strong ties to the Asian American ethnic enclaves, many residents there, overwhelmed by the need to survive, were uninterested in the political agenda of the movement (Espiritu 1992; Wei 1993).

Third, the ideological component of the movement was rather weak. Some radical, leftist groups adhered to Marxism-Maoism, but they failed to reach the majority of the Asian American population (Wei 1993). Lastly, its very small size at the time, 878,000 in 1960 and 1,369,000 in 1970, or less than 1 percent of the U.S. population, made it very difficult to be a formidable force for change (Wei 1993).

Despite these problems, most of which were inborn natures of the Asian American community, the Asian American movement started in the late 1960s and blossomed in the 1970s. Did it continue to grow well into the 1980s, 1990s, and beyond, or did it just vanish after the decline of general social movements in the 1970s? It is debatable whether or not the movement has ended, and if so, when it ended. What we know at least is that there were abundant cases of Asian American protests after the heyday of the movement and that these protests were definitely a continuation, if not a part, of the movement.

Case Studies

In the 1980s and 1990s, Asian Americans continued to get involved in protest politics in relation to a large variety of issues, including college admission, appointment of political officials, images of Asian Americans in popular culture, labor issues, anti-Asian violence, redress and reparations for the internment of the Japanese, civil rights and legal justice, Korean American-African American relations, issues concerning their motherlands, and so on, which can be exemplified by the following cases.

In the mid-1980s, Asian Americans of divergent socioeconomic and ethnic backgrounds were united together in protest of possible quotas in college admissions that worked against Asian American students. These protest activities prompted investigations by federal and university authorities of possible anti-Asian bias at the University of California, Berkeley, and other campuses.

In 1987 Californians for Responsible Government, a coalition of Asian Americans, successfully blocked California Governor George Deukmejian's nomination of conservative Republican Congressman Daniel Lungren to be state treasurer. He was the only member of the Commission on Wartime Relocation and Internment of Civilians to oppose reparations to the Japanese internees. As a result of the coalition's efforts, the California state senate rejected the appointment by twenty-one to nineteen (Wei 1993; Hing 1993).

In the domain of popular culture, a 1988 broad coalition of Asian American organizations, including the Asian American Journalists Association, the Japanese American Citizens League, the Korean American Bar Association, and the Asian Pacific American Legal Center, protested an article published in the *Rolling Stone* magazine that was offensive to Koreans. The article described Koreans as all looking the same, having "the same tea-stain complexion" and "identical anthracite eyes." The protests later resulted in the magazine's editorial apology and the hiring of Asian American interns (Hing 2001).

Asian Americans organized two demonstrations in April 1991 in protest of *Miss Saigon,* a Broadway musical that was seen as filled with racist misperceptions of Asian men as asexual and contemptible and Asian women as submissive and self-effacing. About 500 protestors participated in the first one on April 6 against the use of *Miss Saigon* as a fund-raising event by the Lambda Legal Defense and Education Fund (LLDEF), a national legal organization in support of gay and lesbian rights. The second one, less attended than the first one, was staged on the opening night of the musical on April 11 (Yoshikawa 1994). Also troubled by negative images of Asians in the media and entertainment business, Asian Americans formed the Media Action Network for Asian Americans (MANAA) in Los Angeles in 1992. The MANAA and other Asian American organizations held demonstrations in Los Angeles, San Francisco, New York, Chicago, and Washington, D.C., in protest of the movie version of a novel, *Rising Sun,* in which Japanese men were portrayed negatively as cruel, corrupt, and lurid.

Even though the Asian American labor movement was in decline in the 1980s, Asian workers continued the tradition of labor protests into the 1990s, and many of their activities were against their own organizations or employers of their own race. For instance, restaurant workers, labor activists, and construction workers held their annual New Year's protest outside a restaurant in New York's Chinatown where the Chinese American Planning Council (CPC) had a New Year's banquet fund-raiser. The council, the largest Asian American social service organization in New York City, was accused of underpaying its workers, firing them illegally, and discriminating against senior workers (Cho 1994).

Another example involved Korean Americans in Los Angeles. Workers of Radio Korea, the largest Korean language radio station in the United States, went on strike for better wages and overtime pay. They also demanded union recognition. The strike lasted over four weeks, the longest in Koreatown history, and attracted the attention of Korean American communities across the country. In the end, even with much publicity, the strike failed to achieve any goals and was broken by some of the workers who cut side deals with the management and crossed the picket line (Wong 1994).

In New York, thirteen years after the historic 1982 march by 20,000 garment workers, several hundred garment workers, mostly Chinese Americans, marched in Brooklyn on June 18, 1995, representing the largest demonstration since 1982 (Lin 1998).

There were also cases of protests against anti-Asian violence. On April 29, 1997, Kuanchung Kao, an immigrant from Taiwan, was killed by a police officer in front of his house in Rohnert Park, California. The event outraged the Asian American community in the Bay Area. In August about 300 people, mainly Chinese Americans, held a rally in downtown San Francisco, demanding a more thorough investigation by the Justice Department and the U.S. Commission on Civil Rights (Eljera 1997).

In the sphere of civil rights, there were nationwide campaigns to defend the civil rights of Asian Americans victimized by the legal system, such as Chol Soo Lee, a Korean American imprisoned for a murder he did not commit, and Wen Ho Lee, a Taiwanese American scientist wrongly accused of being a Chinese spy in the late 1990s. The Chol Soo Lee case is particularly noteworthy for sparking a nationwide Asian American campaign in 1977 during which, for the first time in the history of Korean Americans, they formed a multi-ethnic coalition with other Asian American groups. As a result of the campaign's tremendous efforts, collecting more than 10,000 signatures on petitions and raising $175,000, Lee was granted a new trail and released in 1983 (Zia 2000).

Troubled relations with other minority groups were the cause of some Asian American protests. Due to tensions between Korean Americans and African Americans, two Korean American stores in Brooklyn, New York, were boycotted by the African American community starting in January 1990. In September, about 7,000 Korean Americans in New York representing all ages, genders, and occupational backgrounds, attended a mass rally against Mayor Dinkins for not taking action to bring the boycott to an end (Min 1995).

Lastly, Asian Americans also launched campaigns related to issues in their homelands. To name a few, in the early 1980s Korean Americans demonstrated over the Soviet Union's downing of Korean Air flight 007 and the Kwangju massacre, during which thousands of civilians were killed by the South Korean military government. Taiwanese Americans demonstrated against the Taiwanese authoritarian government for the murder of Henry Liu in California in 1984, and Chinese Americans protested against the Chinese communist government for the 1989 Tiananmen Square massacre. Although most of these protest activities were mainly targeted at foreign governments, some of them were also organized to pressure the U.S. government to take action against these foreign governments.

In addition to the cases mentioned above, there were three more cases of Asian American social movements and protests that truly deserve in-depth study because of their massive scope, duration, and historical significance. They were the campaign after the murder of Vincent Chin in 1982, the Redress movement in the 1970s and 1980s, and the campaign following the Los Angeles riots in 1992, involving Chinese, Japanese, and Korean Americans, respectively.

Campaign after the Murder of Vincent Chin

Vincent Jen Chin was murdered on June 19, 1982, in Detroit. A twenty-seven-year-old, second-generation Chinese American (or fifth-generation from his mother's side), Chin went to a local bar in Highland Park with three friends to celebrate his upcoming wedding. While in the bar, two Caucasian American males, Ronald Ebens, a foreman for a Chrysler plant, and his stepson, Michael Nitz, a laid-off worker, called Chin a "Jap" and cursed: "It's because of you mother-fuckers that we're out of work." A fistfight ensued, and then the man-ager expelled both groups from the bar. But the scuffle did not end there. Ebens and Nitz approached Chin and his friends with a base-ball bat taken from the trunk of their car. Chin and his companions fled the scene. Ebens and Nitz drove through the area with a neigh-borhood man whom they paid to hunt Chin and others. Half an hour later, they located Chin outside a crowded McDonald's restaurant. While Nitz held Chin's arms from behind, Ebens swung the bat into Chin's shins, knees, and chest. At least four blows struck him in the head, shattering his skull and causing his death. Two off-duty police-men witnessed the attack, arrested the two assailants at the scene, and called an ambulance for Chin, who had collapsed bleeding on the pavement. He died four days later. Instead of attending his wed-ding, 400 guests came to his funeral (Chan 1991; Espiritu 1992; Wei 1993; Takaki 1998, 481; Zia 2000).

Vincent was the only son of Lily and Hing Chin. Lily Chin was a fourth-generation Chinese American woman, and her husband was a Chinese immigrant, who had arrived in the United States in 1922 at the age of seventeen. During World War II, Hing Chin served in the U.S. Army. After the war, both spouses worked in a laundry. After her husband died of a kidney disease in 1980, Lily Chin found a job in an assembly plant. As for Vincent Chin, he graduated from Oak Park High School and later studied architecture at the Lawrence Institute of Technology. Before he was murdered, he worked as a draftsman for the Efficient Engineering Company (Takaki 1998).

Judging from the racial slurs used at the scene of the crime, the two killers mistook Chin for Japanese and blamed him for layoffs in the automobile industry. Apparently, the killing was a racially motivated "hate crime." After the district attorney's office of Wayne County charged them with second-degree murder (homicide with no pre-meditation), Ebens pleaded guilty to a lesser charge of manslaughter, and Nitz did not contest the charge of having beaten Chin to death. Although in Michigan a manslaughter conviction can carry a maxi-mum sentence of fifteen years in prison, in March 1983 County Cir-cuit Judge Charles Kaufman sentenced both defendants to three years' probation and a fine of $3,000 each, plus $780 in fees to be paid over three years. They did not spend a single night in jail for the crime they committed! Later, Judge Kaufman wrote a letter to a newspaper attempting to justify the sentences, saying that sentences should depend upon the criminal's background, not the crime. For him, there was no reason to impose harsh punishment, because the two killers had stable employment without previous criminal records. Even non–Asian Americans were enraged at the judge's explanation. Another judge in Michigan and one of the policemen who witnessed the crime both said that it should have been first-degree murder (Chan 1991; Espiritu 1992; Wei 1993).

Asian Americans, especially those of Chinese origin, in the Detroit area and throughout the country were infuriated by the sentences. This reminded them of the situation a century earlier when the Chinese were not allowed to testify in court and thus received no protection under the law, reflected in the infamous expression, "not a Chinaman's chance" (Wei 1993). Even in a state of shock, the Asian American community in the Detroit area did not take any immediate action right after the murder, perhaps because they were few in number and unorganized, and—most importantly—they had trust in the U.S. judicial system. The light sentences left them in a state of greater shock and disbelief. This time they did not wait long to react. At first, the murder case was handled by the traditional Chinese American community. After the court's ruling, Lily Chin, the mother of the victim, turned to two traditional Chinese American organizations, the On Leong Association and the Chinese Welfare Council, for help. Soon after that, a meeting of about thirty was held. The attendees were all Chinese Americans, except one Japanese American attorney, the only attorney in town with an Asian background. Because the murder case underscored the need for all Asian Americans to unite across ethnic lines to fight against anti-Asian violence, the initial Chinese American campaign soon became a pan–Asian American endeavor. One week after the first meeting, a second one was attended by more than eighty people, including Japanese, Korean, and Filipino Americans. By the end of the meeting, they had formed the American Citizens for Justice (ACJ) to make sure that justice would be done (Espiritu 1992; Zia 2000).

Initially, the ACJ's protest focused on the lenient sentences only. But, the more they learned about what happened the night of the murder, the more they were convinced that the crime was racially motivated. The ACJ asked the Michigan Court of Appeals to order a retrial and requested that the Department of Justice step in to investigate a possible violation of Chin's civil rights (Chan 1991). To make their voices heard loud and clear, the ACJ organizers employed various methods, including mass rallies, demonstrations, a nationwide letter-writing campaign, appeals to politicians, and a tour to the West Coast by Lily Chin.

In May 1983 the ACJ organized a mass rally in downtown Detroit to protest the lenient sentences given in March. Other Asian American groups joined Chinese Americans in the event and leaders of the Japanese, Korean, and Filipino American communities were invited to speak. With participation by 500 to 1,000 persons, it was the largest rally ever staged by Asian Americans in the history of Detroit. This was Detroit—not New York, San Francisco, or Los Angeles. Given Detroit's rather small Chinese American population (1,213 in 1980) and Asian American population (7,614 in 1980), the magnitude of this rally was historically monumental. Coupled with the national letter-writing campaign and other efforts, the rally proved to be monumentally effective later on (Espiritu 1992).

In support of the struggles in Detroit, Asian Americans across the country sent tens of thousands of letters to government officials and the press. The Department of Justice alone received more than 15,000 letters, a record number in the contemporary history of the department. Monetary assistance to the ACJ was equally impressive. From March 1983 to December 1984, the ACJ received nearly $83,000 from many organizations and businesses around the nation, mainly from California, New York, and people within the state of Michigan. The amount of the donations might not be too impressive, but the widespread support across the nation truly was. The money poured in from Minnesota to Louisiana, from Canada to Florida, and from states in America's heartland (Espiritu 1992).

In addition, the ACJ and other Asian American organizations also launched a campaign to mobilize supporters to pressure local politicians. For example, in response to the ACJ's request, Norman Mineta, a Japanese American congressman from San Jose at the time and secretary of transportation in the George W. Bush administration, and other California congresspersons wrote a letter to urge the U.S. attorney general to take action on the murder, as well as to look into the way it was handled by the Wayne County officials. Mineta declared, "When the word 'Jap' gets painted on a door or a man is murdered, we ought to let the whole world know" (Takaki 1998, 484). In Los Angeles, under constituency pressure, the city council petitioned the Department of Justice to investigate the case. In July 1983 Lily Chin and some members of the ACJ toured the West Coast. They directly appealed to thousands of people in Los Angeles, San Diego, San Francisco, Oakland, San Jose, and Sacramento about the case and its implication to Asian Americans. Many existing Asian American organizations on the West Coast, such as the Asian Pacific Student Union (APSU), the Chinese for Affirmative Action, the Japanese American Citizens League, and the Organization of Chinese Americans protested the lenient sentences and addressed the problem of anti-Asian violence to the public. Lily Chin also visited Denver and Chicago later that year and addressed the founding meeting of the Democratic Party's Asian Pacific American Caucus (Espiritu 1992; Umemoto 2000).

Under tremendous pressure, the Department of Justice asked the FBI to investigate the case. As a result of the investigation, a federal grand jury was convened in September 1983. In November the grand jury indicted Ebens and Nitz on two counts of civil rights violations. In June 1984 they were tried in a U.S. district court. The jury convicted Ebens of violating Chin's civil rights but acquitted him of conspiracy, and acquitted Nitz of both charges. Ebens was sentenced to twenty-five years in prison and told to receive treatment for alcoholism, but was freed after posting $20,000 bond. Ebens's attorney appealed the civil rights conviction, and it was overturned in September 1986 by a federal appeals court on the technicality that one of the ACJ attorneys "improperly coached" several of the prosecution's witnesses. Receiving enormous numbers of letters requesting a retrial, the Department of Justice decided to retry Ebens. This time the trial was held in Cincinnati, because the Justice Department believed that the publicity of the case in Detroit made a fair trial in that venue impossible. Nearly five years after the murder, the Cincinnati jury acquitted Ebens of federal civil rights charges in May 1987. In the end, neither Ebens nor Nitz spent any time in prison for the crime they committed. Lily Chin was so outraged by the final outcome that she left the United States for China (Chan 1991; Espiritu 1992).

Redress Movement

The incarceration of the Japanese along the Pacific Coast began after the Japanese empire attacked Pearl Harbor in Hawaii on December 7, 1941. The U.S. War Department drafted an executive order that granted the army complete power to remove any individuals of Japanese ancestry, aliens and citizens alike, from the Pacific Coast. President Roosevelt signed it immediately after it was presented to him as the infamous Executive Order 9066 on February 19, 1942.

According to the order, the western halves of Washington, Oregon, California, and the southern half of Arizona were designated "military areas" beginning in March, and soon after that more than 40,000 first-generation Japanese (*Issei*) along with their 70,000 American-born children (*Nisei*) were removed from their homes in these areas and incarcerated in as many as ten "relocation camps" built on federal land in deserted places in California, Idaho, Wyoming, Utah, Arizona, Colorado, and as far east as Arkansas. Inside the camps, the detainees lived in barracks behind barbed wire under gun towers and armed guards. They were detained without trials. The whole process of internment was completed in November that year (Chan 1991; Wu 2002). The federal government revoked the mass exclusion orders two years later in December 1944, but there were still 44,000 internees in the camps when the war ended on August 14, 1945. These uprooted people had no place to go and were afraid to return to the outside world. By December 1, 1945, every camp but Tule Lake was closed, and this California camp still held 12,545 detainees. By March 1, 1946, it still had 2,806. Finally the last one was evicted that month (Chan 1991; Daniels 1993).

It is difficult to trace precisely the beginning of the Redress movement. Right after the incarceration in 1942, a handful of the Japanese protested with verbal defiance or civil disobedience. During the period of internment, there were protests involving thousands of internees over various issues within camps in Arizona, California, and Utah. Even though their struggles were not directly aimed at the injustice of the incarceration, they were defiant actions against injustice inside the camps. Ever since the camps were closed, there have been efforts to redress the wrongdoing of the government. In 1948 the Japanese American Citizens League (JACL), a national organization composed of mainly second-generation Japanese Americans, lobbied for the passage of the Evacuation Claims Act. The act was passed, but it provided only minimal compensation to the victims for property loss, on average only $340 for each claim (Wei 1993). The more organized efforts to redress the wrongs done to them did not emerge until the late 1960s, when small groups of Japanese Americans in Southern California, San Francisco, and Seattle began to discuss the issues of reparation and redress. It was no coincidence that the Asian American movement was born at the same time.

The JACL was the lead organization, or the locomotive, of the Redress movement. In 1970 the first of a series of resolutions calling for redress was introduced at the JACL biennial convention in Chicago. It was introduced repeatedly at every convention in the

1970s. In 1974 at the Portland convention, a National Committee for Redress was formed. In 1976 President Ford apologized to all Japanese internees and terminated Executive Order 9066 on February 19, 1976. But little progress was made by the JACL until 1978. In April 1978 the National Committee for Redress, under the leadership of Clifford Uyeda, met in San Francisco and recommended the adoption of a $25,000 compensation payment per victim and the creation of a Japanese American foundation for the benefits of the Japanese American community. The following summer the guidelines were adopted at the JACL convention held in Salt Lake City. After some members of the JACL met with four Japanese American members of Congress (Hawaii Senators Daniel Inouye and Spark Matsunaga and California Congressmen Norman Mineta and Robert Matsui) in January 1979, the National Committee for Redress met in San Francisco in early March to hammer out strategies to pursue redress. The committee voted in favor of legislation over a lawsuit, as well as in favor of legislation for the creation of a federal commission over legislation directly for compensation (Tateishi 1991).

While the Japanese American community elites worked with Japanese American members of Congress as the "insiders," mass community support for redress continued throughout the 1970s. For instance, the first "Day of Remembrance" was held on Thanksgiving weekend in 1978, just a few months after the historic JACL convention, in the state of Washington. Thousands of Japanese Americans attended the event, commemorating the camp experiences. It was followed by many more Days of Remembrance in subsequent years in many other places (Kitano and Maki 2003). As a result of these efforts for redress inside and outside Washington, D.C., a bill was passed by Congress to create a federal commission to investigate the whole issue of internment. In July 1980 President Carter signed Public Law 96–317 to form the Commission on Wartime Relocation and Internment of Civilians (CWRIC). After hearing testimony from more than 750 witnesses and after 18 months of research and investigation, the commission issued its report, *Personal Justice Denied,* to the government in February 1983. In the report the commission concluded that the detention of the 110,000 people of Japanese ancestry was "a grave injustice" because it was not justified by military conditions but was the result of "race prejudice, war hysteria and a failure of political leadership." In its final report, the commission made a five-point recommendation, including a proposal that each surviving victim be compensated $20,000 as redress for the injustice (Tateishi 1991; Chan 1991).

In spite of the commission's unequivocal conclusions and the promptness of the introduction of relevant legislation to Congress in 1983, the bill was not passed until 1987 by the House and 1988 by the Senate to ask the government to issue an official apology to Japanese Americans and to compensate each surviving detainee with $20,000. In August 1988 President Reagan signed the bill into the Civil Liberties Act, authorizing $1.25 billion to compensate about 70,000 survivors of the camps. Central to the final approval was the contribution of the Japanese American members of Congress who carefully prepared each step (Chan 1991; Wei 1993). However, the whole story of the redress did not end there in 1988. The appropriation of the redress payment was delayed in Congress. Finally in November 1989 President Bush signed the appropriations bill and the government began to make redress payments in October 1990, 48 years after the incarceration (Chan 1991; Daniels 1991).

Korean Campaigns following the Los Angeles Riots

On April 29, 1992, twelve Simi Valley jurors, including ten Caucasian Americans, one Latino American, and one Asian American, acquitted all four Caucasian American officers of the Los Angeles Police Department charged with beating African American motorist Rodney King after a traffic stop. The beating was videotaped and shown repeatedly on news programs around the country. The jury's decision triggered demonstrations, violence, arson, and looting in San Francisco, Las Vegas, Seattle, Atlanta, and many other cities in the United States. The worst violence happened in Los Angeles, where, before the governor ordered 6,000 National Guard troops to restore order, riots engulfed a 60-square-mile area, including South Central Los Angeles and Koreatown for three days, resulting in 58 deaths, 2,400 injuries, and 12,000 arrests. More than 3,000 businesses were damaged or destroyed and property damage totaled $800 million. Korean Americans owned most of these businesses and Koreatown was virtually dismantled (Takaki 1998; Abelmann and Lie 1997; Park 2001).

The Los Angeles riots served as a wake-up call to many Korean Americans who had long been politically apathetic. Just like the year of 1942 for the Japanese, exactly half a century later, the year of 1992 was a defining moment for Korean Americans. Immediately after the riots, many young Korean Americans promptly organized to help the victims. They also staged a series of protests against media bias against Korean Americans and the police department's failure to protect Koreatown.

On May 2, 1992, the day after the riots ended, about 30,000 Korean Americans participated in a solidarity and peace rally at Ardmore Park in Koreatown—the largest gathering of Korean Americans ever in the United States—in protest of the police department's inability to protect them during the riots. In addition to sending letters of protest to the media, on May 3, about 1,000 Korean students rallied at the ABC network's television station to protest its biased coverage that had insinuated that tensions between Korean Americans and African Americans were at the center of the whole event (Min 1995). On May 11, 30,000 Korean Americans marched along the streets in the heart of Koreatown, demonstrating their grief over the death of Edward Lee, an 18-year-old shot in crossfire on April 30. At the end of the march, the protestors gathered at Ardmore Park, where they criticized political officials and the police department for their failures. During the rally, people carried placards such as "Justice for All People of Color" and "More Jobs for the Inner City" displaying a sense of common victimization of Korean Americans together with other minority groups by institutional racism in the society (Park 1994; Park 2001).

From June 17 to July 2, 1992, in actions organized by the Association of Korean American Victims of the Riots, more than 250 Korean American riot victims, mostly first-generation immigrants, marched in front of the city hall, protesting the delays in the approval of aid to rebuild their businesses. The strategy of continuous protest proved to be successful. As a result, they were finally able to meet Mayor Bradley, Councilman Holden, and the city council. Both officials promised to deal with cases of disaster relief applications that had been rejected. The city council also responded positively by establishing an ad hoc Committee on Recovery and Revitalization (Park 1994).

Conclusion

Ever since their first arrival in the middle of the nineteenth century, East Asian Americans, particularly Chinese and Japanese Americans, have been active in protest politics to address their social and economic concerns. Like other minority groups in the United States, East Asian Americans did not have other choices in many cases but to resort to using mass protest as their primary way of political participation. However, their early protest activities were neither very visible nor effective in the American political arena until the birth of the Asian American movement in the late 1960s, which was such a watershed that thoroughly renewed the then century-old Asian protest politics in American society with new members, visions, agendas, and strategies and most importantly, created pan-Asian solidarity for the first time. Influenced by the Asian American movement, East Asian Americans continued their struggles well into the 1980s and 1990s, many of which, especially the campaign after the murder of Vincent Chin in 1982, the Redress movement in the 1970s and 1980s, and the post–Los Angeles riots Korean American campaign in 1992, had profound impacts on East Asian American communities and redefined their relations to the mainstream society as well as other minority groups.

All three struggles had their share of historical significance. While the Asian American movement in the late 1960s and 1970s enlivened the old-fashioned, fragmented Asian protest politics in American society, the pan-Asian campaign to seek justice for Vincent Chin in turn redefined the weakening Asian American movement in the 1990s by providing new opportunities to reunite Asian Americans with different ethnic, class, gender, generational, and ideological backgrounds. The Redress movement was truly a defining moment for Japanese Americans who, especially second- and third-generation Japanese Americans, finally stood up to confront the bitterness of the racism they suffered during World War II. Similarly, the Los Angeles riot was such a turning point in the history of Korean Americans who, especially 1.5-generation (those who immigrated to the United States at a young age and were raised and received an education in the States) and second-generation Korean Americans, became politicized for the first time and participated in many post-riot campaigns, unfolding a new chapter in their political participation. In sum, all three tragedies redefined being Asian American in American society and energized political activism among Asian Americans, especially those of younger generations.

Despite the historical significance and far-reaching impact of these protest movements on East Asian Americans themselves, their ultimate effect was a mix of successes and failures. First, it is evident that due to a variety of political, social, economic, and demographic factors, the early protest activities of the Chinese and Japanese seldom produced any victories, especially in the sphere of labor justice. The Asian American movement in the late 1960s and 1970s had its moments of sweet success and bitter failure, largely depending upon whether or not the struggles were in collaboration with other minority groups. The movement's two signature events, the San Francisco State College strike and the International Hotel campaign, are cases in point: while the former, as a collective effort of several minority groups, victoriously gained the establishment of ethnic studies programs, the latter, primarily an Asian American-based struggle, failed completely.

As for the three more recent cases in the 1980s and 1990s, there were also successes and failures. Whether it was the Asian Citizens for Justice mass rally in May 1983 in Detroit, or the Day of Remembrance in November 1978 in the state of Washington, or the mass rallies in May 1992 in Koreatown, all protests had their share of impacts at the moment, but some of them were more influential than others. Among them, it is clear that the Redress movement was the most successful. However, ironically, it was not their protest activities per se that brought victories to the Japanese American victims of internment at the end, but their lobbying and "insider" politics that brought final success to the Redress movement.

Regardless of how significant the impacts of these movements and protests were on policy issues, the many East Asian American organizations that were established prior to and as a result of the Asian American movement have provided East Asian Americans another important way to participate in mainstream American politics to address their concerns.

References

Abelmann, Nancy, and John Lie. 1997. *Blue Dreams: Korean Americans and the Los Angeles Riots.* Cambridge, MA: Harvard University.

Chan, Sucheng. 1991. *Asian American: An Interpretive History.* New York: Twayne.

Cho, Milyoung. 1994. "Overcoming Our Legacy as Cheap Labor, Scabs, and Model Minorities: Asian Activists Fight for Community Empowerment." In *The State of Asian America: Activism and Resistance in the 1990s.* Edited by Karin Aguilar-San Juan. Boston: South End.

Daniels, Roger. 1991. "Redress Achieved, 1983–1990." In *Japanese Americans: From Relocation to Redress.* Rev. ed. Edited by Roger Daniels, Sandra C. Taylor, and Harry H. L. Kitano. Seattle: University of Washington.

———. 1993. *Prisoners without Trials: Japanese Americans in World War II.* New York: Hill and Wang.

Delgado, Ray. 2002. "Rising from Rubble." *San Francisco Chronicle* (July 24).

Eljera, Bert. 1997. "S. F. Rally Spotlights Kao Killing." *Asian Week* (August 22): 12–13. Included in *Asian Americans: Experiences and Perspectives.* Edited by

Timothy P. Fong and Larry H. Shinagawa. Upper Saddle River, NJ: Prentice Hall, 2000.

Espiritu, Yen Le. 1992. *Asian American Panethnicity: Bridging Institutions and Identities.* Philadelphia: Temple University.

Fong, Timothy P. 2002. *The Contemporary Asian American Experience: Beyond the Model Minority.* 2d ed. Upper Saddle River, NJ: Prentice Hall.

Franks, Joel. 1993. "Chinese Shoemaker Protest in 19th Century San Francisco." In *Asian Americans in the United States.* Volume 1. Edited by Alexander Yamato, Soo-Young Chin, Wendy L. Ng, and Joel Franks. Dubuque, IA: Kendall/Hund.

Geron, Kim. 2003. "Serve the People: An Exploration of the Asian American Movement." In *Asian American Politics: Law, Participation, and Policy.* Edited by Don T. Nakanishi and James S. Lai. Lanham, MD: Rowman and Littlefield.

Hing, Bill Ong. 1993. *Making and Remaking Asian America through Immigration Policy, 1850–1990.* Stanford, CA: Stanford University.

———. 2001. "Still Not Laughing." *Asian Week* (April 20).

Hohri, William. 1991. "Redress as a Movement towards Enfranchisement." In *Japanese Americans: From Relocation to Redress.* Rev. ed. Edited by Roger Daniels, Sandra C. Taylor, and Harry H. L. Kitano. Seattle: University of Washington.

Kitano, Harry H. L., and Mitchell T. Maki. 2003. "Japanese American Redress: The Proper Alignment Model." In *Asian American Politics: Law, Participation, and Policy.* Edited by Don T. Nakanishi and James S. Lai. Lanham, MD: Rowman and Littlefield.

Kordziel, Beverly. 2001. "To Be a Part of the People: The International Hotel Collective." In *Asian Americans: The Movement and the Moment.* Edited by Steve Louie and Glenn K. Omatsu. Los Angeles: UCLA Asian American Studies Center.

Lien, Pei-te. 2001b. *The Making of Asian America through Political Participation.* Philadelphia, PA: Temple University.

Lin, Jan. 1998. *Reconstructing Chinatown: Ethnic Enclave, Global Change.* Minneapolis: University of Minnesota.

Min, Pyong Gap. 1995. "Major Issues Relating to Asian American Experiences." In *Asian Americans: Contemporary Trends and Issues.* Edited by Pyong Gap Min. Thousand Oaks, CA: Sage.

Nakanishi, Don. T. 1985–1986. "Asian American Politics: An Agenda for Research." *Amerasia Journal* 12 (2): 1–27. Included in *Asian American Interethnic Relations and Politics.* Edited by Franklin Ng. New York: Garland, 1998.

Ng, Franklin. 1998. *The Taiwanese Americans.* Westport, CT: Greenwood.

O'Brien, David J., and Stephen S. Fugita. 1991. *The Japanese American Experience.* Bloomington: Indiana University.

Okihiro, Gary Y. 1994. *Margins and Mainstreams: Asians in American History and Culture.* Seattle: University of Washington.

Omatsu, Glenn. 1994. "The 'Four Prisons' and the Movements of Liberation: Asian American Activism from the 1960s to the 1990s." In *The State of Asian America: Activism and Resistance in the 1990s.* Edited by Karin Aguilar-San Juan. Boston: South End.

Park, Edward J. W. 2001. "The Impact of Mainstream Political Mobilization on Asian American Community: The Case of Korean Americans in Los Angeles, 1992–1998." In *Asian Americans and Politics: Perspectives, Experiences, Prospects.* Edited by Gordon H. Chang. Washington, DC: Woodrow Wilson and Stanford, CA: Stanford University.

Park, Winnie. 1994. "Political Mobilization of the Korean American Community." In *Community in Crisis: The Korean American Community after the Los Angeles Civil Unrest of April 1992.* Edited by George O. Totten III, and H. Eric Schockman. Los Angeles: University of Southern California, Center for Multiethnic and Transnational Studies.

Takaki, Ronald. 1998. *Strangers from a Different Shore: A History of Asian Americans.* Updated and rev. ed. Boston: Back Bay.

Tateishi, John. 1991. "The Japanese American Citizens League and the Struggle for Redress." In *Japanese Americans: From Relocation to Redress.* Rev. ed. Edited by Roger Daniels, Sandra C. Taylor, and Harry H. L. Kitano. Seattle: University of Washington.

Turnbull, Spence K. 2003. "Wen Ho Lee and the Consequences of Enduring Asian American Stereotypes." In *Asian American Politics: Law, Participation, and Policy.* Edited by Don T. Nakanishi and James S. Lai. Lanham, MD: Rowman and Littlefield.

Umemoto, Karen. 1989. "'On Strike!' San Francisco State College Strike 1968–1969: The Role of Asian American Students." *Amerasia Journal* 15 (1): 3–41. Included in *Contemporary Asian America: American Multidisciplinary Reader.* Edited by Min Zhou and James V. Gatewood. New York: New York University, 2000.

———. 2000. "From Vincent Chin to Joseph Ileto: Asian Pacific Americans and Hate Crime Policy." In *The State of Asian Pacific America: Transforming Race Relations, A Public Policy Report.* Volume IV. Edited by Paul M. Ong. Los Angeles: LEAP Asian Pacific American Public Policy Institute and UCLA Asian American Studies Center.

Wang, Zuoyue. 2002. "Chinese American Scientists and U.S.-China Scientific Relations: From Richard Nixon to Wen Ho Lee." In *The Expanding Roles of Chinese Americans in U.S.-China Relations: Transnational Networks and Trans-Pacific Interactions.* Edited by Peter H. Koehn and Xiao-huang Yin. Armonk, NY: M. E. Sharpe.

Wei, William. 1993. *The Asian American Movement.* Philadelphia: Temple University.

Wong, Kent. 1994. "Building an Asian Pacific Labor Alliance: A New Chapter in Our History." In *The State of Asian America: Activism and Resistance in the 1990s.* Edited by Karin Aguilar-San Juan. Boston: South End.

Wu, Frank H. 2002. *Yellow: Race in America beyond Black and White.* New York: Basic.

Yip, Steve. 2000. "Serve the People—Yesterday and Today: The Legacy of Wei Min She." In *Legacy to Liberation: Politics and Culture of Revolutionary Asian Pacific America.* Edited by Fred Ho. Brooklyn, NY: Big Red Media, and San Francisco: AK.

Yoshikawa, Yoko. 1994. "The Heat Is on *Miss Saigon* Coalition: Organizing across Race and Sexuality." In *The State of Asian America: Activism and Resistance in the 1990s.* Edited by Karin Aguilar-San Juan. Boston: South End.

Zia, Helen. 2000. *Asian American Dreams: The Emergence of an American People.* New York: Farrar, Straus and Giroux.

3

Participation in Ethnic Interest Groups

n addition to participating in various forms of mass protest, including boycotts, strikes, marches, and demonstrations, East Asian Americans have been involved in interest-group politics as well to fight for racial equality and social justice in American society. While Chapter 2 reviewed the long history of Asian American protest politics and social movements, this chapter is devoted to investigating the organizational bases of East Asian American politics and how these bases are employed to pursue the common interests of the East Asian American community.

Known as a nation of joiners, Americans have taken interest-group politics for granted as one of the most typical characteristics of American political life. The number of interest groups in the American political system has been constantly on the rise over the past five decades. For instance, 22,000 groups were listed in the 2004 edition of the *Encyclopedia of Associations,* up about 50 percent since 1980 and 400 percent since 1955 (Hunt 2004; Edwards, et al. 1999). Following this long-standing tradition of American politics and its recent trend of explosive growth, Asian Americans have also organized hundreds of interest groups of their own to play the game of American pluralist democracy.

An interest group can be defined as an "aggregate of individuals who interact in varying degrees in pursuance of a common interest" (Bill and Hardgrave 1981, 121). A political interest group, therefore, is an interest group that pursues its shared interest as policy goals in the political process. Depending on the type of interest being pursued, American interest groups can be roughly classified as economic interest groups (including labor, business, agricultural, and consumer groups), environmental interest groups, and equality interest groups (Edwards, et al. 1999). Even though some East Asian American interest groups fall into the first two categories, the majority of them belong to the category of equality interest groups. Like other minority rights groups that see ethnic equality as their main policy goal, these East Asian American groups are referred to in this chapter as ethnic interest groups.

Mainstream American interest groups generally have used four strategies to achieve their policy goals: lobbying, litigation, electioneering, and going public (Edwards, et al. 1999). Asian American interest groups are no exception. However, if the conventional strategies of lobbying legislatures and executives and filing lawsuits in the judicial system fail to work, Asian American interest groups, like many other equality interest groups, are also willing to take more radical and confrontational approaches, which was the main focus of the preceding chapter. This chapter focuses on East Asian Americans' involvement in lobbying, litigation, and public education through issue advocacy. East Asian American activities in the realm of electioneering, including promoting voter registration, mobilizing voters to support candidates and referendum issues, and raising campaign funds and making campaign contributions are examined in Chapter 4.

History of Early Ethnic Interest Groups

Similar to their history of mass protests, East Asians began forming associations to achieve collective goals at the very beginning of their stay in the United States in the mid-nineteenth century. In the next hundred years or so, Chinese, Japanese, and Koreans established organizations mainly within their respective ethnic enclaves aimed at fighting for inclusion and against injustice for their own members. Although organizations of this sort were rare in their countries of origin, East Asians' group-oriented cultures provided them with ideas and principles for organizing overseas. Confronted by mounting hostility in the New World, East Asian community organizations developed rapidly from weak regional and family-based associations to umbrella mutual aid organizations and finally to more powerful and organized political interest groups, especially in the case of the Chinese and the Japanese.

However, there was little interethnic communication among the three groups and thus no agenda for pursuing the collective interests of Asians as a whole. Political organizations of a truly pan-Asian nature were not created until the birth of the Asian American movement in the late 1960s when a pan-Asian ethnic identity first took shape, and as a part of the larger civil rights movement these organizations engaged in struggles for racial equality and social justice in the following decades.

Chinese

Among the three ethnic groups, the Chinese established the largest array of ethnic organizations in terms of number, size, and variety. Soon after their arrival, Chinese immigrants founded various community organizations in the New World, which were largely mutual aid associations created to benefit their members in various ways. The most important of these in American Chinatowns were associations made up of people from the same regions in China —called *huiguan* ("meeting place") in Chinese. As early as 1851 in San Francisco, the first two regional associations, the *Sanyi* (*Sam Yup* in Cantonese) *Huiguan,* including people from three Cantonese districts and the *Siyi* (*Sze Yup*) *Huiguan,* made up of people from four districts, were established. These were groups of people who formed very strong "we-group" identifications through shared dialects.

Next to these regional associations in terms of social significance were numerous family or clan associations composed of people who shared the same surnames and presumably the same ancestors. Clans with popular surnames formed their own family associations exclusively for family members, while those with less popular surnames came together to create coalition associations. For regional associations or family associations alike, the bottom-line organizing principle was to create an organization sizable enough to be powerful either by combining people from several districts in a region back home or, if necessary, by joining people with different surnames.

The kinds of mutual aid provided by these regional and family associations included securing housing and employment for members and offering resources and moral support for important social and religious rites (e.g., funerals, festivals, marriages, and births, etc.). Another significant type of mutual aid organization in Chinatowns was the rotating credit association in which funds were pooled together from members and the total sum was given to just one member each month on a rotating basis until every member received the money. This kind of association was financially so important that it helped new arrivals start businesses (Chan 1991).

All the community organizations discussed above can be loosely categorized as "interest groups," but they were hardly "political interest groups" in a modern-day sense because their collective interests were not transformed into any sort of policy goals in the American political process.

In addition to associations based on geographical or family origins, there were other associations existent among Chinese immigrants, such as fraternal organizations (*tang* in Chinese or "triad," a term used by Western scholars) requiring sworn brotherhood, and guilds for protecting economic interests. Both types of organization were far from being political interest groups by today's standards.

As more and more associations came into existence, the Chinese community became more hierarchical. In 1862, six existing *huiguan,* Sze Yup, Ning Yeung, Sam Yup, Yeong Wo, Hop Wo, and Yan Wo, in San Francisco formed a loose federation of representatives from each *huiguan*. It was called a *gongsuo* ("public hall") by the Chinese and popularly known as the "Six Chinese Companies" in the outside world.

As the largest Chinese organization at the time, the Six Chinese Companies represented a social as well as a political interest group. While it helped settle interregional conflicts and provided social services in the areas of education (including a Chinese language school) and health, it also challenged anti-Chinese laws and fought against harassment and violence toward Chinese. In addition to litigation, the main strategy the Six Chinese Companies used was to lobby people who occupied key positions. For instance, with the help of a Protestant missionary, the companies hired a lawyer-lobbyist to represent the Chinese in Sacramento on an ongoing basis (Lien 2001b). During the 1868 negotiations between the United States and China with regard to the Burlingame-Seward Treaty, the companies lobbied for legal provisions to protect Chinese immigrants by contacting an adviser to the treaty negotiators about the need for federal legislation to protect Chinese lives and property in the United States. The outcome of the negotiations marked a major political victory for the companies in that the completed treaty recognized the "free migration and emigration" of Chinese to the United States and the rights of Chinese to "enjoy the same privileges, immunities, and exemptions in respect to travel or residence, as may there be enjoyed as the citizens or subjects of the most favored nation" (Takaki 1998, 114).

In 1876 the Six Chinese Companies sent a letter to President Ulysses Grant citing contributions made by Chinese immigrants to the United States, and a representative from the companies gave an address to Congress in the same year about the hardship experienced by Chinese laborers. In the next year, the companies sent a letter to the mayor of San Francisco denouncing mob violence against the Chinese, and at the federal level, the companies published a pamphlet, *Memorial of the Chinese Six Companies to the Congress of the United States,* and made possible the publication of books written by mainstream authors who were friends of the Chinese community (Takaki 1998; Lien 2001b).

Twenty years after the establishment of the Six Chinese Companies, Chinese leaders organized themselves into another umbrella organization that came closer to the present-day model of political interest groups. As the Chinese Exclusion Act became effective in 1882, at the request of the Chinese consul general in San Francisco, Chinese leaders, mostly merchants, founded a more formal Chinese Consolidated Benevolent Association (CCBA), or *Zhonghua Huiguan,* in order to deal with the prevailing hostility in the larger society. It was an all-male hierarchy encompassing many fraternal, regional, family, business, and charitable organizations. This new organization was known as the "Chinese Six Companies," slightly different from the old nickname of its predecessor, in the outside world. Other than being a powerful organ for self-governance in the ethnic enclave, its main task at the time was to fight against anti-Chinese legislation through litigation. To achieve this goal, it hired a large number of Caucasian American lawyers in the next half-century to represent its members in courts (Chan 1991; Wei 1993).

Other CCBAs emerged very rapidly in other places, including New York in 1883, Honolulu and Vancouver in 1884, Lima, Peru, in 1885, Portland, Oregon, around 1886, and Seattle a few years later (Chan 1991). Thus the CCBA had grown from a regional association into a national and even an international network of many regional subsidiaries, advocating the interests of Chinese immigrants as a whole. Until recently, CCBAs elsewhere looked to the original one in San Francisco for leadership in dealing with all issues of the Chinese American community (Chan 1991).

When the Chinese Exclusion Act expired in 1892, it was replaced with an even stricter one, the Geary Act. Under the new law, all Chinese in the United States were required to register or be subject to immediate deportation. In response to rising hostility in the larger society, the Chinese under the CCBA's auspices took more defiant actions by exercising noncompliance throughout the United States and challenging the constitutionality of the new act in court. About $60,000 was raised for this legal purpose. After three Chinese, Fong Yue Ting, Wong Quan, and Lee Joe (selected in advance by the CCBA) were arrested, the U.S. Supreme Court took the case almost immediately. In *Fong Yue Ting v. United States* (1893), the Supreme Court held that the U.S. government had the right to exclude aliens from its territory and foreign-born Chinese were neither recognized nor eligible to be naturalized as citizens of the United States. Due to this legal setback, the CCBA's handling of the post-Geary Act crisis was viewed as ineffective by many native-born Chinese (Chan 1991; Lien 2001b).

The CCBA also led the Chinese community to fight against segregation of their children from the Caucasian Americans. After a claim filed by a Chinese parent in San Francisco for equal protection for his daughter was denied by a federal court in 1902, in addition to issuing thousands of protesting letters against the city's policy, the CCBA hired a former Baptist missionary to lobby the legislature for changing the unjust practice (Lien 2001b).

The CCBA was born as a response to the passage of the Chinese Exclusion Act in 1882; it was also instrumental in the demise of the act about sixty years later. After China became America's ally during World War II, the U.S. Congress began considering a bill to repeal the law, which was supported by the Chinese throughout the nation who lobbied intensively for the cause. The CCBA of New York lobbied Congress, referring to the Chinese Exclusion Act as a serious violation of the fundamental principles of equality and an obstacle to improving the relationship between the two nations (Takaki, 1998).

Ever since its founding, the CCBA, as the dominant organizational force, has been involved in many activities in American Chinatowns and made profound impacts on those communities. Moreover, it is noteworthy that due to its strong ties to Chinese consuls representing the Republic of China on the mainland before the 1949 communist revolution and on Taiwan after that (Chan 1991), the CCBA has been involved—sometimes very deeply—in affairs affecting China, other than those domestic issues concerning Chinese Americans. One of the most notable cases was that after 1949 the CCBA sided with Taiwan's nationalist government to support the campaign to overthrow the communist government on the mainland. One year later, when the Chinese communists' intervention in the Korean War triggered anti-Chinese sentiments in the United States, fearful that what happened to the Japanese during World War II could happen to them, Chinese Americans, led by the CCBA and other organizations, declared their loyalty to the United States and intensified anticommunist campaigns among Chinese American communities across the country (Takaki 1998).

In contrast to the Chinese Consolidated Benevolent Association, a primarily community-based, mutual aid organization, the Chinese Equal Rights League (CERL) of New York was probably the first Asian American civil rights organization ever established. While the former was created right after the passage of the Chinese Exclusion Act in 1882, the latter was formed in the wake of the 1892 Geary Act. Even with this striking similarity, the obvious difference between their names indicates the difference between the CERL and the CCBA in prioritizing organizational tasks. The CERL was founded by Chinese American citizens naturalized before 1882, but their rights associated with citizenship were not recognized by the U.S. government (Lien 2001b).

The CERL employed a variety of tactics, including protesting, lobbying, and litigation, to achieve its goals. It published a pamphlet, *Appeal for the Chinese Equal Rights League to the People of the United States for Equality of Manhood,* when it was founded and mobilized 1,000 non-Chinese supporters and 200 Chinese merchants in a mass rally three weeks later against the Geary Act. It also successfully lobbied Congressman George W. Smith to introduce a bill to permit Chinese naturalization. In the sphere of litigation, collaborating with the CCBA, the CERL sponsored a test case to challenge the constitutionality of the Geary Act in court (Lien 2001b).

The second phase of the formation of Chinese American political organizations emerged with the growth of the native-born population of Chinese Americans. The membership of the CCBA and the CERL was mainly Chinese immigrants. As the number of native-born Chinese Americans increased near the end of the nineteenth century, the composition of Chinese American organizations underwent fundamental changes. Frustrated by the ineffectiveness of the CCBA's traditional elites in handling the Geary Act challenge and inspired by the CERL's activities in New York, a group of second-generation Chinese Americans began forming their own political organizations. In 1895 the Native Sons of the Golden State was founded in San Francisco with its main goal of fighting for citizenship rights. Although more America oriented, the members pursued equality and justice not only for themselves but also for the Chinese community as a whole. They participated in the 1905 boycott of American goods in China (discussed in Chapter 2) to fight against discriminatory exclusion laws. They also lobbied Congress and government officials for the same purpose, with both triumphs and failures. In 1907 they attempted but failed to force the repeal of the act of March 2, 1907, which stipulated that any American woman who married an alien automatically took the nationality of her husband. In 1913 they successfully stopped a proposal to disenfranchise Chinese Americans in the California senate (Lien 2001b; Fong 2002).

Between 1912 and 1913, Chinese Americans in Oakland, Los Angeles, Fresno, and San Diego organized local chapters under the umbrella organization of the Native Sons of the Golden State, making it a statewide organization. To accommodate branches being formed outside the state, the Native Sons renamed itself the Chinese American Citizens Alliance (CACA) in 1915 with the stated goals of elevating its status within the Chinese community, ending racial discrimination, accelerating the process of assimilation into the mainstream society, and urging the Chinese to participate in politics. In the following years, the CACA became a national organization after accepting the membership of local chapters created in twelve cities outside California, including Portland (Oregon), Chicago, Boston, Houston, New York, and Washington, D.C. (CACA website).

The members of CACA fought on against discriminatory acts. By writing petition letters to and testifying before Congress, they were victorious in amending the 1924 Immigration Act to grant entry to alien wives married before its passage. They proclaimed that they were involved in practically all pieces of national legislation that affected the Chinese. They were also active in areas of litigation, lobbying, and voter education. The CACA provided legal and financial assistances to those who were involved in cases of immigration exclusion; published the *Chinese Digest,* the first English-language Chinese American newspaper in the United States, beginning in 1935; and, although the majority of the Chinese were not eligible to vote until 1943, encouraged its members and others who were eligible to vote. Thus the CACA was likely the first Chinese American political organization to engage in voter education. Although mainly an America-oriented organization, the CACA collaborated with the CCBA in support of China during World War II. Overall, despite its efforts to promote the interests of the Chinese as a whole and of the motherland, as a citizen-only organization, the CACA was never the backbone of the Chinese organizational network (Lien 2001b; Fong 2002).

Japanese

Like Chinese Americans, Japanese Americans have had a long tradition of using formal organizations for achieving collective goals in the New World. Given similarities in cultural backgrounds and historical experiences, it is not surprising that the Japanese organizations were similar to those of the Chinese in many aspects, such as organizational type, structure, development, and goals. Although some differences did exist, overall, the Chinese and the Japanese were more similar than different in terms of their associational life.

Similar to the Chinese regional associations (*huiguan*), the most common and earliest community organizations created by Japanese immigrants in the United States were the *kenjinkai*, or prefectural associations. Though the *kenjinkai* existed in Hawaii as well, given the unique nature of plantation life, they were not as important as their counterparts in the continental United States, where the *kenjinkai* provided mutual aid and social functions to their members. Compared with the Chinese *huiguan,* the *kenjinkai* were more loosely organized with less control over their members, because new arrivals from Japan were less dependent on the *kenjinkai* to find housing and jobs than Chinese newcomers were on their *huiguan.* More often than not, this was because Japanese labor contractors were the ones who helped newly arriving Japanese immigrants find jobs (Chan 1991).

Other types of organizations existed besides those based on members' mutual geographic origins. Like the guilds of the Chinese, a number of economically oriented organizations were also formed by the Japanese. The first Japanese American trade association, the Shoemakers' League, was formed in 1893 by twenty or so Japanese shoemakers with help from the Tokyo Shoemakers' Alliance. Soon, organizations based upon other professions mushroomed one after the other in the subsequent years. Among them, the ones that affected the largest number of Japanese immigrants were agriculture-related trade associations. Japanese farmers established many central agricultural associations, local agricultural cooperatives, and organizations for farm labor contractors, mostly in California. Later, these trade associations combined to form the Japanese Chamber of Commerce, an umbrella economic organization, in 1915 (Chan 1991). There were also underworld entrepreneurs in the Japanese community, but their activities were not as luridly conspicuous as those of the Chinese Triads. Because many Japanese immigrants were Buddhists, they also formed religious organizations that played a significant role in the social life of the community (Chan 1991). Nonetheless, similar to the early Chinese organizations, none of these groups were political interest groups.

The Chinese and the Japanese organizations also share a strikingly similar pattern of organizational development. As recounted above, the CCBA was formed at the request of the Chinese consul general in San Francisco in 1882 in the wake of anti-Chinese agitation. Similarly, the Japanese consul general also urged Japanese community leaders to establish a more formal, umbrella community organization, the Japanese Association of America (JAA), in 1908 to deal with the anti-Japanese hostility in California at the time. The JAA became the most important organization and a semi-official organ of the Japanese government in the pre–World War II history of the Japanese. It was composed of a national headquarters in San Francisco; branches in the three West Coast cities of Portland (formed in 1911), Seattle (1913), and Los Angeles (1915); other branches in Colorado, Utah, Texas, Illinois, and New York; and dozens of local chapters. In total, there were 100 affiliated organizations (Chan 1991). Apparently, the JAA was a more widespread organization than the CCBA.

In addition to being a powerful self-governing body in the Japanese community, the JAA also led the community to fight against discriminatory laws in the same way as the CCBA did. While the CCBA was mainly concerned with the exclusion laws, due to the large population of Japanese farmers in California, the JAA put an emphasis on the alien land laws that prohibited Asian aliens, mostly Japanese, from buying or leasing agricultural lands. Between 1917 and 1923, the JAA got itself into a number of lawsuits concerning naturalization and the alien land laws. Similar to the CCBA, it provided its members with legal and financial assistance by hiring Caucasian American lawyers and raising money to pay court expenses. More specifically, the JAA's headquarters in San Francisco and its branch in Los Angeles each formed a land litigation committee to deal with land-related cases in Northern and Southern California, respectively. It was such a vigorous effort because agriculture was the cornerstone of the economy of Japanese immigrants at the time. Together, they sponsored four types of test cases, but in the end, the California Supreme Court upheld most of the prohibitions of the laws. Additionally, the JAA published and distributed English-language pamphlets hoping to influence American public opinion regarding the Japanese community (Chan 1991; Lien 2001b).

Furthermore, given the significance of agriculture for the Japanese community at the time, the JAA was heavily involved in agriculture-related activities. For instance, the JAA set up farmers' cooperatives that gave Japanese immigrant farmers advantages in purchasing seeds, fertilizer, and tools, and providing marketing mechanisms for their products. These associations also sent experts to help farmers in their jurisdiction by giving lectures and advice and representing them in labor disputes. Also, they published agriculture-related works such as the "Report of Investigation on Arable Land" (1918) and in response to California's alien land laws, the "Report of the Investigation on Agricultural Land Outside the State" (1926) (O'Brien and Fugita 1991). In this regard, the JAA was very different from the CCBA, which was an exclusively urban organization.

While the native-born Chinese established the more America-oriented Chinese American Citizens Alliance (CACA) in 1915 to have a political organization concerned more with citizen rights than immigrant rights, in 1930 the second-generation Japanese, or *Nisei,* created the Japanese American Citizens League (JACL), the most important political organization of the community even to the present day, for the same purposes. The JACL was certainly not formed overnight. It took tremendous efforts by both the first-generation Japanese, or *Issei,* and *Nisei* leaders in the 1920s to make possible its establishment. Between 1918 and 1920, *Nisei* college students and professionals, most of whom considered themselves more American than Japanese, began forming study groups in the wake of anti-Japanese sentiments in the mainstream society. These study groups in the San Francisco Bay Area eventually combined themselves into a patriotic group called the American Loyalty League. In 1922 a similar but separate *Nisei* organization, the Seattle Progressive Citizens League, was founded in the Pacific Northwest. At the time, *Issei* leaders urged the *Nisei* to organize to fight against the adversities associated with the alien land laws. In 1923 a statewide American Loyal League was formed in California. *Issei* leaders in the Bay Area were instrumental in its formation. Traditional elites of the Japanese Association of America selected delegates from *Nisei* in San Francisco, Fresno, San Jose, Turlock, Oakland, Berkeley, Lodi, Florin, Monterey, and Sacramento to attend its founding convention. During the height of its influence, in 1926, the organization had sixteen chapters throughout California. Later on, leaders of the California-based American Loyalty League and the Seattle Progressive Citizens League met formally to discuss the possibility of creating a national organization for *Nisei*. In April 1929 they approved a proposal that a founding convention of this new group, the Japanese American Citizens League, would be held in Seattle the next summer. In the meantime, there was a debate over the name of the new organization. Should it be "Japanese-American" to emphasize the ethnic ties, "American" only to stress its Americanism or "Japanese American" with the word "Japanese" simply an adjective modifying "American"? In the end, the delegates agreed with the latter alternative but decided that local chapters would have the right to make their own selection of the name. For example, the Fresno chapter kept its old name of American Loyalty League (Takahashi 1997).

Subsequently, the JACL was founded in the summer of 1930, and in the next decade it expanded rapidly from 8 to 50 chapters with about 5,600 dues-paying members (Takahashi 1997). Influenced by its members' social skills and familiarity with and trust in American democracy, the JACL's operating strategies were conservative and accommodationist, rather than radical and confrontational (Lien 2001b; Takaki 1998). Such a preference for accommodation was vividly reflected in the following passage of the organization's official creed: "Although some individuals may discriminate against me, I shall never become bitter or lose faith, for I know that such persons are not representative of the majority of the American people. True, I shall do all in my power to discourage such practices, but I should do it in the American way—above board, in the open, through the courts of law, by education, by proving myself to be worthy of equal treatment and consideration" (O'Brien and Fugita 1991, 40). Evidently, it recognized that although Japanese Americans would encounter discrimination, they had to surmount it the "American" way.

Just like its Chinese counterpart, the CACA, the JACL was also a citizen-only organization. It placed a clear emphasis on loyalty to the United States, which was expressed in its creed as well: "Because I believe in America, and I trust she believes in me, and because I have received innumerable benefits from her, I pledge myself to do honor to her at all times and all places; to support her constitution; to obey to her laws; to respect her flag; to defend her against all enemies, foreign and domestic; to actively assume my duties and obligations as a citizen, cheerfully and without any reservations whatsoever, in the hope that I may become a better American in a greater America" (O'Brien and Fugita 1991, 40). In addition, the 1936 JACL Convention condemned dual citizenship, and *Nisei* were asked to display their loyalty by contributing to the social, economic, and civic welfare of the nation as intelligent voters and public-spirited citizens

(Takaki 1998). Despite these efforts, the loyalty of Japanese Americans was seriously questioned by the mainstream society a few years later after the Japanese attack on Pearl Harbor in 1941.

Due to the emphasis of the JACL on Americanism, there were generational tensions between the JACL and the old-fashioned *Issei* leaders. However, the JACL's relationship with the Japanese Association of America was a paradoxical one. Because its initial leadership was composed of *Nisei* in their late twenties and early thirties who were still closely tied to the JAA, not only did the JACL work cooperatively with the JAA, but it also developed policies that paralleled the JAA's emphases on legal and legislative change and public relations. Internationally, the JACL also followed the JAA's policies to maintain close ties with the Japanese consulate until 1941 and oftentimes helped the *Issei* defend Japanese aggression in Asia (Fong 2002; Takahashi 1997).

Working with the JAA during the prewar period, the JACL, along with its representatives in Washington, D.C., launched a few successful campaigns to push for the passage of favorable legislation, as well as challenge discriminatory laws. In 1935 the passage of the Nye-Lea Bill granted the right of naturalization to about 500 World War I veterans of Asian ancestry, mostly *Issei*. The next year marked the repeal of the Cable Act that deprived any American-born woman of her citizenship if she married a person ineligible for citizenship—the first time that one of America's discriminatory naturalization acts was successfully repealed (Takahashi 1997).

In the 1940s, the JACL campaigned intensely in California. In the 1946 election, a proposition for the validation of the alien land law was on the state ballot at the same time the controversy over the enforcement of the law had become increasingly heated. To defeat it, the JACL reminded the general public of contributions by Japanese Americans, especially the loyalty demonstrated by the *Nisei* soldiers, who fought for the United States on the European battlefields during the war. As a result, the proposition was rejected by a sound margin of 18 percent. The JACL had a greater success ten years later when it sponsored its own proposition for the repeal of the alien land law in California after the U.S. Supreme Court ruled the law unconstitutional in 1948, and the California Supreme Court ruled that the state laws could not deny landownership to aliens. Although the law was already enjoined by court order from being enforced at the time, the JACL sought its removal from the statute books and used this opportunity to launch a public education campaign against racial discrimination. In the end, the repeal was supported by a wide margin of 30 percent or so (Takaki 1998).

At the national level, in 1952 the JACL was instrumental in the passage of the McCarran-Walter Act that annulled the racial restriction imposed by the 1790 naturalization law and prevailed in an override of a veto by President Truman. The JACL lobbied vigorously for the legislation by stressing the importance of granting citizenship to the parents of the *Nisei* soldiers as recognition of their contributions. This legislative success was partly attributed to the JACL's strategy of building a cross-racial civil rights coalition with African Americans and Caucasian American liberals (Takaki 1998; Kitano and Daniels, 1988; Lien 2001b).

Different from its Chinese counterpart, the Chinese American Citizens Alliance that never became the backbone of the Chinese community, the JACL eventually took the leading role from the hands of the Japanese Association of America. The attack on Pearl Harbor was a watershed event for the leadership of the Japanese organizations. The JACL did not grow into the most powerful Japanese American organization until after the attack and the following incarceration of the Japanese on the West Coast. After the outbreak of war, JACL membership almost tripled. When Executive Order 6099 was issued, the JACL urged the community to comply and criticized a small number of *Nisei* who defied pre-evacuation restrictions. In the meantime, many JACL leaders volunteered to join the military (Lien 2001b; Takahashi 1997). In the postwar era, the JACL gradually took the leadership position as the JAA was losing its influence before its final dismantling.

Koreans

Given its much smaller population and shorter history in the New World, the Korean community created the smallest array of ethnic organizations among the three groups. Between 1902 and 1905, approximately 7,000 Korean laborers immigrated to Hawaii to work on the plantations. As soon as they arrived there, they formed *tong-hoe*, or village councils, on each plantation as self-governing bodies. They also organized the *Sinmin-hoe*, or New People Society, in 1903 mainly to protest against the Japanese presence on the Korean Peninsula. In 1907 different *tong-hoe* combined themselves into a larger organization called the Hanin Hapsong Hyop-hoe, or United Korean Society, in Honolulu with branches throughout the Hawaiian Islands (Chan 1991).

The first Korean American organization that came into existence on the continental United States was the Chinmok-hoe, or Friendship Society, established in 1903. Two years later, the Kongnip Hyophoe, or Mutual Assistance Society, was founded and soon published the first Korean-language newspaper. In 1909 the Hawaii-based United Korean Society, California's Mutual Assistance Society, and other mainland organizations merged into an umbrella ethnic organization, the Taehan Kookmin-hoe, or Korean National Association (KNA), in San Francisco. This merger was prompted by a need to protect the life of a Korean, Chang In-hwan, who assassinated Durham W. Stevens in San Francisco in 1908. Stevens, a Caucasian American appointed by the Japanese government as an adviser to the Foreign Affairs Department of Korea, made a few remarks that were printed in the *San Francisco Chronicle* to defend the 1905 Japanese occupation of Korea. Infuriated by the remarks, Chang shot Stevens to death and was sentenced to twenty-five years in prison. After the merger, the newly founded KNA proclaimed itself to be the organization that represented all Koreans in the Western Hemisphere and it had seventy-eight branches in Hawaii alone (Chan 1991; Lien 2001b; Kitano and Daniels 1988).

Compared with their Chinese and Japanese counterparts, the Koreans were quick to organize, taking only seven years, from 1902 to 1909, to establish their nationwide organization, the KNA. This is simply because the Korean community was very small at the turn of the twentieth century, as well as because the community was already highly politicized due to its deep concern with the situation of its motherland. Because of the unique origin of its founding, the KNA placed great emphasis on Korean independence. To achieve this goal, the KNA launched diplomatic and educational campaigns, organized mass rallies, and raised funds. Despite its heavy involvement in homeland independence, the KNA was also a mutual aid community organization with one of its stated goals being to promote the welfare of Koreans in the United States. Therefore, the KNA also provided welfare to its members, set up schools, and printed textbooks and newsletters (Chan 1991; Lien 2001b).

However, the KNA was not the most important community organization among Korean Americans, unlike the CCBA and the JAA, which comfortably enjoyed leadership status in their respective communities. Because many Korean immigrants became Christians before their departure from home to the New World, they organized Korean churches soon after their arrival. Only half a year after their arrival in Hawaii, they held their first church service and established

a Korean Evangelical Society. In 1905 they established a Korean Epis-
copal Church, and by 1918 there were a total of 39 Korean churches
for roughly 3,000 Korean Christians on the islands. The first church
service on the mainland was held in Los Angeles in 1904, where the
Korean Methodist Church was formed one year later. During the first
two decades of the twentieth century, more than a dozen churches
were set up for the still very small Korean population of 1,000 or so
in the West Coast (Chan 1991).

Being the most important community institutions, the Korean
churches performed not only religious functions, but also political,
social, and cultural functions as well. Because of the deep resentment
of Korean immigrants against Japanese occupation of their homeland, the churches had become the political center of the community, where many organized activities such as fund-raising and political discussions took place for the cause of Korean independence.
Given the importance of both religion and politics, Christian minis-
ters and expatriate political leaders, often the same persons, constituted the leadership of Korean communities (Chan 1991).

Regardless of the importance of the KNA and the churches within
Korean American communities, the small Korean American population (e.g., only 7,030 in 1950 and 69,150 in 1970) meant that their
influence in the broader mainstream society was minimal until the
1970s, when more Koreans came to the United States after the immigration reforms associated with the 1965 Immigration Act. Ever since
the 1970s, the Korean American population has rapidly expanded, to
more than 1 million people in 2002. However, even in this much
larger community, the church organizations still play a central role in
many aspects of Korean American community life.

The preoccupation of Korean immigrants with homeland politics
and the significance of Korean churches really made their ethnic
organizations markedly different from those of the Chinese and
Japanese. First, because the Korean organizations put greater emphasis
on the issue of Korean independence than the emphasis placed by the
CCBA and the JAA on immigrant and citizen rights, the Korean organizations were the least America-oriented among the three groups, with
the Japanese organizations being the most Americanist. Second, while
the traditional elite class of the Chinese and the Japanese communities was mainly composed of merchants and farmers, respectively, the
Korean leaders were religious and political leaders who were naturally
much less concerned with the economic interests of the community.
However, it seems that this difference in the leadership composition
has little to do with organizational performance. Last, although there

were also religious (mostly Buddhist) organizations among the Chinese and the Japanese, they were not at all comparable to the Korean churches in terms of size and community influence.

Between the Chinese and the Japanese organizations there were more similarities than differences. One of the striking similarities was the same pattern of organizational restructuring within the boundaries of each community. As a result of generational differences, American-born members of both communities began forming their own organizations when the community was in crisis. Generally speaking, while the foreign-born-led organizations were more concerned with self-governance of the community, mutual aid, and homeland-related issues, the native-born-led organizations placed greater emphasis on racial equality and social justice in the larger society. This kind of generational difference in organizational goals continued to grow into the Asian American movement era, with the former becoming more conservative and then outdated as years went by and the latter more liberal and progressive.

As illustrated in the previous chapter, the Asian American movement starting in the late 1960s served as a turning point in the history of Asian American protest politics. Given the intimate relationship between protest politics and interest-group politics (with the latter being the organizational bases for the former), it is easy to see how the Asian American movement also represented a watershed that marked the beginning of the second phase of Asian American participation in interest-group politics. Asian American college students established scores of campus-based organizations at the beginning of the movement. As the movement proceeded, there was an urgent need for Asian American community activists to establish new generation organizations to provide more solid organizational bases for the growth of the movement than those of the student-led organizations. As a consequence, dozens of national and regional organizations sprung up during and after the development of the movement. However, several pre-1960s community organizations did not vanish in the new era. Some of them remained powerful only within the boundaries of their ethnic enclaves, while others of them continued to grow and even become more influential than before.

While some of these new-wave organizations are national organizations with a headquarters or office in Washington, D.C., to represent ethnic interests and facilitate lobbying activities in the national capital, others are grassroots organizations formed at regional levels, especially in those areas with a high concentration of Asian Americans. Even though some of them are ethnic-specific organizations, similar to those traditional ethnic organizations before the 1960s that place great emphasis on the particular interests of their ethnic communities, others are panethnic organizations working to build up pan-Asian consciousness and identity to serve the collective interests of all Asian Americans. While some of these groups are organized around civil rights issues, others are formed around a variety of other issues, such as voter education, women's rights, legal advocacy, anti-Asian violence, social/community service, labor, health, and homeland politics. Last, while some of these newly founded organizations are built for permanence and likely to remain active beyond the present time, others are clearly ad hoc, single-issue organizations with a very short life span.

National Ethnic Interest Groups

During the initial phase of the Asian American movement, the majority of newly founded organizations were campus and community-based groups mainly on the West Coast. However effective and influential these organizations might be, their regional status set limits to their development. As the movement continued to grow in the 1970s and 1980s, East Asian Americans, as well as Asian Americans as a whole, began creating more and more nationwide organizations to exercise more influence on the national political scene. Of these, some are ethnic-specific umbrella organizations and some are panethnic Asian American organizations.

National Ethnic-Specific Interest Groups

Among a handful of nationwide intraethnic organizations, the Japanese American Citizens League has been the most established and influential Asian American organization. Founded in 1930, the JACL is one of a few pre–World War II Asian American organizations that survived the entire postwar era and still exist today. Internally, within the Japanese community, the JACL took over the leadership position as the old-fashioned Japanese Association of America faded into history after the World War II incarceration of the Japanese. Externally, on the national political scene, as demonstrated in the previous chapter, the JACL successfully led the Redress movement in the 1970s and 1980s, during which the group demonstrated its organizational capacities in lobbying and "insider" politics.

Inside the Chinese American community, two long-standing nationwide organizations that were formed in the late nineteenth century are still existent today: the Chinese Consolidated Benevolent Association (CCBA) and the Chinese American Citizens Alliance (CACA). Formed in 1882, the CCBA remains a nationwide umbrella organization with branches in many American cities. However, due to demographic changes within the Chinese American population during the postwar years, the CCBA remains powerful primarily within the boundary of the Cantonese-dominated Chinatowns. In those new Chinatowns in suburban America populated mostly by immigrants from Taiwan and mainland China in recent decades, the traditional CCBA has very little influence. During the Asian American movement, the authority of the CCBA's traditional elites was deemed too conservative and challenged by some new-generation community activists (Wei 1993). In recent years, the CCBA has been involved mainly in community services and activities related to issues of homeland politics, such as Chinese democracy and Taiwanese independence.

Headquartered in San Francisco, the CACA was established as early as 1895 by a group of second-generation Chinese Americans, but it was never a leading organization in the Chinese community before World War II, and it became even less active in the realm of civil rights in the postwar era. For instance, according to its official website, its last civil-rights-related activity took place in 1952 when its members appeared before President Harry Truman's Commission on Immigration and Naturalization to protest against the unfairness of the Walter-McCarran Act (CACA website). In the following decades, it seems that the only political activity in which the CACA got involved was its participation in a pan-Asian coalition to petition for a hearing before the U.S. Commission on Civil Rights in the midst of the campaign finance controversies in the 1990s (Lien 2001b).

Among the contemporary Chinese American national organizations, the only one that somewhat parallels the JACL is the Organization of Chinese Americans, Inc. (OCA). Established in 1973, right after the birth of the Asian American movement, the OCA is the first and only national Chinese American civil rights organization headquartered in Washington, D.C. Since its founding year, the OCA has developed into a sizable organization with fifty local chapters across the nation. One of its stated goals is to build national support and work in coalition with other Asian American national groups to monitor legislation and policies affecting Chinese Americans and Asian Americans (OCA website). Although the OCA is not as influential within and renowned outside the Chinese American community as the JACL with respect to the Japanese American community, because of lack of competing organizations of such caliber, it is considered the leading Chinese American organization by many other Asian American organizations.

In addition, it is important to note that in recent decades, there have been an increasing number of people from Taiwan and their American-born offspring who choose to identify themselves separately as Taiwanese rather than Chinese in the United States. People on Taiwan are mainly composed of two groups, although both belong to the Han Chinese family: (1) mainlanders, referring to those who moved to Taiwan after the Chinese civil war and the communist triumph in the late 1940s and their Taiwan-born offspring, and (2) Taiwanese, referring to those who lived on the island before the end of World War II and their children. It is mainly people from the latter group who claim to be Taiwanese Americans in the United States. With rapid growth of their population as well as their Taiwanese identity, Taiwanese Americans began forming political organizations of their own in the 1980s. Most of their organizations possess political agendas that focus on Taiwan's politics, security, and international status rather than on American politics, with a few exceptions, such as the Taiwanese American Citizens League (TACL).

Similar to the JACL and the OCA, the TACL was formed as a civil rights organization in Monterey Park, California, in 1985. It became a national organization in 1989 with twelve chapters across the nation in 1996 (Ng 1998). However, by 2002, it had only seven chapters in New York, Houston, Atlanta, and four California areas. According to its mission, the TACL is devoted to enhancing "the quality of life for Taiwanese Americans" by "building an understanding of Taiwanese American heritage, encouraging pride in Taiwanese American identity, helping to contribute to a Taiwanese American culture . . ., networking with other Taiwanese Americans, Asians and Pacific Islanders, minority and other citizens . . . to gain respect from and equality with all Americans, and helping to instill in our community a greater sense of citizenship, stressing both the responsibility and rights that come with it " (TACL website). To realize these goals, the TACL successfully lobbied to have Taiwanese Americans counted as a separate category in the 2000 census. It also organized a political internship program, summer and winter leadership camps, a voter registration drive, and seminars to increase the electoral participation of the Taiwanese American community and awareness of some key civil rights issues concerning their community (Ng 1998). Nonetheless, because many Taiwanese Americans are extremely preoccupied with homeland politics, domestic political organizations such as the TACL are hardly able to garner the same amount of support from the community as those homeland-oriented Taiwanese American organizations.

There are two contemporary national Korean American organizations: the Korean American Coalition (KAC) and the National Association of Korean Americans (NAKA). Established in 1983, the Korean American Coalition in Los Angeles (KACLA) was initially a regional civil rights organization to serve the interests of Korean Americans in the greater Los Angeles area. When the Los Angeles riots struck the Korean American community in 1992, the KACLA emerged as the organizational voice of the entire community and took on the leadership position in the post-riot reconstruction. One year later, the KACLA embarked on a vigorous plan for national expansion. It took the following four years to set up an office in Washington, D.C., and four chapters in Northern and Southern California. Today, headquartered in Los Angeles, the KAC is a fully developed national organization with offices in the national capital and Orange County, California, and thirteen chapters throughout the United States (KAC website).

Also in response to the situation of lacking a national voice to speak on the behalf of Korean Americans after the devastating Los Angeles riots, the National Association of Korean Americans was founded in 1994 as a civil and human rights organization. With its founding convention held in New York, where there is no branch of the KAC, the NAKA set up its headquarters in Washington, D.C., with four chapters in New York, the New England area, Los Angeles, and San Francisco. It has the following objectives:

- To help safeguard the civil rights of Korean Americans and others in the United States.
- To promote cooperation and better understanding between the Korean American community and other racial/ethnic groups in the United States.
- To develop Korean American culture and help articulate the shared values of Americans as a community, and
- To contribute to the peaceful, independent reunification of Korea. (NAKA website)

To further these aims, among other things, the NAKA organizes public forums and cultural programs, conducts policy analysis and makes recommendations, and networks with delegations and visitors from Korea. From the above objectives and programs, it is clear that the NAKA is different from the KAC at least in one aspect: the former puts specific emphasis on homeland politics. More specifically, its recent activities in Washington, D.C., included a Korea Peace Forum on United States-North Korea relations held on July 24, 2003, at the Russell Senate Office Building, and from July 24 to July 27, 2003, a series of Korea Armistice to Peace Treaty events were also organized as a campaign to peacefully resolve the North Korean nuclear crisis (NAKA website). These homeland-oriented activities are not unusual among Korean Americans and are probably even more common among Chinese Americans and Taiwanese Americans. The only exceptional group is Japanese Americans, who have maintained a rather distant relationship with their homeland after the internment during World War II.

Chinese Americans have had a long tradition of getting involved in homeland-related issues, be it Chinese domestic politics or U.S. policy toward China, ever since the beginning years of the CCBA. The most recent example of Chinese American homeland-oriented interest groups is the Committee of 100, formed in 1990 right after the Tiananmen democratic movement by a number of prominent Chinese Americans, including Chang-Lin Tien, the late chancellor of the University of California, Berkeley, the architect I. M. Pei, the cellist Yo Yo Ma, and others, to promote better relations between the United States and China. Participants of their past annual conventions, usually held in Washington, D.C., met members of Congress, senior officials, and well-established scholars, and sessions of these conventions were devoted to topics concerning United States-China relations (Watanabe 1999). The Committee of 100 is also active in protecting the rights of Chinese Americans. For instance, after the release of Wen Ho Lee, a Taiwanese American scientist wrongly accused of being a Chinese spy, in September 2000, the committee issued its concerns:

> The Committee of 100 remains deeply concerned about two remaining issues. First, there is "racial profiling," particularly as practiced by federal personnel at the national laboratories and in the defense industry. Americans of Chinese decent are unjustly singled out solely because of their ancestry. Second, the Committee fears that the anti-Chinese hysteria . . . which led to Dr. Lee's indictment and prosecution may reappear wherever tensions or disagreements arise between China and the United States. (Wang 2002, 225)

Although the committee is not a hierarchical national political organization with local chapters, given the national reputation of some of its members, its activities are visible on the American political scene.

Among all East Asian American ethnic groups, Taiwanese Americans are perhaps the most involved in homeland politics. Over the past two decades or so, they have created a plethora of Taiwanese American organizations devoted to Taiwan's internal politics, independence, security, and relations with the United States. These political organizations together constitute the Taiwan Lobby that has worked hard to influence not only Congress and the federal government, but also state and local governments at the grassroots level. These organizations include the Taiwanese Chamber of Commerce of North America, the Center for Taiwanese International Relations, the World United Formosans for Independence, and the Formosan Association for Public Affairs—probably the most organized of all (Chi 2002).

The Taiwanese Chamber of Commerce of North America (TCCNA) was established in 1988 as a nonprofit organization, whose membership in 2000 consisted of 32 local chambers of commerce throughout North America with more than 3,500 individual members. Even though this nationwide organization is primarily devoted to promoting business interests for its members through networking, it also tries to improve Taiwan's relations with the United States. Because many of its local members have kept good relations with politicians in their localities, the latter goal is often pursued at these state and local levels in a less visible way than that at the national level (Chi 2002).

Quite different from the TCCNA, the Center for Taiwan International Relations (CTIR) is a research-oriented lobbying organization. Formed in Washington, D.C., in 1988, the center has maintained that the sovereignty of Taiwan belongs to the people of Taiwan themselves, not to the People's Republic of China. To promote this assertion, the CTIR has produced policy analyses, contacted government officials, testified before Congress, and provided information about Taiwan's international status to members of Congress and the media. Furthermore, it has a branch office in New York City to deal specifically with the issue of Taiwan's entry into the United Nations (Chi 2002).

Headquartered in Dallas, Texas, the World United Formosans for Independence (WUFI) was established in 1970 and is one of the oldest Taiwanese American political organizations in the United States. It has branches not only in the United States but also in Taiwan, Japan, Europe, Canada, and South America, among other places. Its organizational title suggests that, like the CTIR, it has a primary mission to promote Taiwan's independent status from the People's Republic of China. To realize this goal, the WUFI provides speakers, organizes conferences, and publishes the *Taiwan Tribune*, a long-standing newspaper that was once influential in the Taiwanese American community and on college campuses in the 1970s and the 1980s before Taiwan's process of democratization began (Chi 2002).

The most active Taiwanese American lobbying organization with tremendous influence is the Formosan Association for Public Affairs (FAPA). Its lobbying power is marked by *Los Angeles Times* commentator Jim Mann: "The main legislation concerning Taiwan on Capitol Hill is called the Taiwan Security Enhancement Act, which would strengthen U.S. defense links to Taiwan. When that bill passed the House a few months ago, the most active organization was not Cassidy [a Washington-based lobbying company hired by the Taiwanese government] but a nonprofit grassroots group called the Formosan Association for Public Affairs" (Mann 2000).

Founded in 1982 in Los Angeles and modeled after the American Israel Public Affairs Committee (AIPAC), the FAPA is a Washington-based, nationwide nonprofit organization with five full-time workers in the headquarters and fifty-two local chapters throughout the United States in 2004 (FAPA website). This lobbying organization has three goals:

- To promote international support for the right of the people of Taiwan to establish an independent and democratic country and to join the international community.
- To advance the rights and interests of Taiwanese communities throughout the world.
- To promote peace and security for Taiwan. (FAPA website)

To advance the above goals, the FAPA supplies information on issues about Taiwan to government officials at all levels, members of Congress and their aides, the media, and the American public (Chi 2002).

National Panethnic Interest Groups

One of the first pan-Asian American organizations, most of which were campus based in the early years, was the Asian American Political Alliance (AAPA) founded at the University of California, Berkeley, in 1968. Soon after that, the same organization was created across the bay at the San Francisco State College, serving as the lead pan–Asian American student organization during the monumental strike at the college that same year. In the following year, Asian American students in the Midwest and on the East Coast formed their own AAPAs or other similar organizations (Espiritu 1992). As the result of conscious efforts toward panethnic coalition building, Asian Americans have created a number of pan-Asian organizations since the Asian American movement era. While some of these groups are organized around civil rights issues, others focus on a variety of other issues, such as voter education, legal advocacy, anti-Asian violence, and health.

However, the AAPA was not really an organized pan-Asian group. The first major pan-Asian political organization was the Asian American Voters Coalition. Founded in 1986, the coalition included Chinese, Japanese, Korean, and other Asian American national and regional organizations (Lien 2001b). Following this precedent, a few other electorally oriented pan-Asian American organizations came into existence later in the 1990s, including the first National Asian Pacific American Voter Registration Campaign formed by an OCA-led coalition of nineteen Asian American national organizations in 1996; the Asian Americans for Campaign Finance Reform (AAFCFR), created as a response to the campaign finance controversies in the mid-1990s; and the 80–20 Initiative, the first national Asian American political action committee (PAC) organized to, among other things, mobilize Asian American voters for bloc voting (Lien 2001b). These electorally oriented organizations are further studied in the next chapter.

During the same period of time, fourteen national Asian American national organizations, including many well-established, ethnic-specific and pan-Asian American groups, formed a coalition to petition for a hearing before the U.S. Commission on Civil Rights to respond to the prevailing patterns of racial stereotyping and scapegoating of Asian American communities. Specifically, they requested that "the investigations, statements and policy choices of Congress, political parties, and public officials, and reportage by the news media be fair, informed, accurate, and free of racial and anti-immigrant bias" (Lien 2001b, 75).

Given the significance of litigation in Asian American history, as well as in the American political system, Asian American communities can hardly survive without legal advocacy groups. At the national level, there are two organizations of this kind: the National Asian

Pacific American Legal Consortium (NAPALC), created by three regional legal Advocacy groups in 1993 (Lien 2001b); and the National Asian Pacific American Bar Association (NAPABA).

Closely related to the legal advocacy groups is the National Network against Anti-Asian Violence (NNAAV), a national anti-Asian violence group formed in the wake of anti-Asian violence in the larger society in the 1980s. It took the form of a large coalition of many national and regional antiviolence and legal groups across the nation in 1990. The activities of the network include courtroom monitoring, meeting with prosecutors, public education, and hate crime prevention (Lien 2001b).

There are two national health advocacy groups in the Asian American community: the Asian and Pacific Islander American Health Forum (APIAHF) and the Association of Asian/Pacific Community Health Organizations (AAPCHO). In 1990 these two groups pressed Congress to introduce and pass the Asian Pacific Islander Health Act of 1990 (H.R. 4992). According to the bill sponsored by Congressman Norman Mineta, $1 million were allocated to improve the collection of data on health needs of Asian Americans (Espiritu 1992).

Lastly, pan-Asian American organizational efforts can be best demonstrated by the formation of quite a few panethnic civil rights and policy research organizations, including the Asian Pacific American Institute for Congressional Studies (APAICS), the only national Asian Pacific American public policy institute in Washington, D.C.; the Asian American Institute (AAI); the Asian Pacific Partners for Empowerment and Leadership (APPEAL); the Leadership Education for Asian Pacifics (LEAP); the National Asian Pacific American Women's Forum (NAPAWF); the National Asian Pacific Center on Aging (NAPCA); and so on. These organizations and some national intraethnic organizations, such as the JACL, the OCA, and the KAC, had formed single-issue, ad hoc coalitions to be more effective on the American national political scene before. However, in the midst of the campaign contribution controversies in the mid-1990s, Asian American communities realized the need to establish a national pan-Asian American coalition on a more permanent basis. In 1997 this idea became reality. As a broad coalition of twenty-one nationwide Asian Pacific American organizations, the National Council of Asian Pacific Americans (NCAPA) was established, marking the most significant achievement of pan-Asian American coalition building in Asian American history (Lien 2001b).

Regional Ethnic Interest Groups

The Asian American national ethnic interest groups have been supplemented by many grassroots organizations formed at regional levels, especially in those areas with a high concentration of Asian Americans. For example, in Southern California alone, there were more than 250 pan-Asian American organizations in 1997 (Lai 2003). It is noteworthy that few of the regional Asian American groups are organizations at the state level; even some early examples in the state of California such as the CACA were not statewide organizations. One key reason for the absence of such statewide organizations is that the Asian American population is very unevenly distributed, with its center of population gravity located in the urban areas, and thus it would make little difference in terms of membership size and organizational power to organize any groups at the state level. By the same token, even many of the national organizations are not truly national per se. Chances are that each of them represents a coalition of several local organizations across urban America. Among Asian American regional organizations, while some are panethnic, most are ethnic-specific community groups.

Regional Ethnic-Specific Interest Groups

One of the most nationally renowned regional organizations is the American Citizens for Justice (ACJ) formed by concerned members of the Chinese American community in Detroit after the murder of Vincent Chin to ensure that justice would be done. As demonstrated in the preceding chapter, the ACJ leaders used a variety of methods to further this aim, including mass rallies, demonstrations, a nationwide letter-writing campaign, and appeals to politicians.

While the ACJ was created as a response to a community crisis that happened in Detroit, several regional community organizations were formed among Korean Americans in Southern California one decade later as a response to the Los Angeles riots of 1992. In addition to the formation of the two previously mentioned national Korean American organizations, the KAC and the NAKA, community leaders of Koreatown established not one but two political organizations as a reaction to the riots: the Korean American Republican Association (KARA) and the Korean American Democratic Committee (KADC), as the first two partisan political organizations in the Korean American community (Park 2001).

Because the all-powerful JACL constitutes the backbone of Japanese American organizational life with numerous local chapters providing services to its members throughout the nation, regional Japanese American organizations other than JACL chapters are rather insignificant.

Regional Panethnic Interest Groups

Panethnic Asian American organizations at regional levels are numerous, especially in areas with large Asian American populations, and quite divergent in terms of function, extent of influence, and organizational life span. One type is focused on combating anti-Asian violence. Many such groups were created after the establishment of the ACJ in many American cities, including the Bay Area's Break the Silence Coalition and Asian Network for Equality and Justice, Boston's Asians for Justice Coalition, New York's Committee against Anti-Asian Violence (CAAAV), just to name a few. Most of these organizations became inactive after a while.

Another type of these pan-Asian community organizations is the legal advocacy group, including such examples as the Asian Pacific American Legal Center (APALC) of Southern California, the Asian Law Caucus (ALC) in San Francisco, and the Asian American Legal Defense and Education Fund (AALDEF) in New York (Lien 2001b). They also function as electorally oriented organizations devoted to voter registration and education, like the Los Angeles-based Center for Asian Americans United for Self Empowerment (CAUSE). Over the years, these groups have made enormous contributions to many lives in their respective communities.

Still another type of regional organization consists of social agencies. One good example of this kind would be the Asian Pacific Planning Council (APPCON) in Los Angeles. Formed in 1976, the APPCON is the largest umbrella social service organization of more than forty social agencies in Southern California. Because its members have connections with different levels of funding in the County of Los Angeles, the APPCON has been very effective in lobbying for grant proposals on behalf of its member agencies and has become one of the accepted representatives of the local Asian American community (Espiritu 1992). Not many of the above-mentioned Asian American organizations, national and regional alike, are typical "political interest groups" by definition because of their organizational goals and the strategies used to achieve them. Among those organizations that approximate the model of a political interest group, three national Asian American organizations stand out and deserve more detailed investigation. They are the Japanese American Citizens League, the National Council of Asian Pacific Americans, and the Formosa Association for Public Affairs.

Case Studies

The Japanese American Citizens League, the National Council of Asian Pacific Americans, and the Formosa Association for Public Affairs represent a national ethnic-specific organization, a national panethnic organization, and a national organization focusing on homeland politics, respectively. Though they differ in quite a few aspects, such as organizational age, ethnic composition, and objectives, they share one thing in common: because of their lobbying potential or their already demonstrated effectiveness in the national political arena, they are all well-recognized organizations and viewed as the representatives of their respective communities.

Japanese American Citizens League (JACL)

The oldest and largest national Asian American civil rights organization, the Japanese American Citizens League was founded in 1930 with 8 chapters. Some 74 years later, it has 112 chapters across the nation and 8 regional districts with over 24,000 members in 23 states. Headquartered in San Francisco, the JACL has 5 regional offices in Los Angeles, Fresno, San Francisco, Seattle, and Chicago, plus an office in Washington, D.C. It publishes the *Pacific Citizen,* an organizational newspaper distributed nationally from its Los Angeles office. Each year the JACL allocates grants, called Legacy Fund grants, to its chapters and district councils to assist them in achieving the mission of the organization (JACL website).

The JACL calls on its membership to advance the following general purposes (given the shorthand slogan "protect, preserve, participate, and promote"):

- Protect the rights of Japanese Americans as its primary and continuing concern. It shall strive to secure and uphold civil and human rights for all people.
- Preserve the culture and values of Japanese Americans in a multicultural society.
- Participate in the development of understanding between all social and ethnic groups.
- Promote, sponsor, and encourage programs, projects, and activities designed to further and to encourage members to perform faithfully their duties and obligations to the United States of America. (JACL website)

Originally, the JACL's founding mission was to protect the civil rights of Japanese Americans, but today it is also committed to protecting the rights of the entire Asian Pacific American community. The JACL began recognizing the need for vigilance to uphold the rights of all Asian Americans after the 1982 murder of Vincent Chin in Detroit, where he was mistaken as a Japanese. To advance its mission, the JACL has maintained nine advocacy programs dealing with specific programs and issues facing the Asian Pacific American community, including programs concerning hate crimes, defamation, discrimination, workplace discrimination, voter registration, affirmative action, media portrayals, legislative initiatives, and community relations (JACL website).

Among its major achievements, the JACL was instrumental in lobbying for passage of the landmark 1964 Civil Rights Act, the culmination of the Civil Rights movement in the 1960s (JACL website), and in the 1970s and 1980s it successfully led the Redress movement to compensate Japanese Americans for their internment during World War II. As clearly depicted in the previous chapter, the Redress movement has been so far the best example of how Asian American members of Congress, as the insiders, worked with community elites, as the outsiders, to achieve their collective interests. In the 1990s, the JACL often joined other Asian American organizations, especially the OCA, to form a pan-Asian American coalition to deal with issues such as anti-Asian violence and the campaign contribution scandal.

In the new millennium, the national board of the JACL set priorities for 2002–2004. In the area of public affairs, the first of the ten priorities is to develop, strengthen, and expand institutional relationships with organizations in all communities, elected and appointed officials, and policymakers and community leaders on the national, state, and local levels (JACL website).

National Council of Asian Pacific Americans (NCAPA)

To unite various Asian Pacific American advocacy groups under one umbrella, with the help of former Congressman Norman Mineta, the secretary of transportation as of 2005, a series of meetings were held and attended by more than twenty Asian Pacific American organizations as a response to anti-Asian hostility associated with the campaign contribution scandals in the mid-1990s. The consensus reached at these meetings was the need for a national coalition that could bring together Asian Pacific American groups at all levels, represent the collective interests of the greater Asian Pacific American community, and speak with a national voice on Asian Pacific American issues. As a result, the National Council of Asian Pacific Americans (NCAPA) was formally instituted in 1997 in Washington, D.C., with Daphne Kwok, a former executive director of the Organization of Chinese Americans, being the first chairperson. Created as a federation of twenty-one national Asian Pacific American organizations at its founding, the NCAPA now has twenty-seven member organizations, all of which are headquartered in Washington, D.C. (NCAPA website).

As the first national Asian American civil rights organization, the NCAPA has adopted very comprehensive policy principles, which demonstrate the multifaceted purposes of the organization. There are twelve policy principles in total, an abridged version of which is introduced below:

- NCAPA supports efforts to recognize the contributions of Asian Pacific Americans in American society, to promote understanding and appreciation of Asian Pacific American culture, tradition, customs and heritage, and to promote multiracial, multiethnic, and multicultural unity and coalitions.
- NCAPA encourages Asian Pacific Americans to actively participate in the civic, political process by naturalizing, registering, voting, and seeking public office.
- NCAPA supports the appointment of qualified Asian Pacific Americans to positions in federal, state, and local governments.
- NCAPA supports policies and programs to redress past societal injustices to Asian Pacific Americans and to others, to advance the rights and welfare of groups that have been unfairly marginalized in the American society, including, among others, women, the elderly, children, and the disabled, and to ensure equal education, employment, economic opportunities,

and equal access to health care programs for Asian Pacific Americans and all others who face discrimination.

- NCAPA supports immigrant rights and the inclusion of the Asian Pacific Islander categories in all government and private data collection efforts, including statistics and analyses concerning population, education, crime, and income.
- NCAPA condemns the economic exploitation of immigrant workers, hate crimes against Asian Pacific Americans and others, and stereotyping and scapegoating of Asian Pacific Americans and especially racial stereotypes that negatively characterize Asian Pacific Americans as "foreigners." (NCAPA website)

From the above, it is clear that the NCAPA was formed around a large variety of issues, ranging from traditional civil rights and immigrants' rights issues to voter education, political appointments of public officials, women's issues, education, labor, health, census data collection, anti-Asian violence, and scapegoating—all of which reflect an aggregate of the goals of its twenty-seven-member organizations and help explain the NCAPA's involvement in largely varying activities since its inception.

The first signature event of the NCAPA took place in 1997 when it organized an aggressive campaign for the appointment of Bill Lann Lee. Lee was a distinguished civil rights lawyer and former director of the Los Angeles office of the Legal Defense and Educational Fund of the National Association for the Advancement of Colored People (NAACP) before his nomination by the Clinton administration to the position of assistant attorney general for civil rights at the Justice Department. However, some members of the U.S. Senate Judiciary Committee opposed to Lee's past stance on affirmative action barred a full floor vote in the Senate. Consequently, President Clinton appointed Lee as acting assistant attorney general for civil rights at the Justice Department. To deal with this frustrating situation, along with efforts of other Asian American organizations, the NCAPA launched a massive signature-gathering campaign and called for a national action day with rallies to be held in Washington, D.C.; Los Angeles; San Francisco; New York; Philadelphia; and Salt Lake City. Many local Asian American communities were contacted via the Internet and asked to approach those senators on the Judiciary Committee through letter-writing, phone calls, and in-person contacts on the issue that was deemed historically critical by many Asian Americans. In the end, although these campaigns failed to influence the committee members' votes, President Clinton bypassed the Senate confirmation process and exercised his executive power to appoint Lee three years later on August 3, 2000 (Lien 2001b).

The eventual appointment of Lee happened during a highly sensitive period when Asian Americans' civil rights were seriously challenged. There were two incidents of senseless killing during the time: a Filipino American was killed by a white supremacist in Los Angeles in August 1999; and three Asian Americans, a Jewish woman, and a black man were shot to death by a white male in Pittsburgh in April 2000. To demand justice, the NCAPA and other Asian American organizations joined the local civil rights organizations to stage rallies and raise funds. In addition to calling for immediate action to confirm Lee, they also demanded the passage of strong hate crime legislation and serious enforcement of the laws (Lien 2001b).

In October 2003 NCAPA members met with House Democratic Leader Nancy Pelosi (D-CA); Representatives David Wu (D-OR) and Mike Honda (D-CA), the chair and vice-chair of the Congressional Asian Pacific American Caucus (CAPAC); and Representatives Ed Case (D-HI) and George Miller (D-CA) to discuss many policy issues in light of pending legislation, including civil liberties, immigration, native Hawaiian recognition, the economy, health care, and education (NCAPA website).

This series of calls for action by the NCAPA in the preceding years finally culminated in a release of its presidential election year project, *Call to Action: Platform for Asian Pacific Americans National Policy Priorities 2004*, in Washington, D.C., on February 12, 2004, which was endorsed by eighteen leading national Asian Pacific American organizations, including many organizations previously introduced, such as the AAI, AAPCHO, APIAHF, JACL, KAC, NAPABA, NAPALC, and OCA. Policy priorities outlined in this perhaps most important document in Asian American history include issues concerning economic empowerment, community and economic development, education, health care, civil rights, immigration, language access, workers' rights, women, senior citizens, data collection, and technology (NCAPA 2004a). These comprehensive policy concerns were all specified in great detail in this sixty-five-page *Platform* that is divided into five sections: *We, the People of the United States; Promote the General Welfare; Establish Justice; The Door to America's Future; and Working for a Prosperous Future* (NCAPA 2004b). By releasing this document, the NCAPA planned to "assist the leaders of this country in going beyond the stereotypes and addressing the community's issues in platforms and speeches" and urged that "presidential candidates and the political parties should consider these issues carefully" (NCAPA 2004b, 1–3). Less than two weeks after releasing this document, NCAPA officers met with then Democratic presidential candidate Senator John Edwards on February 25 in California to discuss it (NCAPA 2004c). However, neither President George W. Bush nor Senator John Kerry, the Democratic presidential nominee, ever responded to the contents of the NCAPA *Platform*.

Formosa Association for Public Affairs (FAPA)

As the backbone of the Taiwan lobby, not only did the Formosa Association for Public Affairs (FAPA) monitor any Taiwan-related legislation, but it also pushed for passage of legislation in favor of Taiwan, including the following pieces of legislation passed in the 1990s:

- H. Con. Res. 293 of 1990 stating "in determining the future of Taiwan, the will and wishes of the people on the island should be taken into account through effective democratic mechanisms, such as a plebiscite."
- H. Con. Res. 148 of 1996 stating "the United States military forces should defend Taiwan in the event of invasion, missile attack, or blockade by the People's Republic of China."
- H. Con. Res. 212 of 1996 stating "for the efficiency of the United Nations, Taiwan's participation would be desirable and valuable."
- H.R. 2386 of 1997 stating "the United States should help Taiwan defend itself in case of threats or a military attack by the People's Republic of China against Taiwan."
- H. Con. Res. 334 of 1998 stating "Taiwan and its 21,000,000 people should have appropriate and meaningful participation in the World Health Organization." (FAPA website)

Because the passage of all these congressional resolutions would have made a profound impact on the United States-China-Taiwan triangular relationship favorable to Taiwan, they were approved mostly in the face of strong opposition by the White House and harshly criticized by the People's Republic of China (Chi 2002).

Facing the new millennium, the FAPA gave priority to the Taiwan Security Enhancement Act (TSEA), Taiwan's participation in the World Health Organization (WHO) and other international organizations, and reevaluation of the "one China policy" of the United

States. The FAPA made progress in most of these four areas, especially the top two priorities of the TSEA and WHO. The lobbying tactics of FAPA members can be specifically exemplified in their lobbying efforts to push for the passage of the legislation related to the WHO (Chi 2002).

Generally speaking, FAPA members and staff work to achieve their goals simultaneously at both national and grassroots levels. At the grassroots level, members of local FAPA chapters across the country are provided information on the targeted legislation by the Washington-based headquarters and then ask their members of Congress for their support. In the meantime, petition letters prepared by the headquarters are distributed and collected at the local levels. These letters, often in thousands, are sent back to the headquarters and personally delivered by FAPA staff to members of Congress. In addition, local members are encouraged to use materials supplied by the headquarters to write and send letters to the editor and op-ed pieces to local newspapers for publication (Chi 2002).

At the national level, FAPA staff members maintain regular communication with members of Congress and the administration via faxes and e-mails of press releases and reports on the targeted legislation. Moreover, staff members also hold special meetings with congresspersons and their aides, asking them to take specific legislative actions, and organize press conferences to detail the legislation and FAPA actions. They also send letters to the editors of major newspapers and magazines. For example, in 1998 and 1999 three such letters were printed in the *Washington Post,* five in the *Washington Times,* and one in the *Economist* (FAPA website).

Specifically, the lobbying effort in the case of the WHO legislation began in Cleveland, Ohio. As Taiwan is not a member of the WHO as a result of China's opposition, the FAPA chapter president in Cleveland made a request to his friend U.S. Representative Sherrod Brown to change the situation. In response, Brown introduced a resolution in the House to support Taiwan's participation in the WHO in February 1999. Meanwhile, FAPA headquarters asked its members across the nation to contact their respective members of Congress for cosponsorship of the resolution. In addition to extensive efforts made at the local levels, the headquarters staff specifically targeted members of the Foreign Relations Committee in the House and constantly provided them with updated information about new developments. For example, a virus broke out in Taiwan that summer and killed over fifty children, which could have been prevented if Taiwan was a WHO member. Consequently, the executive director of the FAPA,

Coen Blaauw, wrote an article on the issue to promote Taiwan's membership. Representative Brown then sent this article on his letterhead to the *Washington Post*. After the *Post* printed it, the FAPA sent a copy to all congressional aides with a cover letter specifying the necessity of Taiwan's entry into the international organization. Finally, Brown's resolution (H.R. 1794) was passed in the House that summer and passed in the Senate later on (Chi 2002).

In 2000 the FAPA created a more lobby-oriented sister organization, the Formosan Association for Public Relations (FAPR). As a nonprofit, tax-deductible organization, the FAPA is only allowed to spend a maximum 20 percent of its yearly expenses on lobbying. The FAPR was thus formed to focus exclusively on lobbying activities. The FAPR is an I.R.S.-designated 501(c)(4) organization that is legally able to conduct unlimited lobbying without affecting its tax-exempt status, as long as its targeted legislation is related to its founding purpose. Coupled with the potential lobbying influence of the newly established FAPR, the FAPA could become more effective in lobbying on Capitol Hill in the future. Furthermore, with a growing population of half a million or so Taiwanese Americans, it appears that the FAPA could raise significant amounts of funds and continue to increase its membership. Eventually, the FAPA hopes to establish a Taiwanese American Political Action Committee (PAC) in the Taiwanese American community (Chi 2002).

Conclusion

This chapter is an overview of how East Asian Americans have been involved in interest-group politics in varying forms of lobbying, litigation, and public education through issue advocacy to fight for racial equality and social justice in American society. The history of East Asian Americans' participation in interest-group politics can be roughly classified into three periods by two historical turning points.

The first phase was from their first arrival in the New World in the mid-nineteenth century to the Asian American movement in the late 1960s. During this early period, the Chinese, the Japanese, and the Koreans established organizations within their respective ethnic communities, serving only the interests of their own members. Their community organizations began with weak regional and family-based associations, then expanded to umbrella mutual aid organizations, and finally became powerful and organized political interest groups. However, during these early years, there was little effort devoted to building interethnic coalitions across the Chinese, Japanese, and Korean communities.

The second phase of East Asian Americans' participation in interest groups came with the birth of the Asian American movement in the late 1960s. Political organizations of a truly pan-Asian American nature were not created until the movement brought pan-Asian American ethnic identity and unity into the minds of many Asian American campus and community activists. Nonetheless, there were more intraethnic groups than interethnic groups during the second phase of the development of East Asian American interest groups.

The beginning of the last phase was marked by the murder of Vincent Chin in 1982 and other anti-Asian violence in the subsequent years. More and more panethnic Asian American groups have come into existence since, culminating into the formation of several national large-scale coalitions, such as the National Council for Asian Pacific Americans.

Among the three East Asian American groups, the Japanese Americans have had the most established and visible organizations because of their historical experiences and organizational strategies, while the Korean American community, given its much smaller population size in the early years, has the shortest history of formal organizations. As to key organizational concerns of these groups, while participating in many America-related activities, Chinese, Taiwanese, and Korean Americans have been more involved in homeland-related issues than Japanese Americans, who are the most assimilated into mainstream America among the East Asian American groups.

In terms of organizational strategies, just like other interest groups in the American political system, the East Asian American organizations have adopted similar strategies of lobbying, litigation, and public education to achieve their goals. In addition, as their population has dramatically increased, East Asian American organizations are more electorally involved than ever in activities of promoting voter registration, mobilizing voters to support candidates and referendum issues, and raising campaign funds and making campaign contributions, all of which are discussed in the next chapter.

References

Bill, James A., and Robert L. Hardgrave. 1981. *Comparative Politics: The Quest for Theory.* Lanham, MD: University Press of America.
CACA website: http://cacanational.org. Accessed April 20, 2004.

Chan, Sucheng. 1991. *Asian American: An Interpretive History.* New York: Twayne.

Chi, Tsung. 2002. "From the China Lobby to the Taiwan Lobby: Movers and Shakers of the U.S.-China-Taiwan Triangular Relationship." In *The Expanding Roles of Chinese Americans in U.S.-China Relations: Transnational Networks and Trans-Pacific Interactions.* Edited by Peter H. Koehn and Xiao-huang Yin. Armonk, NY: M. E. Sharpe.

Edwards, George C., III, Martin P. Wattenberg, and Robert L. Lineberry. 1999. *Government in America: People, Politics, and Policy.* 8th ed. New York: Longman.

Espiritu, Yen Le. 1992. *Asian American Panethnicity: Bridging Institutions and Identities.* Philadelphia, PA: Temple University.

FAPA website: http://www.fapa.org. Accessed September 2004.

Fong, Timothy P. 2002. *The Contemporary Asian American Experience: Beyond the Model Minority.* 2d ed. Upper Saddle River, NJ: Prentice Hall.

Fugita, Stephen S., and David J. O'Brien. 1991. *Japanese American Ethnicity: The Persistence of Community.* Seattle: University of Washington.

Hunt, Kimberly N., ed. 2004. *Encyclopedia of Associations: An Associations Unlimited Reference. Volume 1: National Organizations of the United States.* 41st ed. Detroit, MI: Gale.

JACL website: http://jacl.org. Accessed April 20, 2004.

KAC website: http://www.kacla.org. Accessed April 20, 2004.

Kitano, Harry H. L., and Roger Daniels. 1988. *Asian Americans: Emerging Minorities.* Englewood Cliffs, NJ: Prentice Hall.

Lai, James S. 2003. "Asian Pacific Americans and the Pan-Ethnic Question." In *Asian American Politics: Law, Participation, and Policy.* Edited by Don T. Nakanishi and James S. Lai. Lanham, MD: Rowman and Littlefield.

Lien, Pei-te. 2001b. *The Making of Asian America through Political Participation.* Philadelphia, PA: Temple University.

Mann, Jim. 2000. "Taiwan's New Era Looks a Lot Like Old One." *Los Angeles Times,* July 12, 2000, A5.

NAKA website: http://www.naka.org. Accessed April 20, 2004.

Nakanishi, Don T., and James S. Lai. 2003. "Introduction: Understanding Asian American Politics." In *Asian American Politics: Law, Participation, and Policy.* Edited by Don T. Nakanishi and James S. Lai. Lanham, MD: Rowman and Littlefield.

NCAPA. 2004a. *National APA Leaders Release Policy Priorities.* Press Release (February 12). Website: *http://www.ncapaonline.org/detail_pressrelease.asp?PID=10*

———. 2004b. *Call to Action: Platform for Asian Pacific Americans National Policy Priorities 2004.* Website: http://www.ncapaonline.org. Accessed April 20, 2004.

———. 2004c. *NCAPA Officers Meet with Presidential Candidate Senator John Edwards.* Press Release (February 25). Website: *http://www.ncapaonline .org/detail_pressrelease.asp?PID=11*

NCAPA website: http://ncapaonline.org. Accessed April 20, 2004.

Ng, Franklin. 1998. *The Taiwanese Americans.* Westport, CT: Greenwood.

O'Brien, David J., and Stephen S. Fugita. 1991. *The Japanese American Experience.* Bloomington: Indiana University.

OCA website: http://www.ocanatl.org. Accessed March 15, 2004.

Park, Edward J. W. 2001. "The Impact of Mainstream Political Mobilization on Asian American Community: The Case of Korean Americans in Los Angeles, 1992–1998." In *Asian Americans and Politics: Perspectives, Experiences, Prospects.* Edited by Gordon H. Chang. Washington, DC: Woodrow Wilson and Stanford, CA: Stanford University.

TACL website: http://ncapaonline.org. Accessed April 20, 2004.

Takahashi, Jere. 1997. *Nisei/Sansei: Shifting Japanese American Identities and Politics.* Philadelphia, PA: Temple University.

Takaki, Ronald. 1998. *Strangers from a Different Shore: A History of Asian Americans.* Updated and rev. ed. Boston: Back Bay.

Wang, Zuoyue. 2002. "Chinese American Scientists and U.S.-China Scientific Relations: From Richard Nixon to Wen Ho Lee." In *The Expanding Roles of Chinese Americans in U.S.-China Relations: Transnational Networks and Trans-Pacific Interactions.* Edited by Peter H. Koehn and Xiao-huang Yin. Armonk, NY: M. E. Sharpe.

Watanabe, Paul Y. 1999. "Asian American Activism and U.S. Foreign Policy." In *Across the Pacific: Asian Americans and Globalization.* Edited by Evelyn Hu-DeHart. Philadelphia, PA: Temple University.

Wei, William. 1993. *The Asian American Movement.* Philadelphia, PA: Temple University.

4

Participation in Electoral Politics

articipatory activities of East Asian Americans in American politics can be generally classified into electoral and nonelectoral politics. Compared with a large variety of nonelectoral political activities, electoral politics, including party politics, is presumed to be the most direct and powerful way for people, especially for members of minority groups in terms of class, race, gender, and other features, to express their views and register their frustration and discontent. As a result, the extent to which each minority group participates in the electoral process is viewed by the mainstream society as a salient indicator of the collective political power of the group. By the same token, electoral politics, especially the actual voting process, is a more important aspect of East Asian Americans' political participation than their participation in protest politics and interest-group politics.

Although Asian Americans have a long-standing tradition of political participation in American politics, they—the so-called quiet Americans—had not been recognized as a visible political force until the 1970s, when they became the fastest growing segment of the U.S. population with high concentrations in several major electoral states, such as California, Texas, and New York. As statistics in the first chapter suggest, between 1960 and 2002 the Asian American population as a whole increased from less than 1 million to more than 11 million. As for East Asian Americans, the combined population of Chinese, Japanese, and Korean Americans was 1.1 million, 1.9 million, 3.3 million, and 4.6 million in 1970, 1980, 1990, and 2002, respectively. As impressive as it may be, the question is whether or not this rapid growth in population as a whole and socioeconomic success for some members of the community have been translated into an increase in electoral and party participation and thus an increase in political power for Asian Americans? Why or why not? To answer these questions, this chapter examines the patterns of participation of East Asian Americans in electoral and party politics by focusing on naturalization and citizenship, registration, voting turnout, voting preferences, political party affiliation, and campaign contributions.

Naturalization and Citizenship

It is no easy task for Asian Americans to become voters. It was the case historically and it is still the case for many Asian American immigrants today. Unthinkable to most other minority groups in the United States, the first hurdle the largely immigrant-dominated Asian American community needs to overcome to be electorally active is naturalization restrictions.

Historically, immigrants from Asia were deprived of citizenship until the 1940s and 1950s. According to the 1790 Naturalization Act, only "free white persons" were eligible to apply for naturalization. This made Asian immigrants a disenfranchised group who were denied the right to become citizens regardless of the duration of their stay in the United States, and as a result, they were also without the right to vote or even run for public office. The laws were modified in 1870 after the Civil War to allow people of African ancestry to apply for citizenship. But, for Asian immigrants, the laws remained the same, and the chance to change them was even slimmer after passage of the infamous Chinese Exclusion Law in 1882. This denial of citizenship was further reconfirmed by the historic Supreme Court case of *Ozawa v. United States* in 1922, which ruled that only white persons and persons of African decent were granted the privilege of naturalization. Only Asians born in the United States were not "aliens ineligible to citizenship" (Wei 1993; Espiritu 1992). Therefore, in those long years prior to World War II, the majority of Asians, mainly Chinese and Japanese immigrants, were not eligible to vote.

Finally, Chinese immigrants became eligible for citizenship in 1943 when the Chinese Exclusion Act was repealed by Congress during the war, and the Japanese and the Koreans were granted the same right to become citizens after the passage of the McCarran-Walter Immigration and Naturalization Act in 1952, which annulled the racial restrictions imposed by the 1790 naturalization law (Wei 1993).

In the subsequent decades, with the continuous arrival of new immigrants, the Asian American community first became an immigrant-dominated society and then a society with more naturalized citizens than U.S.-born citizens. The decade of the 1970s was a critical period in the history of Asian Americans in that, while the U.S.-born population still made up 52 percent of the Asian American population in 1970, the percentage dropped sharply to 30 percent and 24 percent in 1980 and 1996, respectively, making the U.S.-born population a minority for the first time. Even among those with citizenship or who were eligible voters, U.S.-born Asian Americans also became a minority in the mid-1980s when their number was exceeded by that of naturalized citizens. While the percentage of the U.S.-born decreased from 30 percent in 1980 to 21 percent in 1990, the percentage of naturalized citizens increased from 25 percent to 34 percent during the same period (Ong and Lee 2001, Table 6.1).

In 1996 the overall naturalization rate for Asian immigrants was 44 percent, but there were tremendous temporal variations behind this number. In the same year, the naturalization rate was 16 percent, 64 percent, and 88 percent for Asian immigrants who had stayed in the United States for less than ten years, between eleven and twenty years, and over twenty years, respectively (Ong and Lee 2001, Table 6.2). Obviously, the longer they stayed in the country, the more likely they were to be naturalized.

As for intragroup comparisons, it is intriguing to note that both Chinese and Korean immigrants were more likely to be naturalized than Japanese immigrants. For example, in 1990, the naturalization rate for Chinese and Korean immigrants was about 80 percent, while the rate for Japanese immigrants was only 35 percent (Ong and Nakanishi 2003, Table 3.2e). It appears ironic that as the most assimilated group into mainstream American society among the three, the Japanese American community had the lowest rate of naturalization. This is probably because a large number of Japanese nationals were employed by Japanese transnational corporations and came to the United States to work in the American subsidiaries of these companies. They were rather transnational workers than immigrants (Ong and Nakanishi 2003). Although some of them saw themselves as foreigners and still maintained strong ties to the homeland, others were admitted on working visas and thus not allowed to be naturalized even if they had wanted to become citizens.

In comparison to immigrants from other parts of the world, the overall naturalization rate of Asian Americans (44 percent) was between that of non-Hispanic Caucasian Americans (54 percent) and that of Latino Americans (23 percent) in 1996. However, it is noteworthy that, just like that of Latino Americans, the naturalization rate of Asian Americans has been diluted by the constant influx of new immigrants. For instance, among Asian Americans who had stayed in the United States for more than twenty years, 88 percent of them were already naturalized in 1996, 5 percent higher than that of non-Hispanic Caucasian Americans in the same year (Ong and Lee 2001, Table 6.2).

The most recent statistics released in 2004 indicate that the naturalization rate for Asian Americans was 48 percent, 11 percent higher than the corresponding rate for the U.S. foreign-born population as a whole (U.S. Census Bureau 2004). Quite a few factors contributed to the relatively higher rate of naturalization for Asian Americans, including their higher educational attainment, greater distance from their homelands, repressive regimes in their homelands, the ability of citizens to bring in relatives to the United States, and the possibility of losing welfare benefits after 1994. However, the naturalization rate could be even higher, if not for problems Asian immigrants have with lack of English proficiency (see Table 1.8 in Chapter 1), lack of adequate knowledge of the U.S. government and Constitution, and lack of time and money to spend on the lengthy process of naturalization (Lien 2001b). On the issue of lack of money, starting on April 30, 2004, the application fee for naturalization was raised from $310 to $390, including $70 for fingerprinting (*Chinese Daily News*, April 30, 2004, B4), which makes the process of naturalization more difficult, especially for low-income immigrants.

Even though they have a relatively higher rate of naturalization than some other racial/ethnic groups in the United States, Asian Americans still have the smallest percentage of citizens among all the groups. This is because citizens of any group consist of both U.S.-born and naturalized citizens, and Asian Americans have the smallest percentage of U.S.-born citizens within their population. For example, only 59 percent of Asian Americans were citizens in 1998, whereas 61 percent, 98 percent, 96 percent, and 98 percent of Latino, Native, African, and Caucasian Americans, respectively, were citizens in that year (Lien 2001b, Table 3.3). Asian Americans also had a smaller share of the citizenry than all the groups but Native Americans. In 1998 Asian Americans constituted only 2.4 percent of the U.S. citizenry, which is not only much lower than that of Latino (6.8 percent), African (11.8 percent), and Caucasian Americans (78.3 percent), but also lower than their share of the U.S. population of 3.7 percent (Lien 2001b, Table 3.4).

From the above, it is apparent that even after the removal of the legal restrictions on naturalization, the Asian American community is still not a formidable political power, partly due to its small overall population and partly due to the fact that a sizable number of Asian American citizens did not register to vote.

Registration

Ideally, Asian Americans could make the best use of their high population concentrations in the key electoral states of California, Texas, and New York—the states having the largest number of electoral votes—to be a swing vote to influence the results of presidential as well as congressional elections. However, this idea of having powerful electoral leverage would work only if Asian American citizens were not only registered voters but also actual voters who go to the polling places on election day. Otherwise, their strategic advantage would be greatly compromised.

Although Asian Americans have a high naturalization rate, their voter registration rate has been lower than those of other ethnic groups. For example, according to a survey conducted in 1998 by the Census Bureau of the U.S. Department of Commerce, *Current Population Survey: Voter Supplement File,* only 49 percent of surveyed Asian American citizens (or 29 percent of Asian Americans as a whole, including noncitizens) were registered voters, in contrast to 55 percent of Latino Americans and 69 percent of non-Hispanic Caucasian Americans in that year, and a similar pattern can be found throughout all the elections held in the 1990s (Lien 2001b, Table 3.3).

It is difficult to explain why the voter registration rate has been lower for this particular ethnic group, whose members have relatively higher educational attainment and higher incomes than members of other groups, both of which factors are supposedly related to a higher level of political participation. What is more puzzling is the fact that, according to the *Current Population Survey* conducted in 1996, there was no difference at all in the voter registration rate between U.S.-born and foreign-born Asian Americans: both groups had an identical rate of 57 percent (Ong and Lee 2001, Table 6.4). As even for U.S.-born Asian American citizens the registration rate was still lower than other ethnic groups, explanations such as language barriers, age structure, immigrants' sojourn mentality, and political apathy derived from negative political experiences back in the homeland do not have much credibility. Even though it is likely that political orientations can be transmitted from one generation to the next, it is still puzzling why the two generations had an identical registration rate.

One causal relationship associated with the fluctuation of Asian Americans' voter registration rates may be plausibly advanced. It is interesting to observe that the registration rate for Asian Americans in 1998 was the lowest in the 1990s. One possible explanation is that this decline was likely the result of the campaign finance controversies in the mid-1990s that really frustrated many Asian Americans. Whether or not hostility from the mainstream society could be the cause, the persistent pattern of low voter registration rates is one of the aspects of Asian Americans' political participation that requires serious empirical research. Research results of this kind might help Asian Americans successfully to convert their relatively higher incomes and educational backgrounds into a higher registration rate and more votes.

Voting Turnout

Among the three electorally related statistical figures—namely, naturalization rate, registration rate, and voting turnout rate—the last one is the one that really counts in the electoral process. This is particularly true in the case of Asian Americans, because many of them are not citizens; and among those who are citizens, many are not registered to vote; and among registered voters, many do not vote.

It is generally true that Asian Americans are less likely to vote than other ethnic groups. However, the issue of voting turnout is more complicated than it appears to be, because it involves three types of statistics: the percentage of the voting-age population that votes, the percentage of citizens who vote, and the percentage of registered voters who vote.

First, according to the same 1998 survey introduced in the preceding section, the voting percentage of all voting-age Asian American respondents was 19 percent, which is just 1 percent less than Latino American (20 percent) but 28 percent less than the non-Hispanic Caucasian American (47 percent) percentages. Second, in terms of voting turnout among citizens or eligible voters, which is commonly taken as the "voting turnout," the percentage was 32 percent for the Asian Americans in contrast to 33 percent for Latino Americans, and 47 percent for non-Hispanic Caucasian Americans (whose percentage is identical to the first percentage because almost all voting-age non-Hispanic Caucasian Americans were citizens). The last type of statistic is the most intriguing, because the percentage of Asian American registered voters who actually voted was 66 percent, which was 6 percent higher than Latino American turnout (60 percent) and just 2 percent lower than non-Hispanic Caucasian American turnout in 1998. In a similar survey conducted in 1994, the statistics show that in terms of voting turnout among registered voters, Asian Americans' participation (76 percent) was even higher than that of non-Hispanic Caucasian Americans (74 percent) that year (Lien 2001b, Table 3.3).

According to the above 1998 statistics, Asian Americans' electoral participation can be approximately summarized as follows: one out of every five voting-age Asian Americans (19 percent), one out of every three Asian American citizens (32 percent), and two out of every three Asian American registered voters (66 percent) actually went to the polling places to vote. Therefore, relatively speaking, it is not the voting process per se that really caused the problem of lack of voting participation among Asian Americans, but that such a problem is more likely to emerge during the naturalization process and the registration process. All in all, caused by all the above-mentioned problems, Asian Americans contributed only 1.7 percent of the electorate in 1998, while they contributed 2.4 percent of the citizenry and 3.7 percent of the U.S. population in that year (Lien 2001b). The presumed electoral significance of the rapid growth of the Asian American population in recent years has been severely counterweighted by these gaps.

If comparing the voting participation between the U.S.-born and foreign-born Asian Americans, the results of the 1996 *Current Population Survey* suggest that not only was there no difference at all in their registration rates, but also that both groups shared an almost identical voting turnout (45 percent for the U.S.-born population and 44 percent for the foreign-born population) (Ong and Lee 2001, Table 6.4). As for intragroup comparisons, according to results of the 2001 National Asian American Political Survey (PNAAPS, previously discussed in Chapter 1), 44 percent of all the respondents, including noncitizens, cast their ballots in the 2000 presidential election. Even though this percentage is unusually high in contrast to 19 percent in 1998 or other historical figures prior to 1998, it is still useful to examine the intragroup variations. Among the three East Asian American groups, Japanese Americans reported the highest voting turnout at 63 percent, followed by Chinese Americans at 41 percent. The Korean Americans had the lowest turnout at 34 percent (Lien, et al. 2001).

To increase the voter registration rate and turnout, national Asian American organizations launched vigorous voter registration and education drives in Asian American communities throughout the nation. In 1996 the Organization of Chinese Americans (OCA) took the lead with 18 other Asian American national organizations in forming the first National Asian Pacific American Voter Registration Campaign. Across the country, more than 100 Asian American organizations joined the campaign. One of the highlights of the effort was the establishment of a multilingual toll-free number to provide Asian Americans information on voter registration and upcoming voter education activities. In the end, the campaign successfully registered 75,000 new voters. The campaign did not stop there; it continued into the 2000 presidential election. Once again, the OCA, along with many other Asian American organizations, formed another national coalition, Youth Vote 2000, perhaps the nation's largest nonpartisan coalition ever organized to promote voting participation of those between 18 and 30 years old (Lien 2001b). However, among young Asian American voters between 18 and 22 in 2000, only 22 percent were registered voters, even though 71 percent of these registered voters did vote. On May 5, 2004, a large number of Asian American organizations, along with Asian American members of Congress, announced in a press conference held on Capitol Hill the commencement of another national vote campaign for the 2004 presidential election: the Asian and Pacific Islander American Vote (APIAVote) 2004. The campaign activities include a toll-free number to provide assistance in English, Mandarin, Cantonese, Korean, Tagalog, Vietnamese, Laotian, Cambodian, and Hmong, a voter education project to enhance understanding of the importance of voting, and other activities (*Chinese Daily News,* May 6, 2004; APIAVote website).

The Asian American national organizations also recognized that to boost voting turnout of the immigrant community, it was imperative to institute bilingual voting assistance and ballots. When the Voting Rights Act was passed in 1965, it guaranteed the provision of bilingual voting assistance only to Hispanics, American Indians, and Alaska Natives. Although an amendment to the Voting Rights Act in 1975 designated Asian Americans as a language minority eligible to receive bilingual voting assistance, they have to meet two conditions:

(1) they must reside in a jurisdiction where at least 5 percent of the voting-age citizens belong to their language community, and (2) the illiteracy rate (for English) of their citizen population is higher than the national illiteracy rate. Because the benchmark of 5 percent was too high to reach, no Asian American language communities outside Hawaii were eligible under the 1975 amendment. In the summer of 1992, Asian American organizations helped lobby Congress not only to extend the bilingual provisions of the Voting Rights Act for fifteen years, but also to amend the law to require bilingual voting assistance in counties where Asian American communities either meet the 5-percent mark or have more than 10,000 voting-age citizens who speak the same Asian language with limited English ability (Lien 2001b; Fong 2002).

As a result of the new amendment in 1992, ten counties in the nation were required to provide voting assistance in five Asian Pacific languages, namely Chinese, Japanese, Vietnamese, Tagalog, and Ilocano (in Hawaii). Among them, Chinese voting assistance was provided in the three California counties of Alameda, Los Angeles, and San Francisco, while Japanese assistance was provided in Los Angeles County and Honolulu County of Hawaii. Such bilingual voting assistance includes translation of written materials, the hiring of bilingual registrars or deputy registrars and interpreters, and advertisement of the availability of bilingual assistance, but not the translation of the ballot itself (Lien 2001b).

In the summer of 1994 another case involving bilingual voting rights took place at the local level in New York City. The Asian American Legal Defense and Education Fund (AALDEF) there embarked on a campaign for bilingual ballots with candidates' names translated into the Chinese language. The city Board of Elections refused the request for the reason that the ballot machines lacked enough space for that purpose. The AALDEF later claimed victory after the Civil Rights Division of the U.S. Department of Justice ruled the city's decision a violation of the provisions of bilingual voting assistance specified in the Voting Rights Act (Fong 2002). Even with the above victories on national and local fronts, the battle for bilingual voting rights still goes on, with translation of the entire ballot its final end.

Nationwide voting turnout of Asian Americans is indeed important, but it is more important and electorally meaningful to examine the levels of Asian Americans' voting turnout in key electoral states. As discussed earlier, Asian Americans have the highest population concentrations in California, New York, Hawaii, and Texas. Because Hawaii is not a key electoral state in presidential elections and is also an anomaly in the sense that a majority of Asian Americans in the island state are U.S. born, it is excluded from the following interstate comparisons.

California, New York, and Texas altogether share nearly one-quarter of the electoral college votes in the national presidential election, and these three states alone happen to house more than 50 percent of the Asian American population in the United States. According to the 1998 *Current Population Survey* results, while the national average of voter turnout for Asian Americans was 19 percent, the survey showed that 22 percent, 12 percent, and 6 percent of all voting-age Asian American respondents in California, New York, and Texas, respectively, voted in the midterm election that year. If calculated against citizen population, then the voting turnout was 35 percent, 23 percent, and 13 percent in California, New York, and Texas, respectively, in contrast to Asian Americans' national average of 32 percent. In terms of voting turnout percentage for registered voters, the numbers became 69 percent, 64 percent, and 31 percent in the three states in the same order, whereas the national average for Asian Americans as a whole was 66 percent (Lien 2001b, Tables 3.5 and 3.6). All these statistical figures suggest the same pattern: California leads in terms of voting participation, followed by New York, and Texas finishing a distant third with turnouts about half those of New York. This statistical pattern also indicates that Asian Americans in California, a state with the largest number of electoral college votes, have the greatest potential to become a swing vote in the presidential elections.

The above interstate variation in Asian American voting participation is likely to be a function of several factors, including historical experiences of mobilization, devoted political elites, and ethnic interest groups and voter education organizations in each of these key states. Among these factors, the effect of local voter education organizations in particular is probably of greatest significance in contributing to a higher voting turnout.

Echoing the efforts of those national voter education campaigns, quite a few voter education organizations came into existence at the local levels, including Vision 21, Chinese Americans United for Self Empowerment (CAUSE), the Asian American Voter Coalition, the Asian Pacific American Legal Center of Southern California (APALC), the Asian American Legal Defense Education Fund (AALDEF) of New York, the Korean American Coalition (KAC), the Leadership Education for Asian Pacifics (LEAP), and the Chinese American Voter Education Committee of San Francisco. These organizations were involved in activities such as voter education and registration, citizenship classes, and leadership training aimed at increasing political awareness and voting participation of Asian Americans (Lien 2001b; Nakanishi 2000). These local organizations differed from the national registration campaigns in that the former were ongoing campaigns on a regular basis, while the latter were more episodic projects on an ad hoc basis. Among them, the CAUSE in Southern California is one of the most visible local voter education organizations in the Asian American community.

Case Study: Center for Asian Americans United for Self Empowerment (CAUSE)

Based in Pasadena, California, the CAUSE is a nonprofit organization dedicated to advancing the political empowerment of the Asian American community through voter registration and education, community outreach, and leadership development (CAUSE website). At its founding in 1993, the initial title of the organization was Chinese Americans United for Self Empowerment. It later became the CAUSE-Vision 21 after two organizations of similar natures decided to merge in order to better serve the interests of the local community. The latest organizational development happened in 2003, when it changed its name once again to the current Center for Asian Americans United for Self Empowerment to show its transformation to a pan–Asian American organization.

The CAUSE has been very active in Southern California. In the realm of voter registration and education, it has mobilized volunteers to register voters in Los Angeles and Orange Counties and set up a toll-free voter assistance hotline. Given the large concentration of Chinese American population in the area and its own history, the CAUSE mainly targets Mandarin- and Cantonese-speaking Chinese Americans, but it also attempts to recruit volunteers who can speak Hindi, Hmong, Korean, Tagalog, Vietnamese, or other Asian languages.

The most common practice undertaken by the CAUSE to register voters is to set up registration booths at various sites, including ethnic supermarkets, shopping centers, festivals, and college campuses. It has been no easy task for the CAUSE, because the majority of Chinese Americans in Southern California are immigrants deeply preoccupied with homeland politics. Even so, the CAUSE has made its contribution. Between June and October 2000, it helped register 1,884 voters before the November presidential election (CAUSE website). In addition to setting up booths in the community, the CAUSE also provides information about upcoming elections, be they national or local, through ethnic media, although it is hard to gauge the effectiveness of these media efforts.

The result of the toll-free voter assistance hotline was fruitful. In the whole month of October 2000, just shortly before the election, there were a total of 1,834 callers, including 576 asking questions about voting and the election and 1,258 requesting elections materials. Among those 576 callers, 116 had questions about sample ballots, 117 about polling sites, 331 about voting procedure, and 12 about propositions and candidates, while 758 out of those 1,258 callers requesting election materials asked for bilingual voter registration forms, 112 for bilingual absentee ballot applications, 272 for a Chinese voters' guide, and 116 for sample ballots (CAUSE website). It is important to note that more than 90 percent of those callers who requested election materials asked for non-English-language materials. Furthermore, even though no statistics were available on the languages used by the callers, there is little doubt that the absolute majority of these calls were not conducted in English. Therefore, the nature of these calls indicates the desirability of voter education organizations such as the CAUSE for the local community.

The CAUSE has also maintained a good relationship with both mainstream and Asian American political leaders. Its honorary advisory board consists of numerous Californian elected officials at the national, state, county, and city levels, including members of Congress, the governor, secretary of state, state senators, state assembly members, Los Angeles County supervisors and sheriffs, and the mayor of Los Angeles. On April 23, 2004, the organization's eleventh anniversary dinner was attended by a multitude of Asian American elected and appointed officials from all over Los Angeles and Orange Counties, in addition to some mainstream political leaders, making it one of the largest gatherings of this kind in Southern California. At the dinner, the CAUSE unveiled its voter registration and outreach plans for the rest of 2004, a presidential election year, including a video presentation of *Movementality*. "Movementality," a blend of the words "movement" and "mentality," is also the name of a campaign to reach youth voters aged eighteen to twenty-five. Its plans for the 2004 election also included a new voter education public service announcement to be aired on a local television channel in Mandarin, Cantonese, Korean, Japanese, Vietnamese, and Tagalog (CAUSE website).

The CAUSE is a typical example of many local Asian American voter education organizations that have made their mark on Asian

American communities by raising the levels of political awareness and efficacy, and helping develop the political infrastructure of the communities.

Voting Preferences

For whom do Asian Americans vote? Has there been a consistent pattern in their voting preferences over time? Are their votes leaning more toward the Republicans, Democrats, or somewhere between the two? These are critical questions not only for political scientists, but also for political practitioners who are eager to garner as much support as possible from this newly developed political force on the American national political scene.

Limited information is available about Asian Americans' voting patterns in elections held before the 1990s. In the 1984 presidential election, Asian American voters in California, who were more likely to be Democrats than Republicans, were in favor of the Republican Ronald Reagan over the Democrat Walter Mondale by 67 percent to 32 percent, which was congruent with the nationwide voting pattern in favor of Reagan in that landslide victory. In the 1986 gubernatorial election, Californian Asian Americans favored Republican Governor George Deukmejian over Democratic candidate Tom Bradley by 53 percent to 47 percent. In the 1988 presidential election, 54 percent of Asian Americans nationwide voted for the Republican George H. W. Bush in contrast to 44 percent for the Democrat Michael Dukakis (Fong 2002). But, this short-term pattern in favor of Republican candidates failed to persist in the 1992 presidential election in which 39 percent of Californian Asian Americans voted for Bill Clinton, 33 percent for George H. W. Bush and 25 percent for Ross Perot, while nationwide Asian Americans favored Bush over Clinton and Perot by 52 percent to 32 percent to 17 percent (Hing 1993). Based upon this limited information, it appears that while Asian Americans across the country were still in support of the Republicans in early 1992, Asian American support in California began declining.

A similar discrepancy in voting preferences between Asian Americans in California and Asian Americans nationwide reappeared in the 1996 presidential election. According to a three-region exit poll sponsored by the National Asian Pacific American Legal Consortium (NAPALC) in the San Francisco/Oakland Bay Area, Los Angeles County, and New York City, Asian Americans in these three areas supported Bill Clinton over Bob Dole 82 percent to 9 percent, 53 percent to 41 percent, and 71 percent to 21 percent, respectively, while a nationwide survey suggested that Asian Americans favored Dole over Clinton by 48 percent to 43 percent (Fong 2002).

This discrepancy vanished in the 2000 presidential election. Depending on different surveys, the percentages of Asian American voters across the nation who voted for Al Gore and George Bush ranged from 55 percent vs. 26 percent to 66 percent vs. 32 percent, while Californian Asian Americans overwhelmingly favored Gore over Bush by 70.5 percent to 28.5 percent (Lien, et al. 2001; Woo 2001). Moreover, a three-region survey similar to that of 1996 was also conducted in 2000 in the Bay Area (surveying Chinese Americans only), Los Angeles, and New York City, and the results were uniformly in favor of Gore by 82 percent to 16 percent, 60.5 percent to 33.5 percent, and 78 percent to 20 percent, respectively (APALC, et al. 2001).

In the 2004 presidential election, Asian American voters nationwide again favored the Democratic candidate, Senator John Kerry, over President George W. Bush. An exit poll conducted by the AALDEF suggested that 74 percent of Asian Americans on the West Coast and the Midwest voted for Senator John Kerry, whereas 24 percent voted for Bush. The APALC released its exit polling results that showed that Asian Americans across the nation favored Kerry over Bush by 57 percent to 41 percent. The results of mainstream media exit polls (which only included a very limited number of Asian American voters) showed that the percentages of Asian American voters across the nation who voted for Kerry and Bush ranged from CNN's 56 percent vs. 44 percent, the *New York Times's* 58 percent vs. 41 percent, the *Los Angeles Times's* 64 percent vs. 34 percent, to the *Washington Post's* 61 percent vs. 39 percent (APIAVote, *Newsletter.* November 12, 2004).

From the above statistics, it seems that Asian American support for the Republican Party first eroded in California starting in the early 1990s and then in the nation as a whole in the 2000 and 2004 presidential elections. Does this mean that there is already a discernible voting pattern of Asian American voters favoring the Democratic Party? In other words, was the 2000 election a so-called realigning election that marked the beginning of a lasting shift in Asian American support away from the Republican Party to the Democrats? The poll results in the 2004 presidential election seemed to lead to such a conclusion, at least in the case of presidential elections. However, from a longer perspective, it apears that Asian American voting preferences will be largely dependent on the candidates and critical issues before and during the election year. For example, many Californian Asian Americans were irritated by the leading role of Republican governor Pete Wilson in passing Proposition 187 in 1994, which deprived undocumented immigrants of educational and social services. In 1996 the Republican-dominated Congress passed a welfare reform bill that, among other things, limited social services to legal immigrants (Fong 2002). More importantly, Asian American communities were very angry at the Republicans' anti-Asian attacks during the campaign finance controversies in 1996–1997 (Aoki 2001). All these incidents contributed, at least in part, to the shift of Asian American support in California starting in the 1990s and later across the country in 2000. With this in mind, it seems that if some critical issues arise, Asian American voters could break away swiftly from one party to another. Therefore, among the three popular voting-pattern models (namely, party voting, candidate voting, and issue voting) in American politics, the issue-voting model is likely to best fit the case of Asian American voting.

Asian American voting patterns in congressional elections also indicate that Asian American voters can shift party support, actually in a rather oscillating way. For example, in the five U.S. House elections held in the 1990s, a majority of Asian American voters supported Democratic candidates in 1990, 1994, and 1998, whereas they cast a majority of their ballots for Republican candidates in 1992 and 1996 (NCAPA 2004). This pattern of oscillation between the two major parties further affirms that there has not been any discernible pattern of Asian American voting preferences.

Are Asian Americans as an ethnic group truly situated near the center of the American political spectrum? One way to answer this question is to study the spectrum of their political ideology, which is commonly viewed as one of the key correlates of the pattern of voting choices. As previously discussed in Chapter 1 (Table 1.10), according to a survey conducted in 1992, the majority of Chinese (44.6 percent), Japanese (50.3 percent) and Korean Americans (59.5 percent) classified themselves as either very conservative or somewhat conservative. However, another survey suggested that in 2001, just nine years later, Chinese (30 percent), Japanese (34 percent) and Korean Americans (33 percent) were more likely to classify themselves as either very liberal or somewhat liberal. Only 13 percent of Chinese, 24 percent of Japanese, and 31 percent of Korean Americans still considered themselves either very conservative or somewhat conservative. The most drastic change occurred to the size of conservative Chinese Americans, which dropped from 44.6 percent to 13 percent between 1992 and 2001. Another apparent change was that East Asian Americans as a whole were more likely to place themselves as "middle of the road."

Based upon the two survey results, it is apparent that there was a dramatic shift of East Asian Americans in the spectrum of political ideology in the 1990s when more and more of them identified themselves as either more liberal or in the middle. Not surprisingly, this ideological change coincided with the shift of voting support from the Republicans to the Democrats. Although one's political ideology is supposed to be a more lasting attribute than one's voting choices, it is still too early to draw any meaningful conclusion. It is very likely that this shift from being more conservative to being more liberal was also associated with those anti-immigrant and anti-Asian policies of the Republican Party, which is conventionally labeled as being more conservative than the Democrats.

In any event, all the above changes in either voting preferences or political ideology of Asian Americans have had tremendous implications for their relations toward the two major parties, which is discussed in the next section.

Case Study: 80–20 Political Action Committee

In overcoming all the obstacles to their voting participation, many Asian Americans become citizens, registered voters, and then finally actual voters, but voting alone cannot be automatically equated to voting power, unless there is a discernible voting pattern in favor of a particular political party, or so-called bloc voting. To achieve this goal, Asian American leaders founded the first national, nonpartisan Asian American political action committee in 1998, the 80–20 Initiative.

The full name of this organization is the 80–20 Political Action Committee, Incorporated, or 80–20 PAC, with objectives to win equality and justice for all Asian Pacific Americans by forming a swing bloc vote. The name "80–20" suggests the ideal of being able to direct 80 percent of Asian American votes and money to the presidential candidate endorsed by the organization, who best represents the interests of all Asian Americans (80–20 website).

Although the 80–20 PAC is an Asian American organization with representatives from all major Asian American ethnic groups, its six founders are mostly Chinese American leaders, including Chang-Lin Tien, the late chancellor of the University of California, Berkeley; S. B. Woo, former lieutenant governor of Delaware; Michael Lin, former national president of the Organization of Chinese Americans; and Henry Tang, chair of the Committee of 100 (Yao 2002). Among them, S. B. Woo has been the backbone of the organization since its inception. In addition to being former lieutenant governor of Delaware in the 1980s, Woo is a professor of molecular and atomic physics and former national president of the Organization of Chinese Americans (Fong 2002; Woo 2001).

The 80–20 PAC is basically a cyberspace political organization with an e-mail list of 650,000 Asian Pacific American families and individuals throughout the nation. In 2004 it had local chapters in Los Angeles, Houston, New Jersey, and Boston, and a New York-based chapter being organized (80–20 website).

To achieve the general objective of winning equal justice and opportunity for all Asian Americans, the 80–20 PAC expresses its more specific objectives in the following list of items that it asks presidential candidates to accomplish if elected:

- Vigorously prosecute all cases of discrimination.
- Lift glass ceilings on the professional advancement of Asian Americans.
- Appoint qualified Asian Americans to policymaking positions in the judicial and executive branches of the federal government. (80–20 website)

Among these three objectives, the 80–20 PAC has placed the greatest emphasis on lifting glass ceilings for Asian Americans in the workplace.

The 80–20 PAC has developed rather sophisticated strategies to pursue its goals during each presidential election cycle. Prior to the presidential primary, its president writes each of the presidential primary candidates of major political parties and seeks their commitment to support the 80–20 PAC's objectives. In the meantime, it urges Asian Americans on its e-mail list to withhold financial and other forms of support to any candidates who fail to pledge their commitment and only vote for those who have already made their pledge. After the presidential candidates of the major political parties are nominated in the summer during their national conventions, the 80–20 PAC then holds its endorsement convention, whose delegates are composed of equal portions of Democrats, Independents, and Republicans, to endorse the presidential candidate of a political party having helped Asian Americans the most in achieving equal justice and opportunity in the four years of the last election cycle. At the last stage, the 80–20 PAC urges Asian Americans to form a voting bloc for and make contribution to the endorsed presidential candidate (80–20 website).

This series of strategies was first put into practice before the 2000 presidential election. On June 20, 1999, the 80–20 PAC urged all presidential candidates to pledge in writing their support for 80–20's *Declaration Concerning the 2000 Presidential Election* that included two requests: (1) appoint an Asian American to a cabinet-level position, and (2) help Asian Americans break the glass ceiling in workplaces. Democratic candidate Bill Bradley was the first to endorse it. Actually, he made the commitment as early as July 8, 1999, right after the release of the *Declaration*. In response, the 80–20 PAC helped Bradley with his fund-raising events. Vice President Al Gore did not make his commitment until hours before the deadline on February 15, 2000. Because the Republicans refused to endorse its agenda, the 80–20 PAC, with 350,000 Asian Americans on its e-mail list at the time, urged Asian Americans to boycott the party. In August the 80–20 PAC held its first convention in Los Angeles for three days, during which representatives of both parties' presidential candidates lobbied 80–20 delegates. On August 27, twenty-six of the thirty-three delegates decided to endorse Gore. Therefore, the nonpartisan organization began engaging in partisan campaign activities supporting Gore in the following months (80–20 website; Lien 2001b; Fong 2002).

This was the first time the Asian American community sought to deliver a bloc vote. In the end did the 80–20 PAC successfully deliver the bloc vote—80 percent of the total Asian American vote—that it had promised? This is a fundamental issue concerning how much political clout this first Asian American PAC could wield in the 2004 presidential election. As mentioned earlier, depending upon different survey results, about 54 percent to 66 percent of Asian American voters nationwide favored Gore in the 2000 presidential election, with 70.5 percent voting for Gore in California where the 80–20 PAC had launched aggressive recruitment and election campaigns. As far as building an Asian American voting bloc is concerned, it seems that it would most likely be the case in California, the state with the largest number of electoral votes, than in the nation as a whole. However, according to the 2001 National Asian American Political Survey, only about 18 percent of Asian Americans and 39 percent of Chinese Americans had heard of the 80–20 PAC in 2001 (Lien, et al. 2001). In any case, it is extremely difficult to measure empirically the extent to which this voting preference for Gore can be attributed to the efforts of the 80–20 PAC or to other factors such as the anti-Republican sentiment generated after the campaign contribution controversies in the mid-1990s. Equally difficult would be to gauge how much the 80–20 PAC's 2000 agenda contributed to President Bush's historic appointment of two Asian Americans, Elaine Chao as secretary of labor and Norman Mineta as secretary of transportation, to his cabinet in 2001. In any event, it would be wrong to conclude either that the 80–20 PAC delivered all the votes or that it failed to carry any weight at all in the 2000 presidential election.

Learning from the past, the 80–20 PAC became more aggressive in 2004. First, S. B. Woo, president of the 80–20 PAC, sent a questionnaire to presidential candidates of major political parties on December 1, 2003. The purpose of the three questions in this short questionnaire was to know their willingness to enforce Executive Order 11246 for Asian Americans if elected. Issued by President Lyndon Johnson in 1965, Executive Order 11246 prohibits granting federal money to any organizations that practice discrimination. But, for nearly four decades now, it has been enforced for all Americans except for Asian Americans. The results of the questionnaire were more encouraging than they were four years prior. All nine Democratic presidential candidates, except Reverend Al Sharpton, responded positively, including Senator John Kerry, the eventual Democratic presidential nominee, who agreed in writing to enforce Executive Order 11246 for Asian Americans if elected. Because President George W. Bush did not respond, the 80–20 PAC mobilized Asian Americans to send e-mails to Bush asking him to answer 80–20's questionnaire. But Bush never responded. Eventually, the 80–20 PAC decided to endorse John Kerry on October 2, 2004, with reservation. The reason for the organization's reservation can be attributed to the PAC members' lack of satisfaction with both parties' service to Asian Americans (80–20 website). As discussed earlier, Asian American voters nationwide favored Kerry over Bush in the 2004 presidential election. However, as demonstrated in the case of the 2000 election, it is extremely difficult to gauge empirically the degree to which this voting preference can be attributed to the 80–20 PAC's endorsement.

All in all, regardless of how much the 80–20 PAC has been able to empower the Asian American community, what it has done since its founding in 1998 is totally unprecedented, with monumental importance in the history of Asian Americans. However, the likelihood of its future success hinges on the extent to which it is able to overcome two major obstacles. First, being labeled by some as pro-Democrat, the 80–20 PAC needs to bridge the gap between conservative and liberal Asian Americans. Second, although the 80–20 PAC has vigorously recruited non-Chinese Asian Americans, such as, at the leadership level, bringing the former national president of the Korean American Coalition (KAC) and the former president of the National Asian Pacific American Bar Association (NAPABA), a Japanese American leader, to its steering committee, it is still a largely Chinese American organization. Continuing to develop itself into a fully pan–Asian American political action committee will be the key to its future success.

Party Affiliation and Participation

Closely related to the issue of voting preferences are the issues of party affiliation and participation. But, however intertwined these issues are, voting preference for a party in one particular election indicates only a rather momentary choice rather than a long-lasting commitment to the party through activities of affiliation and participation. Although there have been faces of Asian Americans at both the Democratic and Republican national conventions as well as among cabinet members in both the Clinton and Bush administrations, it is more important to study the participation of the general Asian American population in party politics.

Historically, it was not popular for Asian Americans to join either the Democratic or the Republican Party, because neither party treated them well. Although both parties vowed to work for promoting the interests of all disadvantaged racial and ethnic minorities, they had their share of anti-Asian mentality and activities in the past. Some examples include the Democratic Party's use of anti-Chinese sentiment to garner support in California in the post–Civil War era and making the "Chinese Question" a national issue after an electoral victory in 1867, and the Republican Party's instrumental efforts to secure passage of the 1924 Immigration Act that barred Japanese immigration. As a result, the majority of Asian Americans historically had little participation in party politics. One example of their early interactions with political parties took place in the 1930s when the Democratic Party organized the Chinese American Voting League in New York as part of its successful campaign to garner ethnic votes for Franklin D. Roosevelt (Lien 2001b). In the post–World War II period, Asian American activities in party politics were limited to joining some Democratic clubs in Chinatowns on the mainland and a political coalition under the Democratic Party in Hawaii (Wei 1993).

Until recently, the popular image of Asian Americans in the eyes of the mainstream society was that Asian Americans were anything but political. As the "quiet minority," Asian Americans were uninterested, uninformed, and thus uninvolved in politics. If they really had a political agenda, it would be limited to issues concerning how to continue their educational and economic successes. Because a logical conclusion

to be taken from the above popular image is that it would be mean-
ingless and unnecessary to take these apolitical people seriously, political parties usually did not pay much attention to Asian Americans,
except when they needed to solicit donations from them (Hing 1993).

Party Affiliation

Despite the historically troublesome relationship Asian Americans
have had with both major parties and the inattentive attitudes of the
parties toward them, contrary to the popular image of being apolitical, a sizable portion of Asian Americans have affiliated themselves
with political parties.

In a 1984 survey of Californian Asian Americans, 42 percent were
registered Democrats and 41 percent were registered Republicans,
while in a 1986 survey, 50.8 percent were Democrats in contrast to
38.3 percent Republicans. Furthermore, some Asian American party
members displayed strong party loyalties in the 1984 survey results:
19 percent were "strong Republicans" and 10 percent "strong Democrats" (Hing 1993). In 1992 a *Los Angeles Times* exit poll indicated that
42 percent of Asian Americans were Democrats and 40 percent were
Republicans, while the results of two surveys conducted in San Francisco suggested that more Asian Americans there were Democrats
than Republicans by a margin of 43 percent to 23 percent in 1996,
and more Chinese Americans were the case by a wider margin of 52
percent to 17 percent in 2000 (Ong and Lee 2001; APALC, et al. 2001).
All these trivial survey results painted a larger picture that, regardless
of the times or places of these surveys, more than 80 percent of Asian
Americans identified themselves with political parties, and more of
them chose to affiliate with the Democratic Party than the Republican Party.

Nonetheless, in comparison to the above results of the two California statewide surveys conducted in 1984 and 1986, a large survey
of 5,000 Asian Americans in California in 1992 demonstrated that
Asian Americans in general tended to have weak party loyalties and
thus cross party lines quite swiftly and that they were not homogenous in terms of party affiliation. According to the survey results,
both Chinese (37.6 percent vs. 29 percent) and Korean Americans
(49.4 percent vs. 30.4 percent) were more likely to identify themselves as Republicans than as Democrats, while Japanese Americans
affiliated more with the Democratic Party (42.1 percent) over the
GOP (32.8 percent) (see Chapter 1, Table 1.11).

This shift in party affiliation toward the Republican Party was rather short-lived. As discussed earlier, there was a dramatic shift in East Asian Americans' political ideology from being more conservative to more liberal in the 1990s. Therefore, not surprisingly, a similar pattern emerged in their party affiliations. According to the results of the 2001 National Asian American Political Survey, as introduced in Chapter 1, a majority of Chinese (32 percent vs. 9 percent), Japanese (40 percent vs. 12 percent), and Korean Americans (43 percent vs. 22 percent) favored the Democratic Party over the GOP. As the percentage of conservative Chinese Americans dropped from 44.6 percent to 13 percent between 1992 and 2001, the percentage of Republicans among Chinese Americans decreased from 37.6 percent to 9 percent during the same period. There was also a sizable loss of Republican affiliates among the Japanese (from 32.8 percent to 12 percent) and Korean Americans (49.4 percent to 22 percent) in the same decade. The results of some Los Angeles-based polls also showed the same pattern that between 1996 and 2000 the percentage of Asian Americans who identified with the Republican Party dropped from 40 percent to 29.7 percent (Fong 2002).

It is interesting to note that in the 2001 survey, more than half of Chinese Americans (56 percent) and about a quarter of Japanese (28 percent) and Korean Americans (23 percent) either did not think in terms of a party affiliation or were unsure about it (Lien, et al. 2004). It seems that Chinese Americans appeared to have the weakest sense of party affiliation among the three ethnic groups.

Party Participation

While early interactions between the Asian American community and political parties involved exclusively the Democratic Party, such as some Democratic clubs in Chinatowns on the mainland and a political coalition under the Democratic Party in Hawaii in the post–World War II period, the contemporary participation of Asian Americans in party politics mainly centers around the Democratic Party as well. Traditionally, the Democrats have proclaimed themselves to be the party for the underprivileged classes, including racial and ethnic minority groups. As a result of their more aggressive recruiting efforts than those of their rival and their emphasis on the issue of anti-Asian discrimination, the Democrats secured support from Chinese and Japanese American communities in the 1970s (Wei 1993).

As the Democratic presidential candidate in 1976, Jimmy Carter was the first candidate to bring Asian Americans into the national picture of electoral politics by offering them a role in his campaign. Carter rallied support from Asian American communities through the establishment of the Asian/Pacific American Unit (A/PA Unit) on September 7, 1976. The A/PA Unit belonged to the party's Minority Affairs Section that also included other minority units, and was mainly a fund-raising mechanism for campaign donations. Ever since, the Democrats have institutionalized their efforts of seeking support from Asian Americans (Wei 1993).

Asian American participation in the Democratic Party reached another milestone in 1983 when the Asian Pacific Caucus (APC) was founded. Representing Asian American Democrats, the caucus issued an Asian Pacific Caucus platform at the 1984 national convention, and candidates solicited its support during the convention. The APC had a plan to grow itself into a national network with local chapters to recruit more Asian Americans to joint the Democratic Party and influence the party's platform in the 1988 presidential election. However, the APC had a very short life span. On May 17, 1985, the executive committee of the Democratic Party decided to terminate the APC for the reason that the party felt the need to abolish its caucus system to avoid being labeled as the party of special interests (Wei 1993).

Instead of the caucus, Asian American Democrats later established the National Democratic Council of Asian and Pacific Americans (NDCAPA), the first independent national organization for Asian American Democrats. In October 1987 the NDCAPA organized a three-day convention, "Target '88-Margin of Victory," as part of the 1988 presidential campaign. The organization's political clout was demonstrated at this first national convention of Asian American Democrats, which was well attended by high-profile politicians and presidential candidates, including Jesse Jackson, Michael Dukakis, and Paul Simon. In addition to supporting Democratic candidates in general, in subsequent years the NDCAPA also worked closely with the Democratic National Committee to help Asian American candidates and to address Asian American issues as the voice of Asian American Democrats (Wei 1993; Hing 1993; Espiritu 1992).

Although most Asian American elected officials have been Democrats, Asian American political organizations have endeavored to be nonpartisan. For example, the most well-established Japanese American organization, the Japanese American Citizens League, has emphasized nonpartisanship because of its concern with criticisms that bloc voting is against the American way and thus unpatriotic (Takahashi 1997). The 80–20 PAC is not exceptional in that even endorsing candidates, it wants to be a nonpartisan organization, but with a strategy of fluid bloc voting.

Even though the Republican Party has had an image of opposing communism and backing business, which is supposed to attract Asian Americans who are in general anticommunist and belong to the middle class (Fong 2002), there is not much to say about Asian American participation in the Republican Party before the 1980s. At the 1984 National Republican Convention, Anna Chennault, vice chair of the ethnic voter division of Ronald Reagan's presidential campaign, asked the Republicans National Committee to establish an Asian Pacific Caucus similar to that of the Democratic Party. But it was a fruitless effort, because Frank Fahrenkopf, the chair of the committee, thought that a Republican Asian Pacific Caucus was not necessary (Wei 1993).

The GOP became more aggressive in the late 1980s in recruiting Asian Americans and encouraging them to run for office. In 1989 a special Asian American Affairs Office was set up in the Republican National Committee, and in the same year President George H. W. Bush appointed a large number of Asian Americans to high-level positions, including Elaine Chao as deputy secretary of the Department of Transportation. When seeking reelection in 1992, President Bush sent Vice President Dan Quayle to support Asian American candidates by speaking against anti-Asian violence and attending Asian American fund-raising events (Fong 2002). Today, there is an Asian Pacific Islander American Team Leader outreach program in the Republican National Committee with a goal to work with Asian Americans to further the interests of their community (GOP website).

Although the Republican Party has worked to garner support from the Asian American community, the 2004 percentage of Asian Americans among all the delegates to the Republican National Convention (2.17 percent) was only about half of its counterpart to the Democratic National Convention (4.2 percent). However, the Republican Party's figure represented a 40-percent growth from the 2000 figure, whereas the number of Asian American delegates to the Democratic National Convention in 2004 was the largest ever in the party's history (*Chinese Daily News,* August 29, 2004, A2).

A final note on Asian Americans' relations to political parties is that there is no mention at all of Asian Americans in the party platforms of minor political parties, such as the Green Party, the Libertarian Party, or the Reform Party.

Campaign Contributions

Voting and party participation are not the only forms of electorally related activities. Relatively speaking, although Asian Americans have been lacking in voting participation, they have contributed financially to political candidates. One scholar termed this phenomenon an "asymmetrical participation," meaning that Asian Americans "have been a major source of money but a minor source of votes" (Wei 1993, 243). This was why both major parties had begun to reach out to the Asian American community well before the recent rise of its voting power.

Although Asian Americans' voting turnout is proportionally lower than their share of the electorate, ironically, their campaign contributions are proportionally much higher. Furthermore, they have been seen as the most generous campaign contributors, second only to Jewish Americans. However, a common perception persists among politicians that Asian Americans contribute money without asking anything in return. Thus, when they solicit donations from Asian Americans, they do not expect the money to come with any strings attached. This is why it seems that many candidates are not worried about the consequences of failing to fulfill their promises to Asian American donors (Hing 1993), and as a result, Asian Americans often fail to translate their money power into real political power.

In any event, the issue of Asian Americans' campaign contributions has attracted tremendous attention lately, not only from political candidates as expected but also from the mainstream media. This is certainly because of the remarkable contributions made by Asian Americans in federal-level campaigns and campaigns at the state and local levels, but, unfortunately, it is also because of the campaign finance controversies that involved Asian American donors in 1996–1997.

At the Federal Level

Asian American campaign contributions have been very impressive in federal-level campaigns. Although systematic data on the subject is not available, the extent of Asian American contributions at the national level can be demonstrated by the following anecdotal accounts. In 1980, probably because of the operations of the A/PA Unit, mainly a fund-raising machine for the Democrats, Asian Americans donated $2.5 million to Jimmy Carter's presidential campaign.

In 1984 Asian Americans were the second most generous contributor to the Democratic Party, after only the Jewish Americans. In 1988, with the help of Asian Americans, Michael Dukakis raised record amounts of money in California, including more than $100,000 from one fund-raising event held in Los Angeles Chinatown attended by 750 Asian Americans (Wei 1993).

In 1992 President George H. W. Bush raised $1.5 to $2 million by mid-September of that election year from the Asian American community, while Bill Clinton's campaign collected a quarter of a million dollars at a single Asian American fund-raiser in Monterey Park, California, the first suburban Chinatown in the United States (Coleman 2002). In 1996 the Democratic National Committee collected the record amount of $5 million from John Huang, one of the Asian American donors who were later involved in the campaign finance controversies, although over $1 million was returned to the donors because of the controversies. The Republicans were also vigorously seeking donations from Asian Americans at the same time. For example, at an Asian American rally held in California, prominent Chinese American political leader Matt Fong introduced Republican presidential candidate Bob Dole. It was probably the first time both parties began reaching out to the community for financial support (Lai, et al. 2003).

Although many Asian Americans contributed individually, many other Asian American donors operated through organizations. However, given that Asian American political action committees have not been popular in the community, many Asian American donors contributed through other organizational frameworks. For instance, the Pacific Leadership Council, as part of the Democratic Senatorial Campaign Committee, in 1988 collected close to $1.2 million, mostly from Chinese American businesspersons to support Democratic candidates (Espiritu 1992).

An intragroup variation was observable among the three East Asian American groups in terms of the parties they supported financially. A study on contributions to Democratic and Republican candidates in all federal (except presidential) campaigns from 1980 to 1998 showed that Korean Americans were leaning more toward the Republicans. Especially in the years after 1984, about 60 percent of Korean American contributions were made to the Republicans. In contrast, Chinese Americans and Japanese Americans were split between the two parties. According to the dataset of the study, there were 3,254 Chinese American, 1,112 Japanese American, and 1,018 Korean American contributors in 1998, in contrast to 457, 319, and 136, respectively, in 1980 (Lai, et al. 2003).

Another intriguing pattern can be seen in Asian American campaign contributions, as suggested by the same study. It is not surprising that Asian American donors strongly supported Asian American candidates, as exemplified by the year 1998 when about half of their total contributions went to Asian American candidates. And a more interesting pattern is that, understandably, these ethnic contributors seemed more likely to give money to their ethnic candidates than to a broad class of all Asian American candidates. Examples of such cases abound, including that of S. B. Woo, a Chinese American running for the U.S. Senate and the U.S. House seats from Delaware in 1988 and 1992, respectively; Matt Fong, another Chinese American candidate running for the U.S. Senate in California in 1998; Jay Kim, a Korean American running for the U.S. House in Southern California from 1992 to 1998; and Robert Matsui and Norman Mineta, two Japanese American candidates both running for the U.S. House in California during about the same period. Because the support of Asian Americans, especially those of the same ethnic background, for these candidates crossed state borders, they often traveled throughout the country to solicit money from their communities. For instance, Matt Fong collected almost 9 percent of his Asian American contributions outside California. The same study shows that these campaigns coincided very well with the surges of contributions made by the candidate's ethnic group. Therefore, the idea of panethnicity among Asian Americans may have been realized in areas such as political interest groups, but not yet in the area of campaign finance contributions (Lai, et al. 2003; Espiritu 1992).

Moreover, many Asian Americans donate to candidates of their own ethnic group who are running outside their districts or even outside their states, even though funding these nonlocal candidates is strategically not the best way to make use of their financial resources. It is essential that Asian Americans be able to move beyond ethnic politics to concentrate their money on local candidates if they are serious about building their political clout (Lai, et al. 2003).

At the State and Local Levels

Asian Americans have been equally active in making campaign contributions at the state and local levels, especially in California campaigns. They have made contributions to both Asian American and non–Asian American candidates. One well-known example of the latter was during Los Angeles mayor Tom Bradley's 1982 and 1986 campaigns. Asian Americans, representing 6 percent of the state population, contributed 10 percent of Bradley's statewide donations (Lai, et al. 2003).

Just like their counterparts at the national level, many Asian American candidates at the state and local levels also depended on Asian American contributions, including those candidates who ran in non-Asian American majority districts as mainstream candidates. According to the results of a recent survey of Asian American elected officials, nearly one-third of them at the national, state, and local levels depended on Asian American contributions (Lai, et al. 2003). There were two prominent examples in state-level campaigns: Asian American contributions constituted 75 percent and 70 percent of the campaign money of California Secretary of State March Fong Eu and Delaware Lieutenant Governor S. B. Woo, respectively (Espiritu 1992). The most significant case of Asian American contributions to Asian American candidates at all levels is probably the case of Michael Woo in Southern California.

Case Study: Michael Woo's 1985 and 1992 Campaigns

Michael Woo, a third-generation Chinese American, was the most renowned Asian American political figure in Southern California and the ethnic pride of Chinese Americans across the country in the 1990s. Woo collected substantial amounts of financial support from the Asian American community in his 1985 Los Angeles city council campaign. According to campaign disclosure statements, in the six months before the election between January and June 1985, 51.4 percent of his contributors were Asian Americans who contributed 35.4 percent of the total $385,855 raised, absolutely disproportionate to their 5-percent share of the population in the Silver Lake district. Chinese Americans alone constituted 37 percent of the contributors and 26.7 percent of the total fund. Woo was running as a mainstream candidate in this non-Asian American majority district and received 49.1 percent of his campaign money from non-Asian Americans, who accounted for 36.4 percent of all the contributors. Altogether, non-Asian Americans contributed $189,390 to him, whereas in sharp contrast, Peggy Stevenson, Woo's defeated opponent, collected a total of only $1,300 from twelve Asian Americans (Espiritu 1992).

Seven years later in 1992, Michael Woo ran for mayor of the city of Los Angeles against self-financed millionaire Richard Riordan to succeed Mayor Tom Bradley. In spite of the local nature of the mayoral race, Woo received Asian American contributions from seventeen states throughout the country. In total, one-quarter of his campaign contributions were from Asian Americans outside the state. The majority of these Asian American donors were Chinese Americans who were proud of Woo running for mayor of the second largest city in the nation. However, no more than 10 percent of the Asian American contributions came from Japanese, Korean, Filipino, Vietnamese, and Asian Indian Americans (Lai, et al. 2003). Woo's case showed that pan-Asian American ethnicity was still in its infancy in the area of campaign contributions.

Given the high fund-raising capacity of Asian American candidates, they have at times encountered criticism from non–Asian American candidates. For instance, in the 1990 city council race in Cerritos, one of the eighty-eight cities in Los Angeles County, a Korean American candidate, Charles Kim, collected $96,000—nearly double the amount raised by all the other twelve candidates and almost triple the largest amount of fund-raising in the city's history, which was only about $36,000. The absolute majority of Kim's contributors were Korean Americans from outside of Cerritos (Espiritu 1992). Asian American candidates who have practiced this kind of fund-raising are often criticized for playing money-centered politics and inviting outside influences.

Campaign Finance Controversies

As Asian American electoral participation gradually reached a historic high in the mid-1990s with unprecedented growth in votes, party participation, and campaign contributions, the campaign finance controversies suddenly came as a sharp blow, shocking the entire community into spinning. Just as the murder of Vincent Chin was the turning point in the history of Asian American protest politics and group politics, the fund-raising scandal was definitely a watershed event in the history of Asian American electoral participation. Due to this event, said one Asian American scholar, "We were transformed from invisible to infamous" (Wu 2002, 104). It has had profound impacts on the political participation of the entire community in many aspects.

The so-called Asian connection scandal arose from allegations that foreign governments, corporations in Asia, and individuals of Asian background made campaign contributions to U.S. political candidates in attempts to influence U.S. policy decisions. At the center of these allegations were John Huang, Johnny Chung, Charlie Yah-lin Trie, and Maria Hsia, who, all Chinese Americans, raised money for President Bill Clinton and Vice President Al Gore's reelection campaigns and the Democratic National Committee (DNC) (Fong 2002).

The focal point of these allegations was John Huang, because the investigations originated from his work and his files at the DNC. Huang came to the United States from Taiwan as a graduate student. When he became politically active, based in Los Angeles, he headed the banking operations of the Lippo Group, an Indonesia-based conglomerate owned by the Riady family who were also ethnic Chinese. With his political connections, Huang was eventually appointed deputy assistant secretary of the U.S. Department of Commerce during the first term of the Clinton administration. Before the presidential election in 1996, Huang took the newly created position of DNC's vice chair of finance specifically in charge of raising funds from the Asian American community. As mentioned earlier, Huang helped raise the record amount of $5 million for the DNC in that year. One key reason why Huang was involved in the "Asian connection" was because of his connection with the contributions made by an Indonesian couple, the Wiriadinatas. As business associates of the Riady family, the couple gave $450,000 to the DNC. Even though as lawful permanent residents of the United States, the Wiriadinatas were allowed to make donations to U.S. political parties, the couple was suspected of giving the money on behalf of the Riadys, who were not permanent residents (Wu 2002).

Huang was not the only Asian American accused of illegal political contributions. Johnny Chung, a California businessman who raised hundreds of thousands of dollars for the DNC, was also under investigation. With his connections, Chung was permitted to tour the White House. His access to the White House was controversial because some Chinese government officials accompanied him on these tours. Charlie Yah-lin Trie was another suspect. Trie was a restaurant owner in Little Rock, Arkansas, who raised more than half a million dollars for the Whitewater legal defense fund for the Clintons' legal costs. Also in California, Maria Hsia organized a visit by Vice President Al Gore to the Hsi Lai Buddhist Temple in Hacienda Heights of Los Angeles County where campaign donations were collected. Controversy surrounded her case because political donations may not be made on religious property (Wu 2002).

Because all of the above cases were against the Democrats, in response the DNC hired an auditing firm to initiate its own investigation in November 1996 in which about 1,200 contributions made from 1994 to 1996 by Asian Americans were audited. Therefore, Asian American donors, identified by their Asian surnames, became the targets of the probe. They were interrogated on the phone with respect to their citizenship status, income, source of the donations, credit history, and so on. Some of them were told that if they refused to cooperate, their names would be released to the press (Fong 2002; Lien 2001b). Those Asian American contributors under investigation were outraged that they were targeted solely because of their Asian surnames. Asian American communities protested against this racial stereotyping immediately. For example, the Organization of Chinese Americans and the Japanese American Citizens League organized a press conference condemning the auditing by the Democratic Party. Under mounting pressure, the party soon apologized (Gotanda 2001; Fong 2002). In the end, the DNC's auditing resulted in the return of more than $3 million in donations (Wu 2002).

In addition to the audit initiated by the party, these allegations led to quite a few official investigations. Both the Federal Election Commission (FEC) and the Department of Justice conducted an investigation, and at one time the Justice Department devoted 120 attorneys and investigators to these cases. Beginning in summer 1997, both the Senate and the House held numerous public hearings. The most extensive congressional hearings were the ones held by the Senate Governmental Affairs Committee from July through October 1997 to investigate the cases of Huang and Trie. Chaired by Republican Senator Fred Thompson of Tennessee, the committee reached a modest conclusion, after 33 days of hearings with more than 70 witnesses, over 200 interviews, about 200 formal depositions and 400 subpoenas issued, that there was not enough information to substantiate the claims of a Chinese scheme to influence American presidential elections (Wu 2002; Kim 2001).

Criminal prosecutions were also initiated against Huang, Chung, Trie, and Hsia. In 1999 John Huang pleaded guilty to minor campaign contribution charges. He admitted that he raised nearly $1 million in illegal contributions for the Democratic Party, but denied allegations by some Republican members of Congress that he was a spy for China. In the same year, Johnny Chung was convicted of breaking campaign finance laws. He was sentenced to 3,000 hours of community service and five years probation. Also in 1999 Charlie Yah-lin Trie pleaded guilty to a felony charge of causing the DNC to file a false campaign finance report and a misdemeanor charge of using another person's name to make a campaign contribution. He was sentenced to a three-year probation, including four months of in-house detention. In 2000

Maria Hsia was convicted of raising more than $100,000 in illegal contributions to the Democrats. She did not plea-bargain and was later convicted of a felony (Fong 2002; Brookings Institution 1998).

In the meantime, national politicians and media made numerous biased assumptions and reinforced stereotypes against the Asian American community on the basis of the race, ethnicity, and national origin of those convicted. Stunned by unwanted national attention and racial stereotyping, the Asian American community protested and launched a media education campaign. In October 1996 Asian Americans organized a coordinated series of press conferences in Washington, D.C., Los Angeles, and Chicago to criticize the biased image of Asian Americans. In addition, as mentioned in Chapter 3, a broad coalition of fourteen Asian American national organizations petitioned the U.S. Commission on Civil Rights for a hearing and also filed a complaint requesting the commission to consider the racial aspects of the ongoing investigations and reportage by the news media (Lien 2001b; Wu 2002).

These campaign contribution controversies have had far-reaching impacts on Asian Americans' political participation. Consequently, while many Asian Americans began shifting their political preferences from the Republicans to the Democrats because of the latter's harsh attacks on Asian Americans during the investigations, many other Asian Americans simply became politically inactive after these incidents, especially in the area of campaign contributions. Rumors also circulated that Chang-Lin Tien, late chancellor of the University of California, Berkeley, would have been appointed to the position of secretary of energy in 1997, and that the congressional confirmation of Bill Lann Lee as assistant attorney general for civil rights would not have been stalled for years if these controversies had not arisen (Fong 2002). However, there is always a silver lining in every cloud. At least, these controversies prompted Asian American leaders to further realize the need to form national pan–Asian American political organizations. As also mentioned in the preceding chapter, the National Council of Asian Pacific Americans, the first national pan–Asian American coalition, was founded in 1997 in the wake of these campaign finance controversies.

Conclusion

For decades, many Asian Americans have overcome obstacles to their electoral participation, becoming citizens, getting registered, and then casting their ballots on election days. According to limited statistical information, some discernible patterns of Asian American voting behaviors have been observed. A shift of Asian American electoral support from the Republicans to the Democrats was apparent in the 2000 election, and the results of the 2004 election seemed to suggest that this shift represents the beginning of the formation of a long-lasting loyalty to the Democratic Party. In other words, it appears that the 2000 election was really a realigning election for Asian Americans with the Democratic Party.

In addition to being voters, Asian Americans have also been active as party members and campaign contributors, although the campaign finance scandals were quite detrimental to their participation in this area. In sum, although there has been a remarkable increase in their overall involvement in the U.S. electoral system, Asian Americans have not as yet been able to present themselves as a formidable, unified force on the American political scene. This is partly because many members of the community still are politically apathetic and partly because the Asian American community is a rather divergent group with tremendous internal differences and cleavages. But another significant reason behind the lack of Asian American political clout is a lack of adequate representation at all levels of the American political arena. However, more and more Asian Americans have gone beyond the level of voting participation lately and have begun seeking to run for public office or become politically appointed officials.

References

80–20 website: http://www.80–20initiative.net. Accessed January 16, 2005.

Aoki, Andrew L. 2001. "A New Day." In *National Asian Pacific American Political Almanac.* 10th ed. Edited by Don T. Nakanishi and James S. Lai. Los Angeles: UCLA Asian American Studies Center.

APIAVote website: http://www.apiavote.org. Accessed May 4, 2004.

APIAVote. *Newsletter.* November 12, 2004. http://www.apiavote.org/newsletter/newsletter.html. Accessed May 4, 2004.

Asian Pacific American Legal Center, Asian American Legal Defense and Education Fund, Chinese Americans Voters Education Committee, and *Los Angeles Times.* 2001. "The 2000 Asian Pacific American Exit Poll: Los Angeles, New York City, and San Francisco Bay Area; The California Electorate." In *National Asian Pacific American Political Almanac.* 10th ed. Edited by Don T. Nakanishi and James S. Lai. Los Angeles: UCLA Asian American Studies Center.

Brookings Institution. 1998. *Recent Developments in Campaign Finance Regulation.* Website: http://www.brookings.org/gs/cf/headlines/trie.htm. Accessed January 20, 2005.

CAUSE website: http://www.causeusa.org. Accessed April 29, 2004.

Chinese Daily News (World Journal), News Reports. April 30, 2004, B4; May 6, 2004; and August 29, 2004, A2.

Coleman, Kevin. 2002. "Asian Americans and Electoral Politics." In *Asian-American Electoral Politics.* Edited by John W. Lee. New York: Novinka.

Espiritu, Yen Le. 1992. *Asian American Panethnicity: Bridging Institutions and Identities.* Philadelphia, PA: Temple University.

Fong, Timothy P. 2002. *The Contemporary Asian American Experience: Beyond the Model Minority.* 2d ed. Upper Saddle River, NJ: Prentice Hall.

GOP website: http://www.gop.com. Accessed April 27, 2004.

Gotanda, Neil T. 2001. "Citizenship Nullification: The Impossibility of Asian American Politics." In *Asian Americans and Politics: Perspectives, Experiences, Prospects.* Edited by Gordon H. Chang. Washington, DC: Woodrow Wilson and Stanford, CA: Stanford University.

Hing, Bill Ong. 1993. *Making and Remaking Asian America through Immigration Policy, 1850–1990.* Stanford, CA: Stanford University.

Kim, Claire Jean. 2001. "The Racial Triangulation of Asian Americans." In *Asian Americans and Politics: Perspectives, Experiences, Prospects.* Edited by Gordon H. Chang. Washington, DC: Woodrow Wilson and Stanford, CA: Stanford University.

Lai, James S., Wendy K. Tam-Cho, Thomas P. Kim, and Okiyoshi Takeda. 2003. "Campaigns, Elections, and Elected Officials." In *Asian American Politics: Law, Participation, and Policy.* Edited by Don T. Nakanishi and James S. Lai. Lanham, MD: Rowman and Littlefield.

Lien, Pei-te. 2001b. *The Making of Asian America through Political Participation.* Philadelphia, PA: Temple University.

Lien, Pei-te, M. Margaret Conway, Taeku Lee, and Janelle Wong. 2001. "A Summary Report of the Pilot Study of the National Asian American Political Survey." In *National Asian Pacific American Political Almanac.* 10th ed. Edited by Don T. Nakanishi and James S. Lai. Los Angeles: UCLA Asian American Studies Center.

Lien, Pei-te, M. Margaret Conway, and Janelle Wong. 2004. *The Politics of Asian Americans: Diversity and Community.* New York: Routledge.

Nakanishi, Don T. 2000. "Introduction: The Politics of Asian Americans." In *Encyclopedia of Minorities in American Politics. Volume 1: African Americans and Asian Americans.* Edited by Jeffrey D. Schultz, Kerry L. Haynie, Anne M. McCulloch, and Andrew L. Aoki. Phoenix, AZ: Oryx.

NCAPA. 2004. *Call to Action: Platform for Asian Pacific Americans National Policy Priorities 2004.* Website: http://www.ncapaonline.org. Accessed April 20, 2004.

Ong, Paul M., and David E. Lee. 2001. "Changing of the Guard? The Emerging Immigrant Majority in Asian American Politics." In *Asian Americans and Politics: Perspectives, Experiences, Prospects.* Edited by Gordon H. Chang. Washington, DC: Woodrow Wilson and Stanford, CA: Stanford University.

Ong, Paul M., and Don T. Nakanishi. 2003. "Becoming Citizens, Becoming Voters: The Naturalization and Political Participation of Asian Pacific Immigrants." In *Asian American Politics: Law, Participation, and Policy.* Edited by Don T. Nakanishi and James S. Lai. Lanham, MD: Rowman and Littlefield.

Takahashi, Jere. 1997. *Nisei/Sansei: Shifting Japanese American Identities and Politics.* Philadelphia, PA: Temple University.

U.S. Census Bureau. 2004. *Asian Pacific American Heritage Month: May 2004.* Press Release. Website: http://www.census.gov/PressRelease/www/releases /archives/facts_for_features_special_editions/001738.html. Accessed September 2004.

Wei, William. 1993. *The Asian American Movement.* Philadelphia, PA: Temple University.

Woo, S. B. 2001. "What Is the Impact of the 2000 Presidential Election on Asian Pacific Americans?" In *National Asian Pacific American Political Almanac.* 10th ed. Edited by Don T. Nakanishi and James S. Lai. Los Angeles: UCLA Asian American Studies Center.

Wu, Frank H. 2002. *Yellow: Race in America beyond Black and White.* New York: Basic.

Yao, Nancy. 2002. "From Apathy to Inquiry and Activism: The Changing Role of American-Born Chinese in U.S.-China Relations." In *The Expanding Roles of Chinese Americans in U.S.-China Relations: Transnational Networks and Trans-Pacific Interactions.* Edited by Peter H. Koehn and Xiao-huang Yin. Armonk, NY: M. E. Sharpe.

5

Participation in Political Officeholding

oters cast their ballots to select political candidates who can best represent their interests, but the most direct way for a minority group to further its collective interests is to have its members running for political offices or seeking to become politically appointed officials. Compared with participation in protest politics, interest-group politics, and voting and party politics, Asian Americans' involvement in the areas of elected and politically appointed officials is the most recently adopted, and perhaps also the most important, form of political participation. Asian Americans' success in this area is the culmination of years of hard work in the above three areas of political participation. This chapter studies the patterns of such participation at the federal, state, and local levels.

Political victory for Asian American candidates in general in either the electoral process or the political appointment process can be attributed not only to the support of Asian as well as non–Asian American voters, but also to the contributions of numerous Asian American community and organizational leaders. Although some of East Asian American leaders eventually have come out to seek a political career themselves, more of them have worked hard behind the scenes at the community level and contributed greatly to the well-being of the community. Hence, this chapter also provides an examination of these East Asian American community and organizational elites.

Elected Officials

The Asian American story of electoral politics in the early years was mostly a story written by Chinese and Japanese in Hawaii, owing to the unique demographic characteristics of the Aloha State. Their participation in Hawaii's electoral politics began in 1919 when a Chinese, William Heen, was elected the city and county attorney of Honolulu. In that year, Chinese voters made up 4.3 percent of the registered voters. Japanese involvement in electoral politics did not begin until 1922, when a Republican *Nisei*, James Hamada, ran for office in the Hawaii territorial legislature. He did not succeed, nor did several other *Nisei* who tried after him in the 1920s. In 1922 Japanese voters accounted for 3.5 percent of the electorate of the islands. The year 1927 marked the entry of the first Chinese, or Asian in general, to the Honolulu Board of Supervisors and the territorial House of Representatives. The first Japanese electoral victory was delivered in 1930 by Noboru Miyake, who was elected a county supervisor. During the same period, two Japanese, Tasaku Oka and Andy Yamashiro, were elected to the territorial House of Representatives. By 1936, nine (or 23.1 percent) out of thirty-nine elected officials in Hawaii were *Nisei*. In 1938 a Hawaii-born Chinese, Hiram Fong, was elected to the Hawaii House of Representatives and became its Speaker in 1949. In 1940, shortly before the attack on Pearl Harbor, *Nisei* constituted 15.6 percent of all the elected legislators, while their share of the electorate that year was 31 percent (Chan 1991; Lien 2001b).

During the war, there was no presence at all of *Nisei* in Hawaii's legislature, but they won 13.3 percent of the legislative seats in the first election after the war. The Asian presence in Hawaii's politics continued to grow into the late 1940s and early 1950s, when Japanese American veterans of the highly recognized 100th Battalion and 442nd Regimental Combat Team, who fought courageously on the European battlefields, began seeking political careers. During the so-called Democratic Revolution of 1954 in Hawaii, a number of these Japanese American veterans constituted a significant part of the "New Democrats" who managed to dominate both executive and legislative branches of the territorial government that used to be under the control of Caucasian Republican politicians allied with the old plantation power structure. These New Democrats maintained their control in the next three decades, during which Japanese Americans took 55 percent of the leadership positions in the legislature, including president of the senate, Speaker of the House, and chairs of key committees. About 40 percent of them were World War II veterans (Chan 1991; Lien 2001b).

After Hawaii acquired statehood in 1959, Asian American elected officials from Hawaii began their journey from the previously territorial legislature to Capitol Hill in Washington, D.C. Hiram Fong, Speaker of the territorial House from 1949 to 1953, was elected that year as one of the first two U.S. senators from Hawaii. Daniel Inouye, majority leader in the territorial House from 1954 to 1958 and one of the territorial senators from 1958 to 1959, was elected in the same year as the first and only member of the U.S. House of Representatives from Hawaii. Inouye was a Japanese American veteran of the 442nd Regimental Combat Team. Later when Inouye was elected U.S. Senator in 1962, Spark Matsunaga, a returning Japanese American veteran from the 100th Battalion, took his place in the U.S. House of Representatives. When Hawaii was allocated a second seat in the U.S. House in the early 1960s due to population increase, Patsy Takemoto Mink, a Japanese American, won the seat in 1964, becoming the first Asian American woman in the U.S. House of Representatives (Chan 1991). That time period marked the heyday of Asian American participation in Hawaii's electoral politics with all four of the state's seats in the U.S. Congress occupied by them. It is noteworthy that all these elected officials were Democrats except Fong. Although representing the interests of their state, the presence of all these Hawaiian Asian Americans in Congress was symbolically important to the electoral participation of Asian Americans on the mainland.

It was a quite different story on the mainland where far fewer Asian Americans participated in electoral politics in the early years. This was because, living in a more difficult environment than that of Hawaii, the absolute majority of Asian Americans on the mainland had no political ambition to seek public office at any level.

The first mainland Asian American to win a seat in the U.S. House of Representatives was Dalip Singh Saund, a Democrat from California. He was an Asian Indian immigrant who came to the United States in 1920. He was first elected a judge in the town of Westmoreland in the Imperial Valley of California and then he was elected to Congress in 1956 and reelected in 1958. But his poor health forced him to retire before the expiration of his second term (Chan 1991).

At the state level, the earliest recorded case of Asian American electoral participation took place in 1906 when Benjamin Chow ran for a seat in the Massachusetts state legislature. He failed, having won less than 4 percent of the vote. Afterwards, there were other cases of failed attempts until 1946, when Wing F. Ong of Phoenix, Arizona, became the first Asian American elected to a state house of representatives on the mainland. Although one of his parents was U.S. born, Ong was an immigrant who was detained on Angel Island for three months before his entry to the United States in 1918 at the age of fourteen. Long before he was elected in 1946 to Arizona's House of Representatives, he was first exposed to American electoral politics when working as a houseboy for the governor of Arizona. He served two terms but failed twice for a House seat in the 1950s and also lost once for a Senate seat in 1964. In 1966 he was elected to the state senate, but failed to be reelected in 1968 (Lien 2001b; Chan 1991).

Saund's and Ong's successful stories are unique, not only because they were the first Asian Americans ever elected to the U.S. House and a state house, respectively, but also because both were immigrants, in contrast to those Asian American latecomers in electoral politics in the 1960s who were mostly U.S. born. Ong's success was particularly unique in that he managed to triumph in a district with a small Asian American population.

However, beginning in the 1960s and 1970s, the election of Asian Americans to public office was becoming less and less an anomaly on the mainland with the election and appointment of Asian Americans to positions at the federal, state, and local levels in California, Washington, New York, and other states (Nakanishi 1989).

As illustrated in Table 5.1, the tenth (2001–2002) edition of the *National Asian Pacific American Political Almanac* indicates that there were a total of 565 Asian Pacific American elected officials at the federal, state, and local levels in 2001, whereas the number was only 120 in 1978, representing a dramatic increase of 371 percent in 23 years. The most dramatic increase occurred at the local level. While the growth rates of the numbers of Asian Pacific American elected officials were 60 percent and 11 percent at the federal and state levels, respectively, between 1978 and 2001, the number grew from 52 to 487 at the local level, an increase of 837 percent, during the same period of time.

Federal Level

The saga of Asian American representation on Capitol Hill continued into the 1970s. In Hawaii, while Spark Matsunaga was elected to the

Table 5.1
Total Number of Key Federal, State, and Local Asian Pacific
American Elected Officials 1978–2001

Year*	Federal	State	Local	Total
1978	5	63	52	120
1979	6	68	69	143
1980	6	69	98	173
1982	6	59	109	174
1984	5	59	109	173
1995	8	66	157	231
1996	7	66	181	254
1998	7	67	187	261
2000	7	73	248	328
2001	8	70	487	565

Source: The figures from 1978 to 2000 are from James S. Lai, Wendy K. Tam-Cho, Thomas P. Kim, and Okiyoshi Takeda. 2003. "Campaigns, Elections, and Elected Officials." In *Asian American Politics: Law, Participation, and Policy.* Edited by Don T. Nakanishi and James S. Lai. Lanham, MD: Rowman and Littlefield, Table 3.14c. The 2001 figures are from Don T. Nakanishi and James S. Lai, eds. 2001. *National Asian Pacific American Political Almanac.* 10th ed. Los Angeles: UCLA Asian American Studies Center, p. 152.

*Data is not available continuously for every year, because the *National Asian Pacific American Political Almanac,* the only source available for this purpose, is not a yearly publication.

U.S. Senate in 1976 to fill the office previously occupied by Hiram Fong, Daniel Akaka, a Hawaiian and Chinese American, was elected to the U.S. House to fill the position left by Patsy T. Mink, who was not a candidate for reelection that year. Patricia F. Saiki, another Japanese American woman like Mink, but a Republican, was elected to the U.S. House in 1986, representing the district that had been represented by Matsunaga before he was elected a U.S. senator in 1976. When, after serving seven terms in the House, Akaka moved on to the Senate to fill the spot left by Matsunaga in 1990, Mink came back to the House and continued to serve for the next twelve years until she died in 2002. From the above cases involving five Hawaiian politicians, Fong, Matsunaga, Mink, Akaka, and Saiki, it is easy to see that the torch of Hawaiian representation in Congress had been mostly successfully passed on from one Asian American, primarily Japanese Americans, to another.

On the mainland, the growth of Asian American representation in Congress has been impressive in comparison to situations in the past, and other Asian Americans besides Japanese Americans began to flourish. Norman Mineta, mayor of San Jose, California, became the second Asian American from the mainland to win a seat in the U.S. House of Representatives in 1974 and he was soon joined by Robert Matsui, a former member of the Sacramento City Council, in 1978. The first and only Asian American from the mainland to be elected to the U.S. Senate was S. I. Hayakawa from California in 1976, a conservative Republican originally from Canada. He served only one term in the Senate (Chan 1991). In 1992 Jay Kim, a conservative Republican and mayor of Diamond Bar in Southern California, became the first Korean American elected to the House. David Wu, an Oregon Democrat, was the first Chinese/Taiwanese American ever elected a member of the House in 1999. Mike Honda, a Japanese American from San Jose, California, was elected a member of the House in 2001. The most recent newcomer of Asian ancestry in the House is Bobby Jindal, a thirty-three-year-old Republican from Louisiana who was elected in 2004. Jindal is the first Asian Indian American in nearly half of a century to be elected to the House.

Table 5.2 indicates that in addition to the five nonvoting members of the House who are delegates from American Samoa and Guam, a total of thirteen Asian American men and women served in the United States Congress from 1957 to 2004. The majority of them were Japanese Americans who were Democrats from either Hawaii or California. To be more specific, there were eight Japanese Americans; three Chinese Americans, including one Hawaiian Chinese; one Korean American; and one Asian Indian. Six of them were from California, six from Hawaii, and one from Oregon. In terms of party affiliation, there were nine Democrats and four Republicans.

The six members of Congress from Hawaii had different personal backgrounds and career paths from those seven members from the mainland. All of the Hawaiian six were born American citizens. While four of them had law degrees from prestigious universities, including Harvard (Fong and Matsunaga), George Washington (Inouye), and Chicago (Mink), both Akaka and Saiki earned degrees in education from the University of Hawaii. Before entering public service, the majority of them had already served in high positions in Hawaiian politics. After coming to Capitol Hill, all of them supported minority rights (Lien 2001b).

In contrast, four of the seven members of Congress from the mainland were born outside the United States, including Saund

Table 5.2
Asian Pacific Americans Who Have Served in the
United States Congress

Name	Years Served	Ethnicity	Party	State/District
Senate				
Hiram Fong	1959–1977	Chinese	Republican	Hawaii
Daniel Inouye	1963–	Japanese	Democrat	Hawaii
Spark Matsunaga	1977–1990	Japanese	Democrat	Hawaii
S. I. Hayakawa	1977–1983	Japanese	Republican	California
Daniel Akaka	1990–	Hawaiian -Chinese	Democrat	Hawaii
House*				
Dalip Singh Saund	1957–1963	Asian Indian	Democrat	California /29th
Daniel Inouye	1959–1963	Japanese	Democrat	Hawaii at-large
Spark Matsunaga	1963–1977	Japanese	Democrat	Hawaii at-large, then 1st
Patsy Mink	1965–1977 & 1990–2002	Japanese	Democrat	Hawaii/2nd
Norman Mineta	1975–1996	Japanese	Democrat	California /13th, then 15th
Daniel Akaka	1977–1991	Hawaiian -Chinese	Democrat	Hawaii/2nd
Robert Matsui	1979–2004	Japanese	Democrat	California /3rd, then 5th
Patricia Saiki	1987–1991	Japanese	Republican	Hawaii/1st
Jay Kim	1993–1999	Korean	Republican	California /41st
David Wu	1999–	Chinese	Democrat	Oregon/1st
Mike Honda	2001–	Japanese	Democrat	California /15th
House: Nonvoting Delegates				
Antonio Won Pat	1973–1985	Chamorro	Democrat	Guam
Fofo Sunia	1981–1989	Samoan	Democrat	American Samoa
Vicente Blaz	1984–1993	Chamorro	Republican	Guam
Eni Faleomavaega	1989–	Samoan	Democrat	American Samoa
Robert Underwood	1993–2002	Chamorro	Democrat	Guam

Sources: Pei-te Lien. 2001. *The Making of Asian America through Political Participation.* Philadelphia, PA: Temple University, Table 3.1; and James S. Lai, Wendy K. Tam-Cho, Thomas P. Kim, and Okiyoshi Takeda. 2003. "Campaigns, Elections, and Elected Officials." In *Asian American Politics: Law, Participation, and Policy.* Edited by Don T. Nakanishi and James S. Lai. Lanham, MD: Rowman and Littlefield, Table 3.14b.

*Bobby Jindal, a Republican from Louisiana (1st district), was elected to the House in 2004. Jindal is an Asian Indian American.

from India, Hayakawa from Canada, Kim from Korea, and Wu from Taiwan. The three U.S.-born members, Mineta, Matsui, and Honda, were all Japanese Americans from Northern California. Three (Mineta, Matsui, and Kim) of the seven were elected to the House from municipal positions; two (Hayakawa, former president of San Francisco State University, and Wu) had no prior political experience; one (Saund) had served as a local elected judge; and one (Honda) had served in the state legislature. Before entering the political arena, they held jobs in farming (Saund), education (Hayakawa and Honda), business (Mineta and Kim), and law (Matsui and Wu) (Lien 2001b). It is worth mentioning that the only two Republicans in this cohort, Hayakawa and Kim, were extremely conservative, which was probably the reason why both did not serve long in Congress.

Only six Asian American members served in the 108th Congress in 2004. With the death of Robert Matsui, the most senior Asian American member of the House, in January 2005 and the election of Bobby Jindal in November 2004, the number of Asian American members of the 109th Congress remains the same. Even though this representation is much better than in the past, it is still not in proportion to Asian Americans' population share in the nation, which is about 4 percent, corresponding to four senators and seventeen members of the House. One key reason for this underrepresentation is that none of the three mainland Asian American members of the House (Honda, Jindal, and Wu) was elected from a district with more than 10 percent Asian American population. In 1990 all the top ten congressional districts with the largest percentage of Asian Americans, except for the first district in Hawaii represented by Patsy Mink, were represented by members of other races, including five Caucasian Americans, three Latino Americans, and one African American (Lai, et al. 2003; Lien 2001b). The pattern persisted in 2000 and 2004, when neither the congressional districts with the top ten largest Asian American populations on the mainland, nor the top ten fastest growing Asian American districts were represented by an Asian American elected official (Lai, et al. 2003).

The six members of the 109th Congress are Senators Akaka and Inouye and House Representatives Faleomavaega (a nonvoting delegate), Honda, Jindal, and Wu. Among them, Senator Inouye of Hawaii is not only the most senior Asian American member of Congress, in service for more than forty years, but also one of the most senior senators in the United States.

Case Study: Daniel Inouye

Daniel K. Inouye, the third most senior member of the U.S. Senate, is known for his distinguished record as a legislative leader, and as a World War II combat veteran who earned the nation's highest award for military valor, the Medal of Honor. Although he was thrust into the limelight in the 1970s as a member of the Watergate Committee and in 1987 as chairman of the Iran-Contra Committee, he has also quietly made his mark as a respected legislator able to work in a bipartisan fashion to enact meaningful legislation. As the ranking Democrat on the Senate Defense Appropriations Subcommittee, Senator Inouye has been able to focus on defense matters that strengthen national security and enhance the quality of life for military personnel and their families. This reflects his hope for a more secure world and his desire to provide the best possible assistance to the men and women who put their lives at risk to protect the United States. Senator Inouye has also championed the interests of Hawaii's people throughout his career. He was instrumental in engineering the restoration and return of Kahoolawe, the island that had been used for target practice by the U.S. military, to the State of Hawaii. He continues to press for passage of legislation that would establish a process by which Hawaii's indigenous people would be able to form their own sovereign government.

Senator Inouye also continues to push for improved education and health care for all children, additional jobs for Hawaii's economy, health and human services in rural communities, affordable housing, and the protection of the nation's natural resources. He was instrumental in setting the groundwork for the National Park Service's acquisition of approximately 115,000 acres of the Kahuku Ranch in Kau to expand the Hawaii Volcanoes National Park. The initiative is key to protecting rare and endangered bird and mammal species found in the varied habitats of Kahuku Ranch. As a senior member of the Senate Commerce Committee, Senator Inouye has been able to address important issues, such as aviation and maritime transportation, that are crucial for Hawaii, given its location in the middle of the Pacific Ocean. Hawaii is unable to depend on freight trucks and trains the way mainland states can, Senator Inouye notes. Senator Inouye was first elected to the U.S. Senate in 1962 and is now serving his seventh consecutive term. When Hawaii became a state on August 21, 1959, he was elected the first congressman from the new state and was reelected to a full term in 1960. The son of Japanese immigrants, Daniel Inouye was born and raised in Honolulu. Exactly three months after he had celebrated his seventeenth birthday, the Japanese attacked Pearl Harbor on December 7, 1941. Young Dan Inouye, who had some medical training, rushed into service as the head of a first-aid litter team. He saw a "lot of blood." He did not go home for a week.

In March 1943 eighteen-year-old Dan Inouye, then a freshman in premedical studies at the University of Hawaii and long eager to join the U.S. war effort, enlisted in the U.S. Army's 442nd Regimental Combat Team, the famed "Go for Broke" regiment of soldiers of Japanese ancestry.

Inouye was soon promoted to the rank of sergeant and was designated a combat platoon leader during the Italian campaign. He slogged through nearly three bloody months of the Rome Arno campaign with the U.S. Fifth Army.

In the fall of 1944 Inouye's unit was shifted to the French Vosges Mountains and spent two of the bloodiest weeks of the war rescuing a Texas battalion surrounded by German forces. The rescue of the "Lost Battalion" is listed in U.S. Army annals as one of the most significant military battles of the century. Inouye lost ten pounds, became a platoon leader, and was awarded the Bronze Star and a battlefield commission as a second lieutenant, as he and other Japanese Americans continued to fight with unmatched courage that would eventually result with the 442nd being the most decorated unit in U.S. military history for its size and length of service.

Back in Italy as the war was drawing to a close, Inouye displayed "extraordinary heroism" on April 21, 1945, near San Terenzo as he led his platoon through "formidable resistance" to capture a key ridge. His Medal of Honor citation states in part: "With complete disregard for his personal safety, Second Lieutenant Inouye crawled up the treacherous slope to within five yards of the nearest machine gun and hurled two grenades, destroying the emplacement. Before the enemy could retaliate, he stood up and neutralized a second machine gun nest. Although wounded by a sniper's bullet, he continued to engage other hostile positions at close range until an exploding grenade shattered his right arm. Despite the intense pain, he refused evacuation and continued to direct his platoon until enemy resistance was broken and his men were again deployed in defensive positions."

After losing his right arm, Inouye spent twenty months in an army hospital in Battle Creek, Michigan. On May 27, 1947, he was honorably discharged with the rank of captain, and returned home with a Distinguished Service Cross, the nation's second highest award for military valor, along with a Bronze Star, a Purple Heart with cluster, and twelve other medals and citations.

His Distinguished Service Cross was upgraded to the Medal of Honor, and that medal was presented to him by the president of the United States on June 21, 2000.

"Please remember that the story of my experiences during World War II is—by itself—not important," Senator Inouye wrote in 2003 to a girl who had visited him in his Washington office. "Much more significant are the values that the 442nd Regimental Combat Team and other segregated units represented: that patriotism and love of our great country are not limited to any ethnic group, and wartime hysteria must never again lead us to trample on our democratic principles" (U.S. Senate 2004).

With financial assistance from the G.I. Bill, Inouye graduated from the University of Hawaii and the George Washington University Law School. Returning to Hawaii from Washington, Inouye served as a deputy public prosecutor for the City of Honolulu. He broke into politics in 1954 during the "Democratic revolution" with his election to the Hawaii Territorial House of Representatives. In 1958 he was elected to the territorial senate. A year later, Daniel Inouye was elected to the U.S. House of Representatives.

In 1962 then Congressman Leo O'Brien of New York commemorated the third anniversary of Hawaii's admission to the Union by reminiscing about Daniel Inouye's arrival on the national political scene. His recollection of the day Inouye took the oath of office in the U.S. House was recorded in the Congressional Record:

Tuesday last was the third anniversary of the admission of Hawaii. Today is the third anniversary of one of the most dramatic and moving scenes ever to occur in this House. On that day, a young man, just elected to Congress from the brand new state, walked into the well of the House and faced the late Speaker Sam Rayburn. The House was very still. It was about to witness the swearing in, not only of the first Congressman from Hawaii, but the first American of Japanese descent to serve in either House of Congress. "Raise your right hand and repeat after me," intoned Speaker Rayburn. The hush deepened as the young Congressman raised not his right hand but his left and he repeated the oath of office. "There was no right hand, Mr. Speaker." It had been lost in combat by that young American soldier in World War II. Who can deny that, at that moment, a ton of prejudice slipped quietly to the floor of the House of Representatives. (U.S. Senate 2004)

State Level

Asian Americans outside Hawaii have also suffered from a serious lack of representation in government at the state level. The two early cases of Wing F. Ong and Dalip Singh Saund represented extremely rare examples of Asian American electoral participation on the mainland during their time. Although still not salient in the continental states, Asian American electoral participation at the state level has slowly improved since the 1960s.

In 1961 Seiji Horiuchi was the first *Nisei* elected to a state legislature on the mainland. He was an agricultural consultant running as a Republican for office in the Colorado legislature, and he won easily. The following decade witnessed the election of five Asian Americans to the California state assembly (Lien 2001b).

Alfred Song, a trade attorney, was a third-generation Hawaii-born Korean American who became the first Asian American ever elected to the California state assembly in 1962, with a loan of $3,500 and support from many non-Asian American Democrats. Prior to his state-level victory, he was a city councilman in Monterey Park, California. In 1966 he was elected to the state senate. In the same year March Fong Eu, a third-generation Chinese American, was elected to the state assembly, becoming the first Asian American female to win an elective office on the mainland and certainly the first Asian American female ever elected to the state assembly of California, which took place only four years after the first Asian American male was elected to the same legislative body. Prior to her career in the state assembly, having a doctorate degree in education from Stanford University, she was elected in 1956 to the Alameda County Board of Education in the Bay Area. She served in the state assembly for eight years. Another case of electoral participation in the California state legislature was that of Tom Hom, a Republican who had been a San Diego city councilman before he served in the state assembly from 1969 to 1970. In 1973, after three Asian Americans of either Chinese or Korean descent won seats in the state assembly, Paul Bannai, a city councilman from Gardena in Southern California, became the first Japanese American to be elected to the assembly, followed by another Japanese American, Floyd Mori, in 1975 (Lien 2001b).

In 1976 Asian Americans claimed another electoral victory at the state level. This time it occurred in nearby Oregon, where Mae Yih was elected to the state assembly. Also in Oregon, John Lim, an immigrant born and raised in South Korea, was elected to the state senate in 1992 and 1996, but failed when he ran for the U.S. Congress in

1998 (Lien 2001b). Asian American electoral participation at the level of state legislature also flourished in Washington, another West Coast state. Gary Locke, a third-generation Chinese American, served for eleven years from 1982 to 1993 in the Washington state legislature, and Arthur Wong also served there in the 1980s, followed by Paul Shin in 1992, who was adopted by an American and came to the United States at the age of eighteen. Shin ran as a Democrat for a seat in the U.S. Congress in 1994 and for lieutenant governor in 1996, but failed in both attempts (Lien 2001b; Kitano and Daniels 1988).

In California during the 1990s and beyond, Nao Takasugi, a Republican businessman, became the first Asian American elected to the state assembly since 1978. Following Takasugi's electoral victory in 1992, George Nakano from Torrance was elected in 1998 and reelected in 2000 and 2002. In 2000 two Chinese American women, Wilma Chan from Oakland and Carol Liu from Pasadena, were elected to the state assembly by a comfortable margin of votes. They were the first two Asian American women to serve in the California state legislature since the departure of March Fong Eu in 1974 (Fong 2002; Lai 2001; CAUSE website). They were joined by Judy Chu from Monterey Park, chair of the Asian Pacific Islander Legislative Caucus in the assembly in 2004–2005, Alan Nakanishi from Lodi, and Leland Yee from San Francisco in 2002. As of this writing, Chan, Liu, Chu, Nakanish, and Yee are the five Asian Americans in the California state assembly and there is no representation of Asian Americans in the state senate.

In addition to running for office in the state legislatures, Asian Americans also ran for office in the state executive bodies. After serving in the California state assembly for twenty years, March Fong Eu was elected California's secretary of state in 1974, the first Asian American secretary of state in the fifty states, and was repeatedly reelected by wide margins for many years, until she was appointed U.S. ambassador to Micronesia by President Bill Clinton in 1994.

In the meantime, less surprisingly, Asian Americans continued to be electorally victorious in Hawaii. In 1974 a Japanese American, George Ariyoshi, won the governorship, and the lieutenant governorship was won in 1978 by Jean King, the highest-ranking Asian American woman ever to hold state executive office.

In 1984, in a very exceptional case on the East Coast, S. B. Woo, a China-born physics professor without any prior experience of holding a public office, won the lieutenant governorship in Delaware, a state with a small Asian American population. He was the first Asian American on the mainland to be elected a lieutenant governor. Woo failed in his bid for the U.S. Senate in 1988. In 1992 Cheryl Lau, a Hawaii-born third-generation Chinese American woman, was elected Nevada secretary of state, echoing the achievement of March Fong Eu in California. Lau was a music professor who became deputy attorney general of the state before she was elected its secretary. In 1994 Matt Fong, son of March Fong Eu, was elected California state treasurer. But he failed when he ran for the U.S. Senate in 1998. The year 1996 was an extraordinary one in the history of Asian American electoral participation. Gary Locke, after serving eleven years in the state legislature and three years as the chief executive of King County, was elected the governor of Washington—a state where Asian Americans constituted only 4 percent of the electorate. It was quite a history-making event because Locke was the first Asian American on the mainland ever elected a state governor and the first Chinese American governor as well. Overall, he was the third Asian American governor after Hawaii's George Ariyoshi and Ben Cayetano, a Filipino American who was elected in 1994. With high popularity, Locke was reelected by a wide margin in 2000 (Lien 2001b; Chan 1991; Fong 2002).

Table 5.3 provides a large picture of Asian American elected officials in 2001, as state legislators, governors, and lieutenant governors. As noted earlier in Table 5.1, there was not much change in their numbers between 1978 and 2001. While there were sixty-three Asian American elected officials in 1978, the number went up only by about 10 percent in 2001. Out of all fifty states, only eight had elected

Table 5.3
Key Elected Officials at State Level, 2001

State	State Senators	State Representatives	State Governor	State Lieutenant Governor	Total
California	0	3	0	0	3
Colorado	1	0	0	0	1
Hawaii	21	33	1	1	56
Maryland	0	2	0	0	2
Minnesota	1	0	0	0	1
Oregon	1	0	0	0	1
Washington	1	3	1	0	5
West Virginia	0	1	0	0	1
Total	25	42	2	1	70

Source: Based on Don T. Nakanishi and James S. Lai, eds. 2001. *National Asian Pacific American Political Almanac.* 10th ed. Los Angeles: UCLA Asian American Studies Center, p. 152.

officials at the state level, and among these eight states, there was a rather salient regional asymmetry of representation. Sixty-five (or 93 percent) of the seventy elected officials were from the four western states of Hawaii, California, Washington, and Oregon. Hawaii alone contributed fifty-six (or 80 percent) of all seventy elected officials.

In terms of the quality of these state-level positions occupied by Asian Americans, there was also not much difference between 1978 and 2001. The only exception was the case of Gary Locke as the governor of Washington. Among the many Asian American elected officials at the state level, Governor Locke is undoubtedly the only one who is nationally prominent. Although Locke announced in 2003 his plan not to seek reelection, and finished his second term in January 2005, he is still one of a few Asian American public figures who have great political potential in the future.

Case Study: Gary Locke

Gary Locke was elected Washington's twenty-first governor on November 5, 1996, making him the first Chinese American governor in U.S. history. On November 7, 2000, Locke, a Democrat, was reelected to a second term.

Born into an immigrant family on January 21, 1950, Locke spent his first six years in Seattle's Yesler Terrace, a public housing project for families of World War II veterans. He worked in his father's grocery store, became an Eagle Scout, and graduated with honors from Seattle's Franklin High School in 1968. Through a combination of part-time jobs, financial aid, and scholarships, Locke attended Yale University, earning a bachelor's degree in political science in 1972.

After receiving his law degree from Boston University in 1975, he worked for several years as a deputy prosecutor in King County, prosecuting felony crimes. In 1982 Locke was elected to the Washington State House of Representatives, where he served on the House Judiciary and Appropriations Committees, with his final five years spent as chairman of the House Appropriations Committee.

Prior to being elected governor, Locke served as chief executive of King County in 1993 and took on the issues and challenges facing Washington's largest city. Locke and his wife, Mona Lee Locke, a former reporter for the NBC affiliate KING 5 television in Seattle, were married October 15, 1994. The Lockes have two children—Emily, born in March 1997, and Dylan, born in March 1999. (Washington State Office of the Governor).

Local Level

Asian American candidates have been most successful at the local level. As demonstrated in Table 5.1, the number of Asian American elected officials at that level grew from 52 to 487 between 1978 and 2001, representing an increase of 837 percent in 23 years.

Some of the most prominent Asian American elected officials in the nation began their political careers from the municipal or county levels, such as Norman Mineta and Gary Locke. However, Asian American electoral participation at this level did not really begin to grow until the 1960s. In Gardena, California, after Bruce Kaji was elected city treasurer in 1959, Ken Nakapka was elected city councilman in 1966 and mayor in 1972, followed by three more Japanese Americans elected to the city council in the 1970s. Several other *Nisei* were elected mayors in rural California and Idaho in the 1960s. By the late 1960s, Oakland and Berkeley, California, had their first Chinese American city council members, and then Frank Ogawa served on Oakland's city council in the 1970s. The first Korean American to be elected to a school board was Gene Roh in Berkeley in 1973. In 1977 Gordon Lau became the first Chinese American elected to the San Francisco Board of Supervisors (Lien 2001b).

Outside California, when Wing Luke was elected to the Seattle city council in 1962, he became the first Chinese American to win an elective office in the Pacific Northwest. Also in the state of Washington, Carl Ooka was the first *Nisei* elected a county commissioner in Kittitas County in the 1960s. In Arizona, Soleng Tom was elected to the school board of Tucson 1964. On the East Coast, the first Chinese American woman was elected to a school board in 1974. In the South, records show that Chinese Americans were elected mayors or sheriffs in Arkansas, Mississippi, and Louisiana (Lien 2001b).

More and more Asian Americans were elected to office at local levels in the 1980s and 1990s. As indicated in Table 5.1, their total number reached the 100 benchmark in the early 1980s and passed the 200 benchmark in the late 1990s. In the new millennium, it grew even more rapidly with 248 in 2000 and 487 in 2001. The more prominent cases in the 1980s all occurred in California. Carol Kawanami became the first Japanese American woman in the United States elected a mayor, in Villa Park, Orange County, while Lily Chen was elected the mayor of Monterey Park as the first Chinese American woman mayor (Chan 1991). Also in Monterey Park, Judy Chu was later elected councilwoman and mayor. In Los Angeles, Michael Woo was the first Asian American elected to the city council in 1986, while Warren

Furutan was elected to the city Board of Education. In the Bay Area, Thomas Hsieh was elected supervisor of San Francisco (Wei 1993; Kitano and Daniels 1988).

Table 5.4 is a detailed, state-by-state summary of Asian American elected officials at the local level, including city mayors, council members, and school board and higher education board officials. Their numbers total 231 from 20 different states. In addition, there were 256 elected judges from 27 different states (Nakanishi and Lai 2001). As Table 5.4 indicates, even though 20 different states had Asian American locally elected officials, there was still an asymmetric

Table 5.4
Key Elected Officials at Local Level, 2001*

State	City Mayors	County/City Councilmembers	School/Higher Education board Officials	Total
Alaska	0	2	0	2
California	7	30	99	136
Colorado	1	0	0	1
Hawaii	3	24	9	36
Illinois	1	1	0	2
Louisiana	0	1	0	1
Maryland	0	1	0	1
Massachusetts	0	4	0	4
Michigan	0	2	0	2
Nebraska	0	1	0	1
Nevada	0	1	0	1
New Mexico	1	2	0	3
New York	0	0	11	11
North Dakota	0	1	0	1
Ohio	0	0	2	2
Oregon	0	1	1	2
Texas	1	2	0	3
Washington	1	8	11	20
West Virginia	0	1	0	1
Wisconsin	0	1	0	1
Total	15	83	133	231

Source: Don T. Nakanishi and James S. Lai, eds. 2001. *National Asian Pacific American Political Almanac.* 10th ed. Los Angeles: UCLA Asian American Studies Center, p. 152.

*This table does not include 256 Asian American elected judges from 27 states, as of 2001.

representation in favor of the western states. The states of California, Hawaii, and Washington altogether contributed 192 (or 83.1 percent) of the 231 elected officials, of whom nearly 60 percent came from one single state, California, mainly because of its large number of school and higher education board members. The only nonwestern state that had a double-digit number of locally elected officials was New York, where there were eleven school board members, the same as the number in Washington. It is also important to note that even with that many locally elected officials nationwide, only 15 mayors out of thousands of mayors in the country were Asian Americans.

Appointed Officials

In addition to being elected to a public office, seeking to be a politically appointed official is another way for American citizens to serve in the government. However, there is no systematic information about Asian American politically appointed officials, especially at the state and local levels.

In the federal executive branch, political appointment of Asian Americans at cabinet and subcabinet levels did not really occur until the late 1980s, and then it has been basically a story of two persons: Elaine Chao, a Chinese immigrant who came to the United States at the age of eight, and Norman Mineta, a second-generation Japanese American Democrat. In 1989, when the Republican National Committee opened a special Asian American Affairs Office, President George H. W. Bush appointed an unprecedented number of Asian Americans to high-level positions. Among those appointees was Elaine Chao, a Republican. When she was appointed deputy secretary of the U.S. Department of Transportation, she was the only Asian American member at the cabinet and subcabinet levels. Other than Chao, Wendy Gramm, wife of U.S. Senator Phil Gramm from Texas, was appointed to chair the Commodity Futures Trading Commission; Patricia Saiki, former Republican congresswoman from Hawaii, was appointed to lead the Small Business Administration; and Julie Chang Bloch was named ambassador to Nepal (Fong 2002).

In the Clinton administration, Asian Americans as a whole held only 2 of the 250-plus cabinet and subcabinet positions in 1998 (80–20 website). In June 2000 former congressman Norman Mineta was appointed by President Clinton to be secretary of commerce, becoming the first Asian American ever appointed to a cabinet-level office. In July, Bill Lann Lee was appointed assistant attorney general in charge of civil rights without congressional approval, three years after his nomination was stalled in Congress (Fong 2002).

When President George W. Bush took office in 2001, he appointed Elaine Chao secretary of labor and Norman Mineta secretary of transportation. This unprecedented appointment of Asian Americans to two out of fourteen cabinet secretary positions opened a brand-new chapter of Asian American political participation. Both Chao and Mineta stay on in their positions within the cabinet in Bush's second term. Their profiles are introduced below.

Case Study I: Elaine L. Chao

Elaine L. Chao is the nation's twenty-fourth secretary of labor, representing a new generation of American leadership. She was confirmed by the Senate on January 29, 2001.

When President George W. Bush nominated Chao, the first Asian American woman appointed to a president's cabinet in U.S. history, he described her as an individual with "strong executive talent, compassion, and commitment to helping people build better lives."

Secretary Chao was an immigrant to this country at the age of eight. As director of the Peace Corps, she was one of the first Americans to personally embrace the people of the former communist bloc into the family of democratic nations, establishing Peace Corps programs in the Baltic nations of Latvia, Lithuania, Estonia, and the newly independent states of the former Soviet Union. Later, as president and chief executive officer of United Way of America, she restored public trust and confidence after the organization was tarnished by mismanagement and financial abuse, thus preserving the nation's largest institution of private charitable giving.

The experience she gained at the United Way helping communities address their local needs prepared her to mobilize the Department of Labor to promote pathways to economic freedom for individuals and families working to achieve the American Dream. She describes her vision for America's workforce as "one in which everyone can participate . . . where jobs and opportunities are available for those leaving welfare, job training is accessible for those left behind, disability never bars a qualified person from the workplace, and where parents have an easier time balancing the responsibilities of work and home" (U.S. Department of Labor 2004).

Secretary Chao's previous government career includes serving as deputy secretary at the U.S. Department of Transportation, chair of the Federal Maritime Commission, and deputy maritime administrator in the U.S. Department of Transportation. She brings a wealth of business experience to the post, having worked as vice president of syndications at BankAmerica Capital Markets Group and a banker with Citicorp. Prior to her nomination as secretary, she expanded her study of policy as a distinguished fellow at the Heritage Foundation, a Washington-based public policy research and educational institute. She was selected a White House fellow in 1983.

Secretary Chao received her M.B.A. from the Harvard Business School and her undergraduate degree in economics from Mount Holyoke College. She also studied at M.I.T., Dartmouth College, and Columbia University. Serving in many volunteer activities, Secretary Chao has received numerous awards for her professional accomplishments and community service. She is the recipient of twenty-one honorary doctoral degrees from colleges and universities around the world.

Secretary Chao is married to the Senate Majority Whip, Senator Mitch McConnell of Kentucky. (U.S. Department of Labor, Office of the Secretary).

Case Study II: Norman Y. Mineta

Norman Y. Mineta became the fourteenth U.S. secretary of transportation on January 25, 2001. In nominating him, President Bush said, "Norm made a reputation in the halls of Congress as someone who understands that a sound infrastructure in America will lead to economic opportunity for all Americans." "Transportation is key to generating and enabling economic growth, determining the patterns of that growth, and determining the competitiveness of our businesses in the world economy," said Secretary Mineta. "Transportation is thus key to both our economic success and to our quality of life" (U.S. Department of Transportation 2004).

As secretary of transportation, Mineta oversees an agency with 60,000 employees and a $56.3 billion budget. Created in 1967, the U.S. Department of Transportation brought under one umbrella air, maritime, and surface transportation missions.

In response to the terrorist attacks of September 11, 2001, Secretary Mineta oversaw the creation of the Transportation Security Administration (TSA), an agency of more than 60,000 employees that is responsible for protecting Americans as they travel across the country. Starting from a blank sheet of paper on November 19, 2001, Secretary Mineta led a team that met thirty-six mandates set down by Congress, while developing a fully functioning agency that restored air travelers' confidence in aviation security following the terrorist attacks. The Transportation Security Administration was transferred to the Department of Homeland Security on March 1, 2003.

Secretary Mineta also oversaw the Coast Guard's response to the terrorist attacks, including developing the Sea Marshal Program, Maritime Safety and Security Teams, and expanding the number and mission of Coast Guard Port Security Units.

Prior to joining President Bush's administration as secretary of transportation, Mineta served as U.S. secretary of commerce under President Clinton, becoming the first Asian Pacific American to serve in the cabinet. He is the first secretary of transportation to have previously served in a cabinet position. Prior to joining the Commerce Department, he was a vice president at Lockheed Martin Corporation. From 1975 to 1995, he served as a member of the U.S. House of Representatives, representing the heart of California's Silicon Valley. As a member of Congress, Mineta was known for his dedication to the people of his district, for consensus building among his colleagues and for forging public-private partnerships. Mineta's legislative and policy agenda was wide and varied, including major projects in the areas of economic development, science and technology policy, trade, transportation, the environment, intelligence, the budget, and civil rights. He cofounded the Congressional Asian Pacific American Caucus and served as its first chair.

Mineta served as chairman of the House Public Works and Transportation Committee between 1992 and 1994. He chaired the committee's aviation subcommittee between 1981 and 1988, and chaired its Surface Transportation Subcommittee from 1989 to 1991. During his career in Congress he championed increases in investment for transportation infrastructure and was a key author of the landmark Intermodal Surface Transportation Efficiency Act (ISTEA) of 1991, which shifted decisions on highway and mass transit planning to state and local governments. The ISTEA led to major upsurges in mass transit ridership and more environmentally friendly transportation projects, such as bicycle paths. He also pressed for more funding for the department's Federal Aviation Administration (FAA). After leaving Congress, Mineta chaired the National Civil Aviation Review Commission, which in 1997 issued recommendations on reducing traffic congestion and reducing the aviation accident rate.

Many of the commission's recommendations were adopted by the Clinton administration, including changes in the FAA to enable it to perform more like a business.

Mineta and his family were among the 110,000 Japanese forced from their homes and into internment camps during World War II. After graduating from the University of California, Berkeley, Mineta joined the U.S. Army in 1953 and served as an intelligence officer in Japan and Korea. He joined his father in the Mineta Insurance Agency before entering politics in San Jose, serving as a member of its city council from 1967 to 1971 and mayor from 1971 to 1974, becoming the first Asian Pacific American mayor of a major U.S. city. As mayor, he favored greater control of transportation decisions by local government, a position he later championed in the ISTEA.

While in Congress, Mineta was the driving force behind passage of H.R. 442, the Civil Liberties Act of 1988, which officially apologized for and redressed the injustices endured by the Japanese during World War II. In 1995 George Washington University awarded the Martin Luther King Jr. Commemorative Medal to Mineta for his contributions to the field of civil rights. In 2003 Secretary Mineta received the Panetta Institute's Jefferson-Lincoln Award for his bipartisan leadership in addressing the nation's challenges and was selected by the Council of Excellence in Government to receive the Elliot L. Richardson Prize for Excellence and Integrity in Public Service.

Mineta is married to Danealia (Deni) Mineta. He has two sons, David and Stuart Mineta, and two stepsons, Robert and Mark Brantner. (U.S. Department of Transportation).

In addition to these two high-level appointed officials in the cabinet, according to the *National Asian Pacific American Political Almanac, 2001–02,* thirty-five federal appointed officials in 2001 were Asian Americans who held a variety of positions, including director of the Logistics Center at the Federal Aviation Commission, chief information officer of the National Oceanic and Atmospheric Administration Research Center, and commissioner of the U.S. Commission on Civil Rights, just to name a few.

In the federal judicial branch, the percentage of Asian American appointees has remained below their population share. No Asian Americans have ever been appointed to the Supreme Court. Herbert Young Cho Choy, a Korean American, became the first Asian American federal judge in 1971, serving on the U.S. Ninth Circuit Court of Appeal (U.S. Courts for the Ninth Circuit 2005). Between 1985 and 1988 under the Reagan administration, only 0.6 percent of federal judicial appointees to the U.S. district courts were Asian Americans, and no Asian Americans were appointed to the U.S. courts of appeal. Between 1989 and 1992 under the George H. W. Bush administration, no Asian Americans at all were appointed to either one. Between 1993 and 1996 under the Clinton administration, there was an improvement with 1.2 percent of the appointees to the U.S. district courts and 3.4 percent of the appointees to the U.S. courts of appeal being Asian Americans (Lien 2001b). In 1998 only seven (or 0.8 percent) of the 875 active federal judges were Asian Americans (80–20 website). As of January 2003, there were only six active Asian American federal judges, including five U.S. district court judges and one U.S. court of appeals judge, and none of them served as a chief judge. Throughout the history of the U.S. federal judicial branch, there has been a total of fourteen Asian American federal judges: ten serving in the U.S. district courts and four serving in U.S. courts of appeals. Among these, there was only one female U.S. district court judge and only one U.S. district court chief judge (Just the Beginning Foundation 2003).

Community and Organizational Leaders

Most Asian American elected and appointed officials have taken leadership roles in the Asian American community, especially among their respective ethnic groups. However, there is another group of Asian American leaders whose contributions to the community are by no means less than those of the elected and appointed political leaders. They are leaders of Asian American political organizations throughout the nation. Among a plethora of Asian American organizational leaders, seven East Asian American leaders from organizations of great importance are introduced in this section. The introduction to these organizational leaders is then followed by a brief biography of Angela Oh, the most prominent Korean American community leader after the 1992 Los Angeles riots.

Christine Chen of the Organization of Chinese Americans (OCA)

Christine Chen is not only the executive director of the Organization of Chinese Americans (OCA), but also plays a vital role in quite a few other Asian American organizations, including the Asian Pacific Islander American Vote campaign (APIAVote 2000) where she serves as chair, the Conference on Asian Pacific American Leadership (CAPAL), Youth Vote 2000, and the Midwest Asian American Students Union (MAASU). She is also a project coordinator for the "Next GenerAsian" program in charge of the training and development of over 600 students every year.

Because of her contributions at both the grassroots and the national levels, Chen has become a well-recognized voice in Asian American communities across the nation. As a result, she is frequently invited to offer her expertise at various events, such as workshops, panel discussions, press conferences, and so on. In the January 8, 2001, "Women of the 21st Century" issue of *Newsweek,* Chen was one of fifteen women described as "the kind of women who will shape America's new century" (University of Central Florida).

S. Floyd Mori of the Japanese American Citizens League (JACL)

S. Floyd Mori is the national president of the Japanese American Citizens League (JACL). Not only is he a community leader, but he was also a public official. Prior to taking his leadership position at the JACL, Mori was elected a California state assemblyman in 1975 as one of the pioneer Asian American elected officials outside of Hawaii.

Mori developed an interest in politics in the 1970s when he was teaching economics at Chabot College in Hayward, California. In 1973 Mori was elected to the city council of Pleasanton, California, and became its mayor the next year. After spending six years in the state assembly, Mori served as the director of the Office of International Trade in California for one year.

He was also active in Utah. In addition to being a member of several city and regional boards in California, Mori has been the Utah trade representative to Japan and served on the Utah governor's Asian Advisory Board and Small Business Administration Advisory Committee.

Mori received a bachelor's degree and a master's degree in economics, Asian studies, and political science from Brigham Young University (Asian Pacific American Institute for Congressional Studies; Japanese American Citizens League, Hawaii).

Thomas J. Hahn of the Korean American Coalition (KAC)

Thomas Hahn is the chairman of the board of directors of the Korean American Coalition (KAC) in Washington, D.C. Professionally, Hahn is a certified public accountant and certified financial planner and president of an accounting firm, Hahn and Associates, P.C. In addition to his role in the KAC, he has been active in other Korean American organizations. He served as the first treasurer of Advocates for the Rights of Korean Americans, which is a joint advocacy group of the Korean American Association (KAA) and the Korean American Garment Workers (KAGW). He received his B.S. and M.S. in accounting from the University of Maryland and the University of Virginia, respectively. He is also a member of the American Institute of Certified Public Accountants (Korean American Coalition-D.C.).

Karen K. Narasaki of the National Asian Pacific American Legal Consortium (NAPALC)

Karen Narasaki is the president and executive director of the National Asian Pacific American Legal Consortium (NAPALC), the chair of the National Council of Asian Pacific Americans (NCAPA), and the chair of the Compliance/Enforcement Committee of the Executive Committee of the Leadership Conference on Civil Rights. In addition to taking the above leadership positions, Narasaki is also involved in a wide range of other organizations, including the Lawyers Committee for Civil Rights Under Law, the Leadership Conference Education Fund, the Independent Sector, National Immigration Law Center, the National Asian Pacific American Bar Association, the Asian Bar Association of Washington, the Asian Pacific American Legal Center of Southern California, and the Organization of Pan Asian American Women.

Prior to her role in the NAPALC, Narasaki was the Washington, D.C., representative for the Japanese American Citizens League, directing the JACL's national advocacy program. Before that, she served as a law clerk to Judge Harry Pregerson on the United States Court of Appeals for the Ninth Circuit in Los Angeles and later she worked as a corporate attorney in Seattle. She is a graduate of Yale University and the UCLA School of Law.

Narasaki has appeared on several national television networks as well as on National Public Radio shows. Her views have also been featured in national newspapers such as the *New York Times,* the *Washington Post,* the *Wall Street Journal, USA Today,* and the *Los Angeles Times* (National Asian Pacific American Legal Consortium).

Daphne Kwok of the Asian Pacific American Institute for Congressional Studies (APAICS)

Prior to becoming the executive director of the Asian Pacific American Institute for Congressional Studies (APAICS) in April 2001, Daphne Kwok was the first elected chair of the National Council of Asian Pacific Americans for about three and a half years, as well as the executive director of the Organization of Chinese Americans for eleven years, during which she coordinated programs and services for forty-five chapters and thirty-seven college affiliates and focused on issues related to the Asian American community.

Kwok is also active in an array of other Asian American organizations, including the Southeast Asia Resource Action Center, the National Coalition of Asian Pacific American Community Development, and the Asian Pacific American Caucus of the American Political Science Association. In 1996 she was responsible for coordinating an unprecedented national voter registration campaign involving nineteen Asian American organizations, resulting in the registration of more than 70,000 voters. She received a B.A. in East Asian studies and music from Wesleyan University, and later became the first Asian American member of its board of trustees. She earned a master's degree in public administration from New York's Baruch City College (Asian Pacific American Institute for Congressional Studies).

S. B. Woo of the 80–20 Political Action Committee (80–20 PAC)

S. B. (Shien-Biau) Woo is the president of the 80–20 Political Action Committee (80–20 PAC). Woo served as lieutenant governor of Delaware from 1985 to 1989. He also served as a trustee of the University of Delaware and the national president of the Organization of Chinese Americans. Due to his public and community service, Woo is listed in *Who's Who in America,* and was ranked by *A-Magazine* as the sixth of its "25 Most Influential Asian Americans" in 2000.

A retired physics professor who was born in Shanghai, China, and came to the United States at the age of eighteen, Woo received his B.S. in mathematics and physics and Ph.D. in physics from Georgetown College in Kentucky and Washington University in St. Louis, respectively (AsianAmerican.net).

Sandra Chen of the Center for Asian Americans United for Self Empowerment (CAUSE)

Sandra Chen was the first executive director of the Center for Asian Americans United for Self Empowerment. She resigned from the organization in summer 2004.

As executive director, Chen organized hundreds of voter registration drives to help register over 20,000 Asian Americans. Chen's other works include developing outreach programs for seniors and college students to organize their own voter registration activities, setting up a statewide multilingual toll-free voter assistance hotline for Asian American immigrants, and organizing a statewide internship program for Asian American college students in the summer.

In addition to her role at the CAUSE, Chen serves as the director of mentorship for the Asian Professional Exchange and she is also a member of the League of Women Voters—Greater Pasadena, and the advisory boards of the San Gabriel Valley YMCA and the Make-A-Wish Foundation—San Gabriel Valley.

Speaking fluent Mandarin and Cantonese, Chen has appeared on Chinese language media programs to address issues about elections and voter registration. She was named by politicalcircus.com in 2002 one of the site's "Top 30 Most Influential Individuals under 30 Years of Age." Chen received her B.A. in political science from the University of California, Riverside, and a master's degree in urban planning at UCLA (AsianAmerican.net).

Angela E. Oh: A Korean American Community Leader

Angela E. Oh is a trial attorney, specializing in civil rights and criminal defense. Currently, she is the chair of the board of directors of the Korean American Family Service Center in Los Angeles, and a member of the Los Angeles City Human Relations Commission, the Advisory Board of HUD's Community Builder Fellowship Program, and other organizations.

In June 1997 Oh was appointed by President Clinton to serve on a seven-member advisory board to the President's Initiative on Race. Before that, she had served as a lawyer delegate to the Ninth Circuit Judicial Conference, as chair of U.S. Senator Barbara Boxer's Federal Appointments Committee, as president of the Korean American Bar Association of Southern California, and as a board member of the California Women's Law Center.

After the 1992 Los Angeles riots, Oh emerged as the most well-known Korean American community leader. She has given numerous public talks nationally and internationally on issues such as the role of women in law and politics, Asian Americans in politics, the administration of justice, multicultural race relations in the United States, and so on.

Oh received her B.A. and master's degrees in public health from the University of California, Los Angeles, and her J.D. from the University of California, Davis (University of Vermont).

Conclusion

Asian American involvement in political officeholding is the most recently adopted form of their political participation in American politics. In the area of elected office, Asian American political candidates have had most success at the local level. As of 2005, they remain severely underrepresented in the national Congress—especially in the House of Representatives with only four members, including one nonvoting member. The situation at the state level is not any better, with only seventy elected officials in eight states. Worse than that is an asymmetrical representation in favor of four western states, especially Hawaii and California, where the majority of Asian American candidates have been elected. Even though the situation at the local level is much better, there also exists the same problem of regional asymmetry in favor of California and Hawaii.

In the area of politically appointed offices, while the previous situation of underrepresentation has improved at the cabinet level of the federal executive branch, the Asian American presence in the federal judicial branch is not in proportion to their population share.

Overall, there have been some good signs of improvement in Asian American participation in political officeholding, which is partly due to the efforts made by many Asian American organizational and community leaders throughout the years at the national and grassroots levels, whose contributions are not only pivotal to Asian American participation in political officeholding in particular but also to Asian American political participation in all areas.

References

80–20 website: http://www.80–20initiative.net. Accessed January 16, 2005.
AsianAmerican.net. http://www.asianamerican.net/bios/Chen-Sandra.html. Accessed May 4, 2004.
————. http://www.asianamerican.net/bios/Woo-SB.html. Accessed May 4, 2004.
Asian Pacific American Institute for Congressional Studies website: http://www.apaics.org/twaa/twaa_081304.htm. Accessed September 24, 2004
————. http://www.apaics.org/staff.html. Accessed May 4, 2004.
Center for Asian Americans United for Self Empowerment website: http://www.causeusa.org. Accessed April 29, 2004.
Chan, Sucheng. 1991. *Asian American: An Interpretive History.* New York: Twayne.
Fong, Timothy P. 2002. *The Contemporary Asian American Experience: Beyond the Model Minority.* 2d ed. Upper Saddle River, NJ: Prentice Hall.
Japanese American Citizens League, Hawaii, website: http://www.jaclhawaii.org/InfoPages/Speaker%20bios/Flyod%20Mori.pdf. Accessed September 24, 2004.
Just the Beginning Foundation. 2003. website: http://www.jtbf.org/school/JTBF%20ASIAN%20JUDGES%20SUM.pdf. Accessed January 16, 2005.
Kitano, Harry H. L., and Roger Daniels. 1988. *Asian Americans: Emerging Minorities.* Englewood Cliffs, NJ: Prentice Hall.
Korean American Coalition-D.C. website: http://www.kacdc.org/about/people.html. Accessed May 4, 2004.
Lai, James S. 2001. "November 2000 Elections Result in Long-Time Firsts for Asian Pacific Americans." In *National Asian Pacific American Political Almanac.* 10th ed. Edited by Don T. Nakanishi and James S. Lai. Los Angeles: UCLA Asian American Studies Center.
Lai, James S., Wendy K. Tam-Cho, Thomas P. Kim, and Okiyoshi Takeda. 2003. "Campaigns, Elections, and Elected Officials." In *Asian American Politics: Law, Participation, and Policy.* Edited by Don T. Nakanishi and James S. Lai. Lanham, MD: Rowman and Littlefield.
Lien, Pei-te. 2001b. *The Making of Asian America through Political Participation.* Philadelphia, PA: Temple University Press.
Nakanishi, Don T. 1989. "American Quota on Excellence? The Asian American Admissions Debate." *Asian Affairs: An American Review* (November/December). Included in *Contemporary Asian America: American Multidisciplinary Reader.* Edited by Min Zhou and James V. Gatewood. New York: New York University Press, 2000.
Nakanishi, Don T., and James S. Lai, eds. 2001. *National Asian Pacific American Political Almanac.* 10th ed. Los Angeles: UCLA Asian American Studies Center.

National Asian Pacific American Legal Consortium website: http://www.napalc
.org/about/staff/bio-Narasaki.html. Accessed May 4, 2004.

U.S. Courts for the Ninth Circuit. 2005. http://www.ce9.uscourts.gov. Accessed
January 16, 2005.

U.S. Department of Labor, Office of the Secretary. *About Secretary of Labor Elaine
L. Chao.* http://www.dol.gov/_sec/aboutsec/chao.htm. Accessed May 4, 2004.

U.S. Department of Transportation. *Norman Y. Mineta, Secretary of
Transportation.* http://www.dot.gov/affairs/mineta.htm. Accessed May 4, 2004.

U.S. Senate. *Biography of Daniel K. Inouye.* http://www.inouye.senate.gov/
biography.html. Accessed May 4, 2004.

University of Central Florida. http://www.diversity.ucf.edu/programs/
national_conference. Accessed May 4, 2004.

University of Vermont. http://www.uvm.edu/~bocday/angelaoh.html. Accessed
May 4, 2004.

Washington State Office of the Governor. *About the Governor.* http://www
.governor.wa.gov/bios/bio.htm. Accessed May 4, 2004.

Wei, William. 1993. *The Asian American Movement.* Philadelphia, PA: Temple
University.

Conclusion

Participating in mainstream politics is no easy task for East Asian Americans. It took them more than one and a half centuries to stand where they are standing today in the American political arena. Along the way were good moments and bad moments. Sixty or so years ago, at the same time that all Chinese exclusion laws were finally repealed, 111,000 Japanese were put into internment camps for the duration of World War II. Twenty or so years ago, at the same time that the Redress movement led by the Japanese American Citizens League was gaining tremendous momentum after the Commission on Wartime Relocation and Internment of Civilians issued its report, *Personal Justice Denied,* to the U.S. government, the American Citizens for Justice failed to bring justice to the murder case of Vincent Chin. And now, even when Elaine Chao and Norman Mineta are both cabinet secretaries in the George W. Bush administration, the nearly forty-year-old Executive Order 11246, prohibiting any organizations that practice discrimination from receiving federal money, is enforced for all minority groups except Asian Americans.

On September 1, 2004, Secretary of Labor Chao addressed the Republican National Convention held in New York City. At the moment when Asian American delegates among thousands of others were listening to her speech inside the convention hall, Asian American protesters, individually or in groups, were joining thousands of others outside the hall, holding signs and shouting slogans. At that very moment, it was evident that Asian American participation in public officeholding, electoral and party politics, protest politics, and interest-group politics were all at work. Undeniably, the presence of Asian Americans at that particular time and place was indeed a rather encouraging picture. But how about the overall picture across time and space, and more importantly, what will be the picture tomorrow?

Ever since their first arrival in the new land in the mid-nineteenth century, East Asian Americans, particularly Chinese and Japanese Americans, have been active in protest politics and interest-group politics to address their social and economic needs. However, their early participatory activities were neither very visible nor effective until the 1960s, when the Asian American movement was born in the midst of the broader civil rights movement. What did it take for the Asian American movement to come into existence at that particular time and place? It needed to meet two prerequisites common to collective actions and social movements: incentives and opportunities. As East Asians experienced racism and exclusionism in their first century in the New World, their collective historical memory of dismay provided them a strong incentive to advance their political participation when the opportunity came. The opportunity finally came in the 1960s. The Asian American movement emerged later that decade as a result of the general social movement in the mainstream society and enormous demographic changes that dramatically improved both the quantity and quality of East Asian American communities, both of which were valuable resources to foster political participation.

The movement is historically monumental not only because it thoroughly renewed the old-fashioned Asian protest and interest-group politics, but also because it began to create pan-Asian ethnicity and solidarity for the first time ever among Asian Americans who are so heterogeneous in terms of ethnicity, class, gender, and generational and ideological backgrounds. However, despite its historical significance, the movement's impacts on the real world were a mix of successes and failures, largely depending upon whether or not the actions taken were in collaboration with other minority groups. For instance, while the San Francisco State College strike, a collective effort of several minority groups, successfully gained the establishment of ethnic studies programs, the International Hotel campaign, primarily an Asian American-based struggle, failed completely. In terms of Asian American solidarity, many other cases of Asian American protests were even worse than the International Hotel case, in which Asian Americans at least joined forces among themselves. In these other cases, only one ethnic group of East Asian Americans fought alone without help from other groups. Although more successful than the International Hotel case in terms of outcomes, the

Redress movement and the campaign in the wake of the Los Angeles riots in 1992 were two cases in point; while the former was merely a Japanese American movement, the latter involved the participation mainly of Korean Americans.

In contrast with their participatory activities in the realms of protest politics and interest-group politics, East Asian Americans' participation in the spheres of electoral and party politics and political officeholding are more recent phenomena. For the last few decades, many of them have overcome obstacles to become citizens, to register to vote, and then to cast their ballots on election days. However, although there has been a noticeable increase in their overall electoral involvement, East Asian Americans have not yet been able to present themselves as a formidable, unified force in the American national political arena. This is because many members of the community still are politically apathetic and also because the community is a rather divergent group with tremendous internal differences and cleavages.

In the area of elected office, while East Asian American political candidates have had most success at the local level, they are severely underrepresented at the national level, especially in the House of Representatives, as well as at the state level, with only seventy elected officials in eight states as of 2001. One related problem is that there is an asymmetrical representation in favor of the four far western states at both the state and local levels, especially Hawaii and California where the majority of Asian American elected officials can be found. As for the area of politically appointed offices, though the previous situation of underrepresentation has improved at the top level of the federal executive branch, the East Asian American presence in the federal judicial branch is still not in proportion to their population share.

Looking back at the overall picture of East Asian American political participation across time and space, many signs of positive development are evident in all areas of their political participation. However so, as demonstrated throughout the book, East Asian Americans still lack the level of political clout they deserve, mainly because of two reasons. First, a genuine feeling of panethnicity among East Asian Americans or Asian Americans as a whole is not yet fully formulated. Consequently, there is a desperate need for members of the separate communities among them to set aside their differences and forge a group identity and unity to act collectively to defend their interests in the future. In the meantime, work on building intergroup alliances with other minority groups is also vital for East Asian

Americans' future success in political participation. Second, in electoral politics, although many East Asian American elites have vigorously participated as candidates, East Asian American voters have not yet come to represent an electoral power in proportion to their share of the total population. Therefore, overcoming the problem of political apathy and integrating their votes into a voting bloc to become a more powerful swing vote are important for East Asian Americans and Asian Americans as a whole. So, what will be the picture tomorrow? It will be largely determined by the extent to which the above problems can be solved.

Documents

Naturalization Act, March 26, 1790

According to the 1790 Naturalization Act, only "free white persons" with two years of residence were eligible to apply for naturalization. This made Asian immigrants a disenfranchised group who were denied the right to become citizens regardless of the duration of their stay in the United States, and as a result, they were also without the right to vote or even run for public office. The laws were modified in 1870 after the Civil War to allow people of African ancestry to apply for citizenship. Immigrants from Asia had been deprived of citizenship until the 1940s and 1950s.

Chap. III. An Act to Establish a Uniform Rule of Naturalization. (a)

Section 1. *Be it enacted by the Senate and House of Representatives of the United States of America in Congress assembled,* That any alien, being a free white person, who shall have resided within the limits and under the jurisdiction of the United States for the term of two years, may be admitted to become a citizen thereof, on application to any common law court of record, in any one of the states wherein he shall have resided for the term of one year at least, and making proof to the satisfaction of such court, that he is a person of good character, and taking the oath or affirmation prescribed by law, to support the constitution of the United States, which oath or affirmation such court shall administer; and the clerk of such court shall record such application, and the proceedings thereon; and thereupon such person shall be considered as a citizen of the United States. And the children of such persons so naturalized, dwelling within the United States, being under the age of twenty-one years at the time of such naturalization, shall also be considered as citizens of the United States. And the children of citizens of the United States, that may be born beyond sea, or out of the limits of the United States, shall be considered as natural born citizens: *Provided,* That the right of citizenship shall not descend to persons whose fathers have never been resident in the United States: *Provided also,* That no person heretofore proscribed by any state, shall be admitted a citizen as aforesaid, except by an act of the legislature of the state in which such person was proscribed. *(a)*

Approved, March 26, 1790.

Source: Richard Peters, ed. 1845. *The Public Statutes at Large of the United States of America,* vol. 1. Boston: Charles Little and James Brown. Reprinted in Franklin Odo, ed. 2002. *The Columbia Documentary History of the Asian American Experience.* New York: Columbia University, 13–14.

People v. Hall, 1854

The California Supreme Court ruled in the case of People v. Hall *that Chinese could not give testimony against a white person in court. George Hall had been convicted for the murder of a Chinese man, but the Court reversed his conviction on the grounds that it had been based upon testimony given by Chinese witnesses. Chief Justice Hugh Murray ruled that an act passed in 1850 that prohibited American Indian testimony applied to the "Mongolian race." Such prohibition against Chinese testimony was included in California's Civil Procedure Code in 1863 and was not repealed until 1872. The infamous expression "not a Chinaman's chance" originated from this historical situation, meaning no chance at all, because Chinese were not allowed to testify in court and thus received no protection under the law.*

The People, Respondent, v. George W. Hall, Appellant

Section 394 of the Civil Practice Act provides, "No Indian or Negro shall be allowed to testify as a witness in any action in which a White person is a party."

Section 14 of the Criminal Act provides, "No Black, or Mulatto person, or Indian shall be allowed to give evidence in favor of, or against a White man."

Held, that the words, Indian, Negro, Black and White, are generic terms, designating race. That, therefore, Chinese and all other peoples not white, are included in the prohibition front being witnesses against Whites.

Mr. Ch. J. Murray delivered the opinion of the Court. Mr. J. Heydenfeldt concurred.

The appellant, a free white citizen of this State, was convicted of murder upon the testimony of Chinese witnesses.

The point involved in this case, is the admissibility of such evidence.

The 394th section of the Act Concerning Civil Cases, provides that no Indian or Negro shall be allowed to testify as a witness in any action or proceeding in which a White person is a party.

The 14th section of the Act of April 16th, 1850, regulating Criminal Proceedings, provides that "No Black, or Mulatto person, or Indian, shall be allowed to give evidence in favor of, or against a white man."

The true point at which we are anxious to arrive, is the legal signification of the words, "Black, Mulatto, Indian and White person," and whether the Legislature adopted them as generic terms, or intended to limit their application to specific types of the human species. . . .

Can, then, the use of the word "Indian," because at the present day it may be sometimes regarded as a specific, and not as a generic term, alter this conclusion? We think not; because at the origin of the legislation we are considering, it was used and admitted in its common and ordinary acceptation, as a generic term, distinguishing the great Mongolian race, and as such, its meaning then became fixed by law, and in construing Statutes the legal meaning of words must be presumed.

Again: the words of the Act must be construed in *pari materia.* It will not be disputed that "White" and "Negro," are generic terms, and refer to two of the great types of mankind. If these, as well as the word "Indian," are not to be regarded as generic terms, including the two great races which they were intended to designate, but only specific, and applying to those Whites and Negroes who were inhabitants of this Continent at the time of the passage of the Act, the most anomalous consequences would ensue. The European white man who comes here would not be shielded from the testimony of the degraded and demoralized caste, while the Negro, fresh from the coast of Africa, or the Indian of Patagonia, the Kanaka, South Sea

Islander, or New Hollander, would be admitted, upon their arrival, to testify against white citizens in our courts of law.

To argue such a proposition would be an insult to the good sense of the Legislature.

The evident intention of the Act was to throw around the citizen a protection for life and property, which could only be secured by removing him above the corrupting influences of degraded castes. . . .

In using the words, "No Black, or Mulatto person, or Indian shall be allowed to give evidence for or against a White person," the Legislature, if any intention can be ascribed to it, adopted the most comprehensive terms to embrace every known class or shade of color, as the apparent design was to protect the White person from the influence of all testimony other than that of persons of the same caste. The use of these terms must, by every sound rule of construction, exclude every one who is not of white blood. . . .

We are not disposed to leave this question in any doubt. The word "White" has a distinct signification, which *ex vi termini*, excludes black, yellow, and all other colors. It will be observed, by reference to the first section of the second article of the Constitution of this State, that none but white males can become electors, except in the case of Indians, who may be admitted by special Act of the Legislature. On examination of the constitutional debates, it will be found that not a little difficulty existed in selecting these precise words, which were finally agreed upon as the most comprehensive that could be suggested to exclude all inferior races. . . .

We have carefully considered all the consequences resulting from a different rule of construction, and are satisfied that even in a doubtful case we would be impelled to this decision on grounds of public policy.

The same rule which would admit them to testify, would admit them to all the equal rights of citizenship, and we might soon see them at the polls, in the jury box, upon the bench, and in our legislative halls.

This is not a speculation which exists in the excited and overheated imagination of the patriot and statesman, but it is an actual and present danger.

The anomalous spectacle of a distinct people, living in our community, recognizing no laws of this State except through necessity, bringing with them their prejudices and national feuds, in which they indulge in open violation of law; whose mendacity is proverbial; a race of people whom nature has marked as inferior, and who are incapable of progress or intellectual development beyond a certain point, as their history has shown; differing in language, opinions, color, and physical conformation; between whom and ourselves nature has placed an impassable difference, is now presented, and for them is claimed, not only the right to swear away the life of a citizen, but the further privilege of participating with us in administering the affairs of our Government. . . .

For these reasons, we are of opinion that the testimony was inadmissible.

The judgment is reversed and the cause remanded.

Source: Reports of Cases Argued and Determined in the Supreme Court of the State of California [microform]. San Francisco: Marvin and Hitchcock, 1851–1860. Reprinted in Franklin Odo, ed. 2002. *The Columbia Documentary History of the Asian American Experience.* New York: Columbia University, 19–21.

Burlingame-Seward Treaty, July 28, 1868

This treaty was signed in 1868 between China and the United States to legalize the importation of Chinese cheap laborers, who would be under the protection of the American government. The agreement was negotiated by the U.S. Secretary of State William Steward and Anson Burlingame, a former American diplomat to China who was asked by the Chinese emperor to negotiate with the United States. Capitalist interest groups and the Chinese community in California lobbied for the treaty, which recognized "free migration and emigration" of the Chinese to the United States, and the rights of the Chinese in the United States in exchange for the same rights for Americans and American trade privileges in China. However, the U.S. promise to protect the rights of the Chinese was not upheld, as demonstrated in the area of educational rights for Chinese children.

By the President of the United States of America: A Proclamation

Whereas certain additional articles to the treaty now in force between the United States of America and the Ta-Tsing Empire, signed at Tientsin the 18th day of June, 1858, were concluded and signed by their plenipotentiaries at Washington, on the 28th day of July, 1868, which additional articles are, word for word, as follows: . . .

Article IV. The twenty-ninth article of the treaty of the 18th of June, 1858, having stipulated for the exemption of Christian citizens of the United States and Chinese converts from persecution in China on account of their faith, it is further agreed that citizens of the United States in China, of every religious persuasion, and Chinese subjects in the United States, shall enjoy entire liberty of conscience, and shall be exempt from all disability or persecution on account of their religious faith or worship in either country. Cemeteries for sepulture of the dead, of whatever nativity or nationality, shall be held in respect and free from disturbance or profanation.

Article V. The United States of America and the Emperor of China cordially recognize the inherent and inalienable right of man to change his home and allegiance, and also the mutual advantage of the free migration and emigration of their citizens and subjects, respectively, from the one country to the other, for purposes of curiosity, of trade, or as permanent residents. The high contracting parties, therefore, join in reprobating any other than an entirely voluntary emigration for these purposes. They consequently agree to pass laws making it a penal offence for a citizen of the United States or Chinese subjects to take Chinese subjects either to the United States or to any other foreign country, or for a Chinese subject or citizen of the United States to take citizens of the United States to China or to any other foreign country, without their free and voluntary consent respectively.

Article VI. Citizens of the United States visiting or residing in China shall enjoy the same privileges, immunities, or exemptions in respect to travel or residence as may there be enjoyed by the citizens or subjects of the most favored nation. And, reciprocally, Chinese subjects visiting or residing in the United States, shall enjoy the same privileges, immunities, and exemptions in respect to travel or residence, as may there be enjoyed by the citizens or subjects of the most favored nation. But nothing herein contained shall be held to confer naturalization upon citizens of the United States in China, nor upon the subjects of China in the United States.

Article VII. Citizens of the United States shall enjoy all the privileges of the public educational institutions under the control of the government of China, and, reciprocally, Chinese subjects shall enjoy all the privileges of the public educational institutions under the control of the government of the United States, which are enjoyed in the respective countries by the citizens or subjects of the most favored nation. The citizens of the United States may freely establish and maintain schools within the Empire of China at those places where foreigners are by treaty permitted to reside, and, reciprocally, Chinese subjects may enjoy the same privileges and immunities in the United States. . . .

In faith whereof, the respective plenipotentiaries have signed this treaty and thereto affixed the seals of their arms.

Done at Washington the twenty-eighth day of July, in the year of our Lord one thousand eight hundred and sixty-eight.
[seal.] WILLIAM H. SEWARD.
ANSON BURLINGAME.
[seal.]CHIH-KANG.
SUN CHIA-KU.
Source: George P. Sanger, ed. 1871. *Statutes at Large and Proclamations of the United States of America.* Boston: Little, Brown. Reprinted in Franklin Odo, ed. 2002. *The Columbia Documentary History of the Asian American Experience.* New York: Columbia University, 31–32.

An Act to Execute Certain Treaty Stipulations Relating to Chinese (a.k.a. Chinese Exclusion Act), May 6, 1882

With rising anti-Chinese agitation in America in the 1870s, Chinese immigration to America was abruptly ended in 1882 over China's protest by the passage of the law known as the Chinese Exclusion Act. The act reversed some articles of the Burlingame Treaty (1868) and forbade Chinese immigration to the United States for ten years. Moreover, according to the act (the first piece of legislation that specially excluded a particular group of immigrants on the basis of race) Chinese laborers already living in the United States were denied the right to become naturalized citizens. Under the new name of the Geary Law, this act was renewed in 1892 and was finally made a permanent U.S. immigration policy in 1904, followed by China's boycott of American imports in 1905. The act was also applied to immigration from other Asian countries in the following decades and successfully curbed the growth of the Asian population in the United States. The Chinese Exclusion Act was repealed by Congress in 1943 as a gesture of goodwill toward China, a wartime ally of the United States fighting against Japan, and its repeal granted entry to 105 Chinese every year as well as the right of naturalization to eligible Chinese.

Be it enacted by the Senate and House of Representatives of the United States of America in Congress assembled, That from and after the expiration of ninety days next after the passage of this act, and until the expiration of ten years next after the passage of this act, the coming of Chinese laborers to the United States be, and the same is hereby, suspended; and during such suspension it shall not be lawful for any

Chinese laborer to come, or, having so come after the expiration of said ninety days, to remain within the United States.

Sec. 2. That the master of any vessel who shall knowingly bring within the United States on such vessel, and land or permit to be landed, any Chinese laborer, from any foreign port or place, shall be deemed guilty of a misdemeanor, and on conviction thereof shall be punished by a fine of not more than five hundred dollars for each and every such Chinese laborer so brought, and may, be also imprisoned for a term not exceeding one year.

Sec. 3. That the two foregoing sections shall not apply to Chinese laborers who were in the United States on the seventeenth day of November, eighteen hundred and eighty, or who shall have come into the same before the expiration of ninety days next after the passage of this act, and who shall produce to such master before going on board such vessel, and shall produce to the collector of the port in the United States at which such vessel shall arrive, the evidence hereinafter in this act required of his being one of the laborers in the section mentioned. . . .

Sec. 6. That in order to [sic] the faithful execution of articles one and two of the treaty in this act before mentioned, every Chinese person other than a laborer who may be entitled by said treaty and this act to come within the United States, and who shall be about to come to the United States, shall be identified as so entitled by the Chinese Government in each case, such identity to be evidenced by a certificate issued under the authority of said government, which certificate shall be in the English language or (if not in the English language) accompanied by a translation into English, stating such right to come, and which certificate shall state the name, title, or official rank, if any, the age, height, and all physical peculiarities, former and present occupation or profession, and place of residence in China of the person to whom the certificate is issued and that such person is entitled conformably to the treaty in this act mentioned to come within the United States. Such certificate shall be prima-facie evidence of the fact set forth therein, and shall be produced to the collector of customs, or his deputy, of the port in the district in the United States at which the person named therein shall arrive. . . .

Sec. 13. That this act shall not apply to diplomatic and other officers of the Chinese Government traveling upon the business of that government, whose credentials shall be taken as equivalent to the certificate in this act mentioned, and shall exempt them and their body and household servants from the provisions of this act as to other Chinese persons.

Sec. 14. That hereafter no State court or court of the United States shall admit Chinese to citizenship; and all laws in conflict with this act are hereby repealed.

Sec. 15. That the words "Chinese laborers," wherever used in this act, shall be construed to mean both skilled and unskilled laborers and Chinese employed in mining.

Approved, May 6, 1882.

Source: The Statutes at Large of the United States of America, vol. 22. Washington, DC: Government Printing Office, 1983. Reprinted in Franklin Odo, ed. 2002. *The Columbia Documentary History of the Asian American Experience.* New York: Columbia University, 62–63.

An Act to Prohibit the Coming of Chinese Persons into the United States (a.k.a. Geary Act), May 5, 1892

When the Chinese Exclusion Act expired in 1892, it was extended by an even stricter one, the Geary Act, that was introduced by Congressman Thomas Geary from California. Under the new law, Chinese laborers were excluded from becoming naturalized citizens by an additional ten years and all Chinese in the United States were required to register by acquiring certificates of eligibility in one year or face immediate deportation. When the act expired in 1902, the exclusion was extended for another ten years and was made indefinite in 1904. The act was repealed by Congress in 1943.

Chap. 60.—An Act to Prohibit the Coming of Chinese Persons into the United States

Be it enacted by the Senate and House of Representatives of the United States of America in Congress assembled, That all laws now in force prohibiting and regulating the coming into this country of Chinese persons and persons of Chinese descent are hereby continued in force for a period of ten years from the passage of this act.

Sec. 2. That any Chinese person or person of Chinese descent, when convicted and adjudged under any of said laws to be not lawfully entitled to be or remain in the United States, shall be removed from the United States to China, unless he or they shall make it appear to the justice, judge, or commissioner before whom he or they are tried that he or they are subjects or citizens of some other country, in which case he or they shall be removed from the United States to such country: *Provided,* That in any case where such other country of which such Chinese person shall claim to be a citizen or subject shall demand any tax as a condition of the removal of such person to that country, he or she shall be removed to China. . . .

Sec. 6. And it shall be the duty of all Chinese laborers within the limits of the United States, at the time of the passage of this act, and who are entitled to remain in the United States, to apply to the collector of internal revenue of their respective districts, within one year after the passage of this act, for a certificate of residence, and any Chinese laborer, within the limits of the United States, who shall neglect, fail, or refuse to comply with the provisions of this act, or who, after one year from the passage hereof, shall be found within the jurisdiction of the United States without such certificate of residence, shall be deemed and adjudged to be unlawfully within the United States, and may be arrested, by any United States customs official, collector of internal revenue or his deputies, United States marshal or his deputies, and taken before a United States judge, whose duty it shall be to order that he be deported from the United States as hereinbefore provided, unless he shall establish clearly to the satisfaction of said judge, that by reason of accident, sickness or other unavoidable cause, he has been unable to procure his certificate, and to the satisfaction of the court, and by at least one credible white witness, that he was a resident of the United States at the time of the passage of this act; and if upon the hearing, it shall appear that he is so entitled to a certificate, it shall be granted upon his paying the cost. Should it appear that said Chinaman had procured a certificate which has been lost or destroyed, he shall be detained and judgment suspended a reasonable time to enable him to procure a duplicate from the officer granting it, and in such cases, the cost of said arrest and trial shall be in the discretion of the court. And any Chinese person other than a Chinese laborer, having a right to be and remain in the United States, desiring such certificate as evidence of such right may apply for and receive the same without charge. . . .

Approved, May 5, 1892.

Source: The Statutes at Large of the United States of America, vol. 27. Washington, DC: Government Printing Office, 1983. Reprinted in Franklin Odo, ed. 2002. *The Columbia Documentary History of the Asian American Experience.* New York: Columbia University, 89–90.

Theodore Roosevelt Executive Order (a.k.a. Gentlemen's Agreement), March 14, 1907

This executive order was a result of the "Gentlemen's Agreement." The agreement was not a single diplomatic document but rather composed of a series of notes exchanged between the United States and Japan in 1907 to limit Japanese immigration to the United States to nonlaborers. The Japanese, like the Chinese before them, did not escape from being the target of the general anti-Asian sentiment at the time. Under the Gentlemen's Agreement, Japan agreed to stop issuing passports to laborers who wanted to emigrate to the United States. Because Japanese laborers as well as Korean laborers also immigrated to the United States through Mexico, Canada, or Hawaii, President Theodore Roosevelt issued this executive order to stop them from entering the United States through those areas. At the time, Koreans traveled with passports issued by the Japanese government because Korea had become a Japanese protectorate in 1905. Mainly because the United States wanted to maintain good relations with Japan, which was perceived as an apparently more powerful country than China, the United States had not passed any exclusion laws specifically targeted at Japanese immigrants, and this agreement allowed parents, spouses, and children of Japanese residents, including so-called picture brides who were selected in Japan through the exchange of pictures, to come to the United States. Consequently, the Japanese population, in which there was never a severe gender imbalance, continued to grow and in 1910 surpassed the gender-imbalanced Chinese population for the first time in the history of American immigration. However, the growth of the Japanese population was ended by the passage of the Immigration Act in 1924.

Executive Order

Whereas, by the act entitled "An Act to regulate the immigration of aliens into the United States," approved February 20, 1907, whenever the President is satisfied that passports issued by any foreign government to its citizens to go to any country other than the United States or to any insular possession of the United States or to the Canal Zone, are being used for the purpose of enabling the holders to come to the continental territory of the United States to the detriment of labor conditions therein, it is made the duty of the President to refuse to permit such citizens of the country issuing such passports to enter the continental territory of the United States from such country or from such insular possession or from the Canal Zone;

And Whereas, upon sufficient evidence produced before me by the Department of Commerce and Labor, I am satisfied that passports issued by the Government of Japan to citizens of that country or Korea and who are laborers, skilled or unskilled, to go to Mexico, to Canada and to Hawaii, are being used for the purpose of enabling the holders thereof to come to the continental territory of the United States to the detriment of labor conditions therein;

I hereby order that such citizens of Japan or Korea, to-wit: Japanese or Korean laborers, skilled and unskilled, who have received passports to go to Mexico, Canada or Hawaii, and come therefrom, be refused permission to enter the continental territory of the United States.

It is further ordered that the Secretary of Commerce and Labor be, and he hereby is, directed to take, thru *[sic]* the Bureau of Immigration and Naturalization, such measures and to make and enforce such rules and regulations as may be necessary to carry this order into effect.

THEODORE ROOSEVELT.

The White House,

March 14, 1907.

[No. 589.]

Source: CIS Presidential Executive Orders and Proclamations, EO-589, March 14, 1907 [microfiche]. Law Library of Congress, Washington, DC. Reprinted in Franklin Odo, ed. 2002. *The Columbia Documentary History of the Asian American Experience.* New York: Columbia University, 141–142.

Angel Island Poetry, 1910

An immigration station was established on Angel Island in San Francisco Bay in 1910. In the three decades that followed, immigrants from Asia, mostly Chinese, were detained there for interrogation in crowded and unsanitary conditions. The duration of their stay ranged from several months to several years. Overall, approximately 50,000 Chinese came to the United States through Angel Island, and about 10 percent of them were forced to go back to China. During their stay on the island, some detainees carved more than 100 poems on the barrack walls to record their ordeals. The immigration station was finally closed in 1940. These poems were later discovered in the 1960s, and some of them have been saved and have become a treasure of the American history of immigration.

There are tens of thousands of poems on these walls

They are all cries of suffering and sadness

The day I am rid of this prison and become successful
I must remember that this chapter once existed
I must be frugal in my daily needs
Needless extravagance usually leads to ruin
All my compatriots should remember China
Once you have made some small gains,
you should return home early.
—Written by one from Heungshan

In the quiet of night, I heard, faintly, the whistling of
    wind.
The forms and shadows saddened me;
upon seeing the landscape, I composed a poem.
The floating clouds, the fog, darken the sky.
The moon shines faintly as the insects chirp.
Grief and bitterness entwined are heaven sent.
The sad person sits alone, leaning by a window.

America has power, but not justice.
In prison, we were victimized as if we were guilty.
Given no opportunity to explain, it was really brutal.
I bow my head in reflection but there is
nothing I can do.

I thoroughly hate the barbarians because they
do not respect justice.
They continually promulgate harsh laws to
show off their prowess.
They oppress the overseas Chinese and also
violate treaties.
They examine for hookworms and practice
hundreds of despotic acts.

Source: Him, Mark Lai, Genny Lim, and Judy Yung, eds. *Island: Poetry and History of Chinese Immigrants on Angel Island, 1910–1940.* Seattle: University of Washington, 1980. Reprinted with permission of the University of Washington Press.

California Alien Land Law (a.k.a. Webb Act), August 10, 1913

California first enacted an alien land law in 1913 prohibiting "aliens ineligible to citizenship" from buying land or leasing it for longer than three years. This legislation was adopted by eleven other states in the western, northwestern, and even the southern United States from the 1910s to the 1940s. These laws almost exclusively targeted Japanese farmers who represented a majority of all Asian farmers. The land of those who violated the laws were confiscated by the state. Some Japanese had placed their land under the names of their American-born children, but this practice was also prohibited in California by a law passed by the state legislature in 1920. Although the U.S. Supreme Court ruled such laws unconstitutional in 1948, and in 1952 the California Supreme Court declared that the state laws could not deny ownership of land to aliens ineligible for citizenship, California's alien land laws were not formally repealed until 1956.

Chapter 113

An act relating to the rights, powers and disabilities of aliens and of certain companies, associations and corporations with respect to property in this state, providing for escheats in certain cases, prescribing the procedure therein, and repealing all acts or parts of acts inconsistent or in conflict herewith.

The people of the State of California do enact as follows:

Section 1. All aliens eligible to citizenship under the laws of the United States may acquire, possess, enjoy, transmit and inherit real property, or any interest therein, in this state, in the same manner and to the same extent as citizens of the United States, except as otherwise provided by the laws of this state.

Sec. 2. All aliens other than those mentioned in section one of this act may acquire, possess, enjoy and transfer real property, or any interest therein, in this state, in the manner and to the extent and for the purposes prescribed by any treaty now existing between the government of the United States and the nation or country of which such alien is a citizen or subject, and not otherwise, and may in addition thereto lease lands in this state for agricultural purposes for a term not exceeding three years.

Sec. 3. Any company, association or corporation organized under the laws of this or any other state or nation, of which a majority of the members are aliens other than those specified in section one of this act, or in which a majority of the issued capital stock is owned by such aliens, may acquire, possess, enjoy and convey real property, or any interest therein, in this state, in the manner and to the extent and for the purposes prescribed by any treaty now existing between the government of the United States and the nation or country of which such members or stockholders are citizens or subjects, and not otherwise, and may in addition thereto lease lands in this state for agricultural purposes for a term not exceeding three years. . . .

Sec. 5. Any real property hereafter acquired in fee in violation of the provisions of this act by any alien mentioned in section two of this act, or by any company, association or corporation mentioned in section three of this act, shall escheat to, and become and remain the property of the State of California. . . .

Source: The Statutes of California and Amendments to the Codes Passed at the Fortieth Session of the Legislature, 1913. Sacramento: Superintendent of State Printing, 1913. Reprinted in Franklin Odo, ed. 2002. *The Columbia Documentary History of the Asian American Experience.* New York: Columbia University, 160–161.

Supreme Court: *Ozawa v. United States,* November 13, 1922

The U.S. Supreme Court in Ozawa v. United States *declared Japanese ineligible for naturalized citizenship. The 1790 Naturalization Act stipulated that only "free white persons" with two years of residence were eligible to apply for naturalization, and thus deprived Asian immigrants the right to become citizens regardless of the duration of their stay in the United States. However, because the law was not uniformly applied across the country, a handful of Japanese immigrants managed to become citizens after filing petitions in local courts before this monumental case in 1922 that unequivocally disqualified the Japanese. Takao Ozawa was rather a unique case. Ozawa applied for citizenship in Hawaii in 1914. Although he was very assimilated into mainstream American society and was considered by the Supreme Court "well qualified by character and education for citizenship," he was still denied citizenship by the courts from the local level up to the federal level. The ruling of this case and the passage of the Immigration Act in 1924 that barred entry to virtually all Asians had classified Japanese immigrants together with the Chinese and other Asian immigrants in terms of immigration and the right of naturalization.*

Mr. Justice Sutherland delivered the opinion of the court:

The appellant is a person of the Japanese race, born in Japan. He applied, on October 16, 1914, to the United States district court for the territory of Hawaii to be admitted as a citizen of the United States. His petition was opposed by the United States district attorney for the district of Hawaii. Including the period of his residence in Hawaii appellant had continuously resided in the United States for twenty years. He was a graduate of the Berkeley, California, High School, had been nearly three years a student in the University of California, had educated his children in American schools, his family had attended American churches, and he had maintained the use of the English language in his home. That he was well qualified by character and education for citizenship is conceded.

The district court of Hawaii, however, held that, having been born in Japan, and being of the Japanese race, he was not eligible to naturalization under 2169 of the Revised Statutes (Comp. Stat 4358, 6 Fed. Stat. Anno. 2d ed. p. 944), and denied the petition. Thereupon the appellant brought the cause to the circuit court of appeals for the ninth circuit, and that court has certified the following questions, upon which it desires to be instructed:

"1. Is the Act of June 29, 1906, . . . providing 'for a uniform rule for the naturalization of aliens' *[sic]* complete in itself, or is it limited by 2169 of the Revised Statutes of the United States?"
"2. Is one who is of the Japanese race and born in Japan eligible to citizenship under the Naturalization Laws?"
"3. If said Act of June 29, 1906, is limited by 2169, and naturalization is limited to aliens being free white persons, and to aliens of African nativity, and to persons of African descent, is one of the Japanese race, born in Japan, under any circumstances eligible to naturalization?" . . .

It is the duty of this court to give effect to the intent of Congress. Primarily this intent is ascertained by giving the words their natural significance; but if this leads to an unreasonable result, plainly at variance with the policy of the legislation as a whole, we must examine the matter further. We may then look to the reason of the enactment, and inquire into its antecedent history, and give it effect in accordance with its design and purpose, sacrificing, if necessary, the literal meaning in order that the purpose may not fail. . . .

This brings us to inquire whether, under 2169, the appellant is eligible to naturalization. The language of the Naturalization Laws from

1790 to 1870 had been uniformly such as to deny the privilege of naturalization to an alien unless he came within the description "free white person." By 7 *[sic]* of the Act of July 14, 1870 (16 Stat at L. 254, 256, chap. 254, Comp. Stat. 4358, 6 Fed. Stat. Anno. 2d ed. p. 944), the Naturalization Laws were "extended to aliens of African nativity and to persons of African descent." Section 2169 of the Revised Statutes, as already pointed out, restricts the privilege to the same classes of persons; viz.: "To aliens [being free white persons and to aliens] of African nativity and persons of African descent." . . .

On behalf of the appellant it is urged that we should give to this phrase the meaning which it had in the minds of its original framers in 1790, and that it was employed by them for the sole purpose of excluding the black or African race and the Indians then inhabiting this country. It may be true that these two races were alone thought of as being excluded, but to say that they were the only ones within the intent of the statute would be to ignore the affirmative form of the legislation. The provision is not that Negroes and Indians shall be *excluded,* but it is, in effect, that only free white persons shall be *included.* The intention was to confer the privilege of citizenship upon that class of persons whom the fathers knew as white, and to deny it to all who could not be so classified. It is not enough to say that the framers did not have in mind the brown or yellow races of Asia. It is necessary to go farther and be able to say that, had these particular races been suggested, the language of the act would have been so varied as to include them within its privileges . . . .

We have been furnished with elaborate briefs in which the meaning of the words "white person" is discussed with ability and at length, both from the standpoint of judicial decision and from that of the science of ethnology. It does not seem to us necessary, however, to follow counsel in their extensive researches in these fields. It is sufficient to note the fact that these decisions are, in substance, to the effect that the words import a racial, and not an individual, test, and with this conclusion, fortified as it is by reason and authority, we entirely agree. Manifestly the test afforded by the mere color of the skin of each individual is impracticable, as that differs greatly among persons of the same race, even among Anglo-Saxons, ranging by imperceptible gradations from the fair blond to the swarthy brunette, the latter being darker than many of the lighter hued persons of the brown or yellow races. Hence to adopt the color test alone would result in a confused overlapping of races and a gradual merging of one into the other, without any practical line of separation. Beginning with the decision of Circuit Judge Sawyer, in Re Ali Yup (1878)

5 Sawy. 155, Fed. Cas. No. 104, the Federal and state courts, in an almost unbroken line, have held that the words "white person" were meant to indicate only a person of what is popularly known as the Caucasian race. . . .

The determination that the words "white person" are synonymous with the words "a person of the Caucasian race" simplifies the problem, although it does not entirely dispose of it. Controversies have arisen and will no doubt arise again in respect of the proper classification of individuals in border-line cases. The effect of the conclusion that the words "white person" mean a Caucasian is not to establish a sharp line of demarcation between those who are entitled and those who are not entitled to naturalization, but rather a zone of more or less debatable ground outside of which, upon the one hand, are those clearly eligible, and outside of which, upon the other hand, are those clearly ineligible for citizenship. Individual cases falling within this zone must be determined as they arise from time to time by what this court has called, in another connection (Davidson v. New Orleans, 96 U.S. 97, 104, 24 L. ed. 616, 619), "the gradual process of judicial inclusion and exclusion:"

The appellant in the case now under consideration, however, is clearly of a race which is not Caucasian, and therefore belongs entirely outside the zone on the negative side. A large number of the Federal and state courts have so decided, and we find no reported case definitely to the contrary. These decisions are sustained by numerous scientific authorities, which we do not deem it necessary to review. We think these decisions are right, and so hold.

The briefs filed on behalf of appellant refer in complimentary terms to the culture and enlightenment of the Japanese people, and with this estimate we have no reason to disagree; but these are matters which cannot enter into our consideration of the questions here at issue. We have no function in the matter other than to ascertain the will of Congress and declare it. Of course, there is not implied— either in the legislation or in our interpretation of it—any suggestion of individual unworthiness or racial inferiority. These considerations are in no manner involved.

The questions submitted are, therefore, answered as follows:

Question No. 1. The Act of June 29, 1906, is not complete in itself, but is limited by 2169 of the Revised Statutes of the United States.

Question No. 2. No.

Question No. 3. No.

It will be so certified.

Source: Case Argued and Decided in the Supreme Court of the United States, Book 67. Rochester, NY: The Lawyers Co-operative Publishing Company, 1924. Reprinted in Franklin Odo, ed. 2002. *The Columbia Documentary History of the Asian American Experience.* New York: Columbia University, 181–184.

Executive Order 9066, February 19, 1942

President Franklin D. Roosevelt signed Executive Order 9066 authorizing the secretary of war to delegate a military commander to designate certain areas as military areas "from which any or all persons may be excluded." This executive order resulted in the removal of more than 40,000 Japanese from their homes on the West Coast, along with their 70,000 American-born children, and their imprisonment in internment camps. In March, Public Law 503 was passed by Congress, imposing penal sanctions on anyone refusing to carry out Executive Order 9066. The executive order, in actuality, was in direct conflict with the U.S. Constitution because of its encroachment on civil liberties. The War Department revoked the mass exclusion orders in 1944 (effective January 2, 1945), and President Gerald Ford rescinded Executive Order 9066 and apologized to all Japanese American internees in 1976.

Executive Order Authorizing the Secretary of War to Prescribe Military Areas

Whereas the successful prosecution of the war requires every possible protection against espionage and against sabotage to national-defense material, national-defense premises, and national-defense utilities as defined in Section 4, Act of April 20, 1918, 40 Stat. 533, as amended by the Act of November 30, 1940, 54 Stat. 1220, and the Act of August 21, 1941, 55 Stat. 655 (U.S. C., Title 50, Sec. 104):

Now, therefore, by virtue of the authority vested in me as President of the United States, and Commander in Chief of the Army and Navy, I hereby authorize and direct the Secretary of War, and the Military Commanders whom he may from time to time designate, whenever he or any designated Commander deems such action necessary or desirable, to prescribe military areas in such places and of such extent as he or the appropriate Military Commander may determine, from which any or all persons may be excluded, and with respect to which, the right of any person to enter, remain in, or leave shall be subject to whatever restrictions the Secretary of War or the appropriate Military Commanders may impose in his discretion. The Secretary of War is hereby authorized to provide for residents of any such area who are excluded therefrom, such transportation, food, shelter, and other accommodations as may be necessary, in the judgment of the Secretary of War or the said Military Commander, and until other arrangements are made, to accomplish the purpose of this order. The designation of military areas in any region or locality shall supersede designations of prohibited and restricted areas by the Attorney General under the Proclamations of December 7 and 8, 1941, and shall supersede the responsibility and authority of the Attorney General under the said Proclamations in respect of such prohibited and restricted areas.

I hereby further authorize and direct the Secretary of War and the said Military Commanders to take such other steps as he or the appropriate Military Commander may deem advisable to enforce compliance with the restrictions applicable to each Military area hereinabove authorized to be designated, including the use of Federal troops and other Federal Agencies, with authority to accept assistance of state and local agencies.

I hereby further authorize and direct all Executive Departments, independent establishments and other Federal Agencies, to assist the Secretary of War or the said Military Commanders in carrying out this Executive Order, including the furnishing of medical aid, hospitalization, food, clothing, transportation, use of land, shelter, and other supplies, equipment, utilities, facilities, and services.

This order shall not be construed as modifying or limiting in any way the authority heretofore granted under Executive Order No. 8972, dated December 12, 1941, nor shall it be construed as limiting or modifying the duty and responsibility of the Federal Bureau of Investigation, with respect to the investigation of alleged acts of sabotage or the duty and responsibility of the Attorney General and the Department of Justice under the Proclamations of December 7 and 8, 1941, prescribing regulations for the conduct and control of alien enemies, except as such duty and responsibility is superseded by the designation of military areas hereunder.

[signature of Franklin Delano Roosevelt]
THE WHITE HOUSE,
February 19, 1942.

Source: United States Codes Congressional Service, Acts of 77th Congress, 1942. St. Paul, MN: West Publishing Company and Brooklyn, NY: Edward Thompson Company, 1943. Reprinted in Franklin Odo, ed. 2002. *The Columbia Documentary History of the Asian American Experience.* New York: Columbia University, 267–268.

Repeal of Chinese Exclusion Acts (Public Law 199), December 17, 1943

Congress passed Public Law 199 to repeal all Chinese exclusion laws that had barred Chinese immigration since 1882. These laws were repealed in the middle of World War II partly as a goodwill gesture toward China, a wartime ally of the United States fighting against Japan, and partly to counter Japan's propaganda claims that the war was waged against the white race of the United States. The public law also granted an immigration quota of 105 per year and the right of naturalization to the Chinese, while the Japanese and the Koreans remained ineligible for naturalization until 1952.

An Act to Repeal the Chinese Exclusion Acts, to Establish Quotas, and for Other Purposes

Be it enacted by the Senate and House of Representatives of the United States of America in Congress assembled, That the following Acts or parts of Acts relating to the exclusion or deportation of persons of the Chinese race are hereby repealed: May 6, 1882 (22 Stat. L. 58); July 5, 1884 (23 Stat. L. 115); September 13, 1888 (25 Stat. L. 476); October 1, 1888 (25 Stat. L. 504); May 5, 1892 (27 Stat. L. 25); November 3, 1893 (28 Stat. L. 7); that portion of section 1 of the Act of July 7, 1898 (30 Stat. L. 750, 751), which reads as follows: "There shall be no further immigration of Chinese into the Hawaiian Islands except upon such conditions as are now or may hereafter be allowed by the laws of the United States; and no Chinese, by reason of anything herein contained, shall be allowed to enter the United States from the Hawaiian Islands." . . .

Sec. 2. With the exception of those coming under subsections (b), (d), (e), and (f) of section 4, Immigration Act of 1924 (43 Stat. 155; 44 Stat. 812; 45 Stat. 1009; 46 Stat. 854; 47 Stat. 656; 8 U.S.C. 204), all Chinese persons entering the United States annually as immigrants shall be allocated to the quota for the Chinese computed under the provisions of section 11 of the said Act. A preference up to 75 per centum of the quota shall be given to Chinese born and resident in China.

Sec. 3. Section 303 of the Nationality Act of 1940, as amended (54 Stat. 1140; 8 U.S.C. 703), is hereby amended by striking out the word "and" before the word "descendants," changing the colon after the word "Hemisphere" to a comma, and adding the following: "and Chinese persons or persons of Chinese descent:."

Approved December 17, 1943.

Source: United States Statutes at Large Containing the Laws and Concurrent Resolutions Enacted During the First Session of the Seventy-Eighth Congress of the United States, 1943, vol. 57. Washington, DC: Government Printing Office, 1944. Reprinted in Franklin Odo, ed. 2002. *The Columbia Documentary History of the Asian American Experience.* New York: Columbia University, 281–282.

McCarran-Walter Immigration and Nationality Act, June 27, 1952

Nine years after the Chinese were granted the right to become citizens, the Japanese and the Koreans were granted the same right after the passage of the McCarran-Walter Immigration and Naturalization Act, which annulled all the racial restrictions imposed by the 1790 naturalization law. As for immigration, the act set up a racially restrictive quota system of 100 for each quota area in the so-called Asia-Pacific triangle, severely limiting immigration from Asia and the Pacific. President Harry Truman vetoed the bill because of its limited scope, but Congress overrode his veto.

TITLE II—IMMIGRATION

Chapter I-Quota System

Numerical Limitations; Annual Quota Based Upon National Origin; Minimum Quotas

Sec. 201. (a) The annual quota of any quota area shall be one-sixth of 1 per centum of the number of inhabitants in the continental United States in 1920, which number, except for the purpose of computing quotas for quota areas within the Asia-Pacific triangle, shall be the same number heretofore determined under the provisions of section 11 of the Immigration Act of 1924, attributable by national origin to such quota area: *Provided,* That the quota existing for Chinese persons prior to the date of enactment of this Act shall be continued, and, except as otherwise provided in section 202 (e), the minimum quota for any quota area shall be one hundred.

(b) The determination of the annual quota of any quota area shall be made by the Secretary of State, the Secretary of Commerce, and the Attorney General, jointly. Such officials shall, jointly, report to the President the quota of each quota area, and the President shall proclaim and make known the quotas so reported. Such determination and report shall be made and such proclamation shall be issued as soon as practicable after the date of enactment of this Act. Quotas proclaimed therein shall take effect on the first day of the fiscal year, or the next fiscal half year, next following the expiration of six months after the date of the proclamation, and until such date the existing quotas proclaimed under the Immigration Act of 1924 shall remain in effect. . . .

Determination of Quota to Which An Immigrant Is Chargeable

Sec. 202. (a) Each independent country, self-governing dominion, mandated territory, and territory under the international trusteeship system of the United Nations, other than the United States and its outlying possessions and the countries specified in section 101 (a) (27) (C), shall be treated as a separate quota area when approved by the Secretary of State. All other inhabited lands shall be attributed to a quota area specified by the Secretary of State. . . .

(5) notwithstanding the provisions of paragraphs (2), (3), and (4) of this subsection, any alien who is attributable by as much as one-half of his ancestry to a people or peoples indigenous to the Asia-Pacific triangle defined in subsection (b) of this section, unless such alien is entitled to a nonquota immigrant status under paragraph (27) (A), (27) (B), (27) (D), (27) (E), (27) (F), or (27) (G) of section 101 (a), shall be chargeable to a quota as specified in subsection (b) of this section. . . .

(b) With reference to determination of the quota to which shall be chargeable an immigrant who is attributable by as much as one-half of his ancestry to a people or peoples indigenous to the Asia-Pacific triangle comprising all quota areas and all colonies and other dependent areas situate [sic] wholly east of the meridian sixty degrees east of Greenwich, wholly west of the meridian one hundred and sixty-five degrees west, and wholly north of the parallel twenty-five degrees south latitude—

1. There is hereby established, in addition to quotas for separate quota areas comprising independent countries, self-governing dominions, and territories under the international trusteeship system of the United Nations situate wholly within said Asia-Pacific triangle, an Asia-Pacific quota of one hundred annually, which quota shall not be subject to the provisions of subsection (e);
2. Such immigrant born within a separate quota area situate wholly within such Asia-Pacific triangle shall not be chargeable to the Asia-Pacific quota, but shall be chargeable to the quota for the separate quota area in which he was born;

3. Such immigrant born within a colony or other dependent area situate wholly within said Asia-Pacific triangle shall be chargeable to the Asia-Pacific quota;
4. Such immigrant born outside the Asia-Pacific triangle who is attributable by as much as one-half of his ancestry to a people or peoples indigenous to not more than one separate quota area, situate wholly within the Asia-Pacific triangle, shall be chargeable to the quota of that quota area;
5. Such immigrant born outside the Asia-Pacific triangle who is attributable by as much as one-half of his ancestry to a people or peoples indigenous to one or more colonies or other dependent areas situate wholly within the Asia-Pacific triangle, shall be chargeable to the Asia-Pacific quota;
6. Such immigrant born outside the Asia-Pacific triangle who is attributable by as much as one-half of his ancestry to peoples indigenous to two or more separate quota areas situate wholly within the Asia-Pacific triangle, or to a quota area or areas and one or more colonies and other dependent areas situate wholly therein, shall be chargeable to the Asia-Pacific quota.

Source: United States Statutes at Large, 1952, vol. 66. Washington, DC: Government Printing Office, 1953. Reprinted in Franklin Odo, ed. 2002. The Columbia Documentary History of the Asian American Experience. New York: Columbia University, 335–338.

Immigration and Nationality Act, October 3, 1965

The year 1965 marked a watershed in the history of U.S. immigration. The Immigration and Nationality Act, signed by President Lyndon Johnson, abolished the discriminatory, racially based national-origin quota system that had favored European immigrants, and replaced it with a preference system that alloted a quota of 20,000 for each of the countries in the Eastern Hemisphere up to a maximum of 170,000 per year. This act has greatly changed the pattern of immigration into the United States. Emphasizing family reunions and attracting those with professional skills, this reform of U.S. immigration law offered great opportunities for tens of thousands of Asians to enter, leading to a dramatic rise in the Asian American population in the United States in the following decades. Between 1960 and 2000, it increased from less than 1 million to about 10 million. As for East Asian Americans, the combined population of Chinese, Japanese, and Korean Americans went from 1.1 million in 1970 to 1.9 million, 3.3 million, and 4.3 million in 1980, 1990, and 2000, respectively. The most impressive increase occurred in the Korean American population; it increased more than fivefold from 1970 to 1980 and tripled from 1980 to 2000.

An Act to Amend the Immigration and Nationality Act, and for Other Purposes

Be it enacted by the Senate and House of Representatives of the United States of America in Congress assembled, That section 201 of the Immigration and Nationality Act (66 Stat. 175; 8 U.S.C. 1151) be amended to read as follows:

(a) Exclusive of special immigrants defined in section 101 (a) (27), and of the immediate relatives of United States citizens specified in subsection (b) of this section, the number of aliens who may be issued immigrant visas or who may otherwise acquire the status of an alien lawfully admitted to the United States for permanent residence, or who may, pursuant to section 203 (a) (7) enter conditionally, (i) shall not in any of the first three quarters of any fiscal year exceed a total of 45,000 and (ii) shall not in any fiscal year exceed a total of 170,000.

(b) The "immediate relatives" referred to in subsection (a) of this section shall mean the children, spouses, and parents of a citizen of the United States: *Provided,* That in the case of parents, such citizen must be at least twenty-one years of age. The immediate relatives specified in this subsection who are otherwise qualified for admission as immigrants shall be admitted as such, without regard to the numerical limitations in this Act.

. . .

Sec. 2. Section 202 of the Immigration and Nationality Act (66 Stat. 175; 8 U.S.C. 1152) is amended to read as follows:

(a) No person shall receive any preference or priority or be discriminated against in the issuance of an immigrant visa because of his race, sex, nationality, place of birth, or place of residence, except as specifically provided in section 101 (a) (27), section 201 (b), and section 203: *Provided,* That the total number of immigrant visas and the number of conditional entries made available to natives of any single foreign state under paragraphs (1) through (8) of section 203 (a) shall not exceed 20,000 in any fiscal year: *Provided further,* That the foregoing proviso shall not operate to reduce the number of immigrants who may be admitted under the quota of any quota area before June 30, 1968.

. . .

Sec. 3. Section 203 of the Immigration and Nationality Act (66 Stat. 175; 8 U.S.C. 1153) is amended to read as follows:

(a) Aliens who are subject to the numerical limitations specified in section 201 (a) shall be allotted visas or their conditional entry authorized, as the case may be, as follows:

(1) Visas shall be first made available, in a number not to exceed 20 per centum of the number specified in section 201 (a) (ii), to qualified immigrants who are the unmarried sons or daughters of citizens of the United States.

(2) Visas shall next be made available, in a number not to exceed 20 per centum of the number specified in section 201 (a) (ii), plus any visas not required for the classes specified in paragraph (i), to qualified immigrants who are the spouses, unmarried sons or unmarried daughters of an alien lawfully admitted for permanent residence.

(3) Visas shall next be made available, in a number not to exceed 10 per centum of the number specified in section 201 (a) (ii), to qualified immigrants who are members of the professions, or who because of their exceptional ability in the sciences or the arts will substantially benefit prospectively the national economy, cultural interests, or welfare of the United States.

(4) Visas shall next be made available, in a number not to exceed 10 per centum of the number specified in section 201 (a) (ii), plus any visas not required for the classes specified in paragraphs (1) through (3), to qualified immigrants who are the married sons or the married daughters of citizens of tile United States.

(5) Visas shall next be made available, in a number not to exceed 24 per centum of the number specified in section 201 (a) (ii), plus any visas not required for the classes specified in paragraphs (1) through (4), to qualified immigrants who are the brothers or sisters of citizens of the United States.

(6) Visas shall next be made available, in a number not to exceed 10 per centum of the number specified in section 201 (a) (ii), to qualified immigrants who are capable of performing specified skilled or unskilled labor, not of a temporary or seasonal nature, for which a shortage of employable and willing persons exists in the United State.

(7) Conditional entries shall next be made available by the Attorney General, pursuant to such regulations as he may prescribe and in a number not to exceed 6 per centum of the number specified in section 201 (a) (ii), to aliens who satisfy an Immigration and Naturalization Service officer at an examination in any non-Communist or non-Communist-dominated country, (A) that (i) because of persecu-

tion or fear of persecution on account of race, religion, or political opinion they have fled (I) from any Communist or Communist-dominated country or area, or (II) from any country within the general area of the Middle East, and (ii) are unable or unwilling to return to such country or area on account of race, religion, or political opinion, and (iii) are not nationals of the countries or areas in which their application for conditional entry is made; or (B) that they are persons uprooted by catastrophic natural calamity as defined by the President who are unable to return to their usual place of abode.

Source: United States Statutes at Large, 1965, vol. 79. Washington, DC: Government Printing Office, 1966. Reprinted in Franklin Odo, ed. 2002. *The Columbia Documentary History of the Asian American Experience.* New York: Columbia University, 352–354.

San Francisco State College Strike Position Papers, 1968

The San Francisco State (now University) strike in 1968 was a defining event for the Asian American movement. On November 6, 1968, the college's Asian American students, including Chinese, Filipino, and Japanese American students, joined a strike with students of other racial backgrounds under the umbrella of a multiethnic coalition, the Third World Liberation Front. The Front drafted position papers to both faculty and college administration, calling for the establishment of a school of ethnic area studies. In addition, they also demanded open admission to the college. This five-month strike attracted national attention and was the first campus uprising in which Asian American students participated as a collective force. Although their demands were not all met, after causing a shutdown of the campus for five months, the strike finally bore some important fruit in the end: the establishment of the first school of ethnic studies in the nation, including an Asian American studies program.

Third World Liberation Front: School of Ethnic Area Studies

Throughout the entire educational systems in California, a complete and accurate representation of minority peoples' role in the past and the present conditions of this state is nonexistent. In every aspect from lectures to literature the educational facilities do not contain the information necessary to relate any facet of minority peoples' history and/or culture. Such an institutionalized condition of negligence and ignorance by the state's educational systems is clearly an integral part of the racism and hatred this country has perpetuated upon nonwhite peoples. The consistent refusal of State Education to confront its inadequacies and attain an equitable resolution between our peoples, makes it mandatory for minority people to initiate and to maintain educational programs specifically based upon their people's background and present situation at intra and international levels.

The Third World Liberation Front is demanding a school of Ethnic Area Studies specifically organized to establish area studies of nonwhite peoples within the United States. At the present there are being developed area studies of Mexican American, Latin American, Filipino American, Chinese American, and Japanese American peoples.

The school's function is as a resource and an educational program for those minority peoples actively concerned with the lack of their peoples' representation and participation in all levels of California's educational institutions.

The school clearly intends to be involved in confronting the racism, poverty and misrepresentation imposed on minority peoples by the formally recognized institutions and organizations operating in the State of California. The process of such clarification and exposure will be developed through the collection, organization and presentation through ethnic area studies of all information relevant to the historical and contemporary positions of the minority peoples throughout local, state, national and international levels.

As assurance against the reoccurence [sic] of education's traditional distortion and misrepresentation of Third World people's cultures and histories, the School of Ethnic Area Studies is to be developed, implemented, and controlled by Third World people. Whether an area study is at a developmental or a departmental level within the school, the people of an area study will have sole responsibility and control for the staffing and curriculum of their ethnic area study. The operation and development of the School of Ethnic Area Studies is the responsibility and the control of those programs and departments within the School of Ethnic Area Studies.

Intercollegiate Chinese for Social Action Position Paper

San Francisco State, a community college, exists in a moral vacuum, oblivious to the community it purports to serve. It does not reflect the pluralistic society that is San Francisco; it does not begin to serve the 300,000 people who live in this urban community in poverty, in ignorance, in despair. The Chinese ghetto, Chinatown, is a case in point.

1. SF State has a Chinese language department that isolates the "Chinese Experience" as a cultural phenomenon in a language that 83% of the Chinese in the United States do not speak. Realistically, we can expect that a Chinese woman, living in the ghetto, who speaks Cantonese, cannot explain to the scholar that she is dying to [sic] tuberculosis because she speaks a "street language" while the scholar mutters classical poetry in Mandarin. San Francisco State College does not teach Cantonese.

2. Chinatown is a *ghetto*. In San Francisco there are approximately 50,000 Chinese of whom the vast majority live in Chinatown. It is an area of old buildings, narrow streets and alleys, and the effluvia of a great number of people packed into a very small space. At present, more that 5,000 new Chinese immigrants stream into this overpopulated ghetto every year, an area already blessed with a birth rate that is rising, and will rise more. Chinatown is basically a tenement. Tuberculosis is endemic, rents are high and constantly rising, city services are inadequate to provide reasonable sanitation, and space is at such a premium as to resemble the Malthusian ratio at its most extreme conclusion.

There are no adequate courses in any department or school at SF State that even begin to deal specifically with the problems of the Chinese people in this exclusionary and racist environment.

WE, THEREFORE, SUPPORT THE ESTABLISHMENT OF A SCHOOL OF ETHNIC AREA STUDIES and further submit (under separate cover) our proposal for the establishment of a Chinese Ethnic Studies Department within that school that will begin to attack the problems that exist in the Chinese Community and address itself to the problems that exist in the Chinese Community at large—to the problems of acculturation and identity for Chinese people in the United States.

Source: Courtesy Special Collections/Archives, San Francisco State University.

International Hotel Struggle, Manilatown, San Francisco, February 1970

The International Hotel struggle was one of the longest urban struggles since the end of the 1960s, as well as the first struggle that brought a large number of Asian American students into the community as political activists. The hotel was a low-cost residence mainly for retired Chinese and Filipino American workers in San Francisco. In December 1968 the hotel owner attempted to evict the tenants and build a more profitable parking lot. In response, many Asian American students organized to protest in 1969. The hotel soon became a hallmark of the Asian American resistance movement, and the campaign attracted tens of thousands of people from all nationalities in the Bay Area. This pamphlet was an example of the activists' efforts to mobilize supporters. However, all their efforts to save the hotel were in vain. Its residents were finally evicted on August 4, 1977, and the building itself was torn down in 1979. Nothing was built in its space right after the demolition. Following a quarter of a century of negotiations between the community and the city, a plan about how to use the land was finalized and construction on a new fifteen-story hotel began in January 2002. It will be a 105-unit affordable housing development for seniors selected by lottery, with preference given to those who endured the eviction in 1977. Its projected completion will be in summer 2005.

History of International Hotel

The history of the International Hotel is essentially a history of a unique, often forgotten people. The hotel today is a symbol of their past and their future. Located at Kearny and Jackson in San Francisco, the small Filipino community of 1,000 known as Manilatown, faces probable death and extinction.

The International Hotel rests on the periphery of old, crowded Chinatown and of the towering ominous financial district of San Francisco. These clearly visual contradictions surrounding the hotel are merely part of the contradictions implicit within the Hotel crisis, itself.

Manilatown carefully eyes the ex-skyline, as one by one the hotel businesses that have been the home of Manilatown's elderly residents for twenty and thirty years are replaced by parking lots and office buildings.

Manilatown is just one example of an impoverished minority community in which the guise of redevelopment has displaced the poor, damaged traditional organizations and uprooted their cultural heart. Residents are separated, forced into often worse conditions, and acculturated—a massive blow to the identity and culture of a minority.

The Residents

The majority of the residents are elderly men without families, living on welfare checks or pensions. Reminiscing about "old times," they are bleakly aware about their invisible status in America. . . . After decades of menial labor the plight of poverty makes it unlikely that they will ever return to their homelands or families.

Half are in need of medical care. Their rooms average 40–69 square ft; sparsely furnished with a basin, bed, bureau, and chair. Weekly linen is included in the typical $38 monthly rent. Common kitchen facilities exist only in the International and one other hotel. Recreation is too often limited to the local pool hall.

These elderly men are living out their lives in a country which has been historically hostile to them, a country which has exploited the labor of their youth and once again threatens their lives by the destruction of the last vestiges of their community.

Brutal History

The Philippines became a possession of the United States in 1898 as a settlement of the Spanish American War. Taking advantage of the cheap labor source Hawaiian plantation owners recruited young uneducated Filipino laborers under 4-year contracts. They worked 12 hours a day, seven days a week at a dollar a day with room and board. Poor living conditions and violations of the minimum wage caused periodic escapes; most were unsuccessful and ended in prison.

The exploitation of Filipinos ended with the coming of other victims—Chinese and Japanese immigrants. Leaving Hawaii, many of these men were attracted by hopes of better opportunities in California. In cities like San Francisco, San Diego, Los Angeles these men settled in places like Kearny St. because of discrimination, poverty, cultural companionship and the cheap hotels.

The pattern of the Filipinos is similar to those of other Asian groups in America: As immigrants they were confined to menial labor as domestics, sailors, field workers. *Prohibition of interracial marriage combined with the scarcity of Filipino women resulted in extreme loneliness and hardship for many of these men. Furthermore immigrants were limited to a quota of 50 persons annually from the Philippines in a compromise that gave those islands independence in 1934. Filipinos were limited from owning land until 1945.*

Meanwhile during the 1920's and 1930's the area on Kearny St. began to thrive with restaurants and Filipino business. The area expanded to ten blocks as it became a tourist spot and sentimental stop for homesick Filipinos in the American military.

During the depression era (1930–41) Manilatown was a well-knit and well-organized community. To help one another, they used the *bayanihan* system—the sharing of food, housing, and money with those who had none.

With the importation of cheaper Mexican labor and job opportunities in war industries (less discrimination) Filipinos began to return to the city. This weakened the efforts of the Filipino farm workers union who first began activities in 1939. A strong union did not regain strength until Filipino workers were the first to walk out in the 5 year old Delano strike.

Dying Community

Today most Filipino Americans have shared to a degree in the prosperity of the post war days. Large numbers of women have recently been able to immigrate, and the increasing phenomena of Filipino families have increased the population.

With new affluence the young and recent educated immigrant has moved into the suburbs. Many of the poorer have returned to the valley as farm-workers.

Yet the area still serves as a center for those who seek lost relatives, as a launching pad for the new immigrant, as a community for the old and a historic site in the history of Filipinos in America.

Taking a Stand

Growing concern over the fate of Manilatown has sparked some Bay Area Filipino groups into action. In the recent dispute the United Filipino Association with the support of several student groups was in the forefront.

In December 1968, UFA began negotiations to purchase the hotel's lease from the management of International. Then in March 1968 just before the contract was signed a mysterious fire, which many felt was an arson attempt, destroyed one wing on its top floor and killed three elderly persons. Negotiation stopped and the owner refused to negotiate the lease. Eviction notices and plans for a new parking lot on the site of the Hotel suddenly appeared.

Community protests and demonstrations centered around the historic nature of the hotel, the impossibility of finding new homes in a city where the vacancy for low-cost housing is 1%, and human necessity of keeping this community of elderly gentlemen intact.

The controversy which flared led to picketing the offices of Walter Shorenstein, head of the Milton-Meyer Company which owns the property. When tenants were harassed by deteriorating conditions, lack of service and repairs . . . public pressure increased.

The community accused the mayor's office of being hostile, because of Shorenstein's large donations to the Democratic funds.

After months of struggle, the United Filipino Association finally reached a settlement with the reluctant Milton-Meyer Company. *Most see the settlement as extremely unfair.* The $4,000 rent/year, the $23,000 yearly property taxes, the rehabilitation of the hotel, and fire damage repairs were fully assumed by UFA.

Despite the financial debts, volunteers have been able to rehabilitate much of the hotel, set up recreational activities for the tenants.

While much of the continuing renovation takes place during "work sessions" each weekend, more emphasis is now being placed on fundraising.

The fate of the Hotel, Manilatown and low-cost housing for the elderly poor now hangs once more in limbo as the International faces its financial crisis.

   Source: United Filipino Association. *Newsletter.* San Francisco, February 1970. Reprinted in Franklin Odo, ed. 2002. *The Columbia Documentary History of the Asian American Experience.* New York: Columbia University, 365–368.

Recommendations from the Commission on Wartime Relocation and Internment of Civilians, 1983

Japanese Americans began in the late 1960s to seek reparations for the ordeal they had experienced during World War II when thousands of them were removed from their West Coast homes and interned in camps. As a result of their efforts for redress, a bill was passed by Congress to create a federal commission to investigate the whole issue of internment. In July 1980 President Carter signed Public Law 96–317 to form the Commission on Wartime Relocation and Internment of Civilians (CWRIC). After hearing testimony from more than 750 witnesses across the nation and after 18 months of research and investigation, the *commission issued its report "Personal Justice Denied" to the government in 1983. In the report the commission concluded that the detention of the 110,000 people of Japanese ancestry was "a grave injustice" because it was not justified by military conditions but was the result of "race prejudice, war hysteria and a failure of political leadership." The commission also made a five-point recommendation, including a proposal that each surviving victim be compensated $20,000 as redress for the injustice.*

Recommendations

In 1980 Congress established a bipartisan Commission on Wartime Relocation and Internment of Civilians, and directed it to:

1. Review the facts and circumstances surrounding Executive Order Numbered 9066, issued February 19, 1942, and the impact of such Executive Order on American citizens and permanent resident aliens.
2. Review directives of United States military forces requiring the relocation and, in some cases, detention in internment camps of American citizens, including Aleut civilians, and permanent resident aliens of the Aleutian and Pribilof Islands; and
3. Recommend appropriate remedies.

The Commission fulfilled the first two mandates by submitting to Congress in February 1983 a unanimous report, *Personal Justice Denied,* which extensively reviews the history and circumstances of the fateful decisions to exclude, remove and then to detain Japanese Americans and Japanese resident aliens from the West Coast, as well as the treatment of Aleuts during World War II. The remedies which the Commission recommends in this second and final part of its report are based upon the conclusions of that report as well as upon further studies done for the Commission, particularly an analysis of the economic impact of exclusion and detention.

In considering recommendations, the Congress and the nation therefore must bear in mind the Commission's basic factual findings about the wartime treatment of American citizens of Japanese ancestry and resident Japanese aliens, as well as of the people of the Aleutian Islands. A brief review of the major findings of *Personal Justice Denied* is followed by the Commission's recommendations.

I. American Citizens of Japanese Ancestry and Resident Japanese Aliens

On February 19, 1942, ten weeks after the Pearl Harbor attack, President Franklin D. Roosevelt signed Executive Order 9066, empowering the Secretary of War and the military commanders to whom he delegated authority to exclude any and all persons, citizens and aliens, from designated areas in order to secure national defense objectives against sabotage, espionage and fifth column activity. Shortly thereafter, on the alleged basis of military necessity, all American citizens of Japanese descent and all Japanese resident aliens were excluded from the West Coast. A small number—5,000 to 10,000—were removed from the West Coast and placed in "relocation centers"—bleak barrack camps in desolate areas of the Western states, guarded by military police.

People sent to relocation centers were permitted to leave only after a loyalty review on terms set, in consultation with the military, by the War Relocation Authority, the civilian agency that ran the camps. During the course of the war, approximately 35,000 evacuees were allowed to leave the camps to join the Army, attend college outside the West Coast or take whatever private employment might be available to them. When the exclusion of Japanese Americans and resident aliens from the West Coast was ended in December 1944, about 85,000 people remained in government custody. . . .

The federal government contended that its decision to exclude ethnic Japanese from the West Coast was justified by "military necessity." Careful review of the facts by the Commission has not revealed any security or military threat from the West Coast ethnic Japanese in 1942. The record does not support the claim that military necessity justified the exclusion of the ethnic Japanese from the West Coast, with the consequent loss of property and personal liberty.

The decision to detain followed indirectly from the alleged military necessity for exclusion. No one offered a direct military justification for detention; the War Relocation Authority adopted detention primarily in reaction to the vocal popular feeling that people whom the government considered too great a threat to remain at liberty on the West Coast should not live freely elsewhere. . . .

In sum, Executive Order 9066 was not justified by military necessity, and the decisions that followed from it—exclusion, detention, the ending of detention and the ending of exclusion—were not founded upon military considerations. The broad historical causes that shaped these decisions were race prejudice, war hysteria and a failure of political leadership. . . .

The excluded people suffered enormous damages and losses, both material and intangible. To the disastrous loss of farms, businesses and homes must be added the disruption for many years of careers and professional lives, as well as the long-term loss of income, earnings and opportunity. . . .

Less tangibly, the ethnic Japanese suffered the injury of unjustified stigma that marked the excluded. There were physical illnesses and injuries directly related to detention, but the deprivation of liberty is no less injurious because it wounds the spirit rather than the body. . . .

These facts present the Commission with a complex problem of great magnitude to which there is no ready or satisfactory answer. No amount of money can fully compensate the excluded people for their losses and sufferings. Two and a half years behind the barbed-wire of a relocation camp, branded potentially disloyal because of one's ethnicity alone—these injustices cannot neatly be translated into dollars and cents. . . .

It is well within our power, however, to provide remedies for violations of our own laws and principles. This is one important reason for the several forms of redress recommended below. Another is that our nation's ability to honor democratic values even in times of stress depends largely upon our collective memory of lapses from our constitutional commitment to liberty and due process. Nations that forget or ignore injustices are more likely to repeat them.

The governmental decisions of 1942 were not the work of a few men driven by animus, but decisions supported or accepted by public servants from nearly every part of the political spectrum. Nor did sustained or vocal opposition come from the American public. The wartime events produced an unjust result that visited great suffering upon an entire group of citizens, and upon resident aliens whom the Constitution also protects. . . .

The belief that we Americans are exceptional often threatens our freedom by allowing us to look complacently at evil-doing else-where and to insist that "It can't happen here." Recalling the events of exclusion and detention, ensuring that later generations of Americans know this history, is critical immunization against infection by the virus of prejudice and the emotion of wartime struggle. . . .

In proposing remedial measures, the Commission makes its recommendations in light of a history of postwar actions by federal, state and local governments to recognize and partially to redress the wrongs that were done:

- In 1948, Congress passed the Japanese-American Evacuation Claims Act; this gave persons of Japanese ancestry the right to claim from the government real and personal property losses that occurred as a consequence of the exclusion and evacuation. . . .
- In 1972, the Social Security Act was amended so that Japanese Americans over the age of eighteen would be deemed to have earned and contributed to the Social Security system during their detention.
- In 1978, the federal civil service retirement provisions were amended to allow the Japanese Americans civil service retirement credit for time spent in detention after the age of eighteen.
- In four instances, former government employees have received a measure of compensation. In 1982, the State of California enacted a statute permitting the few thousand Japanese Americans in the civil service, who were dismissed or who resigned during the war because of their Japanese ethnicity, to claim $5,000 as reparation. . . .

Each measure acknowledges to some degree the wrongs inflicted during the war upon the ethnic Japanese. None can fully compensate or, indeed, make the group whole again.

The Commission makes the following recommendations for remedies in several forms as an act of national apology.

1. The Commission recommends that Congress pass a joint resolution, to be signed by the President, which recognizes that a grave injustice was done and offers the apologies of the nation for the acts of exclusion, removal and detention.

2. The Commission recommends that the President pardon those who were convicted of violating the statutes imposing a curfew on American citizens on the basis of their ethnicity and requiring the ethnic Japanese to leave designated areas of the West Coast or to report to assembly centers. The Commission further recommends that the Department of Justice review other wartime convictions of the ethnic Japanese and recommend to the President that he pardon those whose offenses were grounded in a refusal to accept treatment that discriminated among citizens on the basis of race or ethnicity. . . .

3. The Commission recommends that Congress direct the Executive agencies to which Japanese Americans may apply for the restitution of positions, status or entitlements lost in whole or in part because of acts or events between December 1941 and 1945 to review such applications with liberality, giving full consideration to the historical findings of this Commission. For example, the responsible divisions of the Department of Defense should be instructed to review cases of less than honorable discharge of Japanese Americans from the armed services during World War II over which disputes remain. . . .

4. The Commission recommends that Congress demonstrate official recognition of the injustice done to American citizens of Japanese ancestry and Japanese resident aliens during the Second World War, and that it recognize the nation's need to make redress for these events, by appropriating monies to establish a special foundation.

The Commissioners all believe a fund for educational and humanitarian purposes related to the wartime events is appropriate, and all agree that no fund would be sufficient to make whole again the lives damaged by the exclusion and detention. . . .

Such a fund should sponsor research and public educational activities so that the events which were the subject of this inquiry will be remembered, and so that the causes and circumstances of this and similar events may be illuminated and understood. A nation which wishes to remain just to its citizens must not forget its lapses. . . .

5. The Commissioners, with the exception of Congressman Lungren, recommend that Congress establish a fund which will provide personal redress to those who were excluded, as well as serve the purposes set out in Recommendation 4. Appropriations of $1.5 billion should be made to the fund over a reasonable period to be determined by Congress. This fund should be used, first, to provide a one-time per capita compensatory payment of $20,000 to each of the approximately 60,000 surviving persons excluded from their places of residence pursuant to Executive Order 9066. . . . After per capita payments, the remainder of the fund should be used for the public educational purposes discussed in Recommendation 4 as well as for the general welfare of the Japanese American community. . . .

Finally, the Commission recommends that a permanent collection be established and funded in the National Archives to house and make available for research the collection of government and private documents, personal testimony and other materials which the Commission amassed during its inquiry.

The Commission believes that, for reasons of redressing the personal injustice done to thousands of Americans and resident alien Japanese, and to the Aleuts—and for compelling reasons of preserving a truthful sense of our own history and the lessons we can learn from it—these recommendations should be enacted by the Congress. In the late 1930's W. H. Auden wrote lines that express our present need to acknowledge and to make amends:

> We are left alone with our day, and the time is short and
> History to the defeated
> May say Alas but cannot help or pardon.

It is our belief that, though history cannot be unmade, it is well within our power to offer help, and to acknowledge error.

Source: Commission on Wartime Relocation and Internment of Civilians, 1983. *Personal Justice Denied, Part Two: Recommendations.* Washington, DC: Government Printing Office. Reprinted in Franklin Odo, ed. 2002. *The Columbia Documentary History of the Asian American Experience.* New York: Columbia University, 419–424.

Appeal Letter from Mother of Vincent Chin, 1983

Vincent Chin, a Chinese American, was murdered by two Caucasian American males in Detroit, Michigan, on June 19, 1982. The two murderers, Ronald Ebens and Michael Nitz, mistook Chin for Japanese and blamed him for layoffs in the automobile industry. After the district attorney's office of Wayne County charged them with second-degree murder, Ebens pleaded guilty to a lesser charge of manslaughter, and Nitz did not contest the charge. Although a manslaughter conviction in the state of Michigan can carry a maximum sentence of fifteen years in prison, in March 1983 County Circuit Judge Charles Kaufman sentenced both defendants to three years' probation and a fine of $3,000 each, plus $780 in fees to be paid over three years. They did not spend a single night in jail for the crime they committed. To protest lenient sentences given to the two killers, Asian Americans organized throughout the country. Despite the continuing efforts of Asian Americans and the involvement of the U.S. Department of Justice to investigate the case further, both killers were ultimately acquitted of federal civil rights charges. Chin's mother wrote this letter to seek help from the Chinese Welfare Council of Detroit.

She was so outraged by the final outcome that she left the United States for China. As a wakeup call, this murder case underscored the need for all Asian Americans to unite together across ethnic lines to fight against anti-Asian violence. As a result, the pan–Asian American campaign to seek justice for Vincent Chin redefined the Asian American movement in the 1980s and the 1990s.

A Letter of Appeal

[translation of original addressed to the Chinese Welfare Council of Detroit]

I, King Fong Yu (the wife of Bing Heng Chin), grieve for my son, Vincent Chin, who was brutally beaten to death by two assailants with a baseball bat. The two killers were apprehended by police and prosecuted in court. During the court proceedings, I, because I am widowed and poor, with no money in my bed, could not retain legal counsel to press the case for my deceased son. As a result, the murderers' attorneys had the say. Yesterday, I read in the newspaper, the sentence was only a fine and probation; and the killers were set free. There was also no compensation for the victim's family. This is injustice to a terrible extreme. My son's blood had been shed; how unjust could this be? I grieve in my heart and shed tears of blood. Yes, my son cannot be brought back—and I can only wait for death. It is just that my deceased son, Vincent Chin, was a member of your council. I therefore plead to you to please help me. Please let the Chinese American community know about this case so they can help me raise funds to hire legal counsel for an appeal. You must help put the killers in prison so my son's soul may rest and my grief be vindicated. This old woman will be forever grateful.

I, King Fong Yu, respectfully submit this letter of appeal.

March 18, 1983.

Reprinted with permission. Helen Zia Collection, Oakland, California.

Resolution on Vincent Chin Decision by Detroit NAACP, March 1983

The lenient sentences given by Judge Charles Kaufman to the two killers of Vincent Chin enraged not only Asian Americans, but also other minority groups. Judge Kaufman wrote a letter to a newspaper attempting to justify the sentences, saying that sentences should depend upon the criminal's background, not the crime. For him, there was no reason to impose harsh punishment, because the two killers had stable employment without previous criminal records. The Detroit Chapter of the National Association for the Advancement of Colored People (NAACP) issued this resolution, deploring the judge's decision and supporting "all efforts to have said sentence rescinded."

RESOLUTION

WHEREAS the Detroit Branch of the NAACP has been active in the Detroit area for over 50 years; and

WHEREAS the Detroit Branch of the NAACP has fought for civil rights and justice for all minorities; and

WHEREAS the Detroit Branch of the NAACP is aware of the brutal and senseless death of Chinese-American Vincent Chin; and

WHEREAS Judge Charles Kaufman has sentenced those responsible for Vincent Chin's death to probation; and

WHEREAS a probationary sentence for the brutal killing of any human by the Court is reprehensible;

NOW, THEREFORE, BE IT RESOLVED that the Detroit Branch of the NAACP deplores the probationary sentence pronounced by Judge Charles Kaufman for the killers of Vincent Chin and support all efforts to have said sentence rescinded and a new sentence rendered mandating appropriate incarceration.

DETROIT BRANCH OF THE NATIONAL ASSOCIATION FOR THE ADVANCEMENT OF COLORED PEOPLE

Reprinted with permission. Helen Zia Collection, Oakland, California.

Civil Liberties Act of 1988 (Public Law 100–383), August 10, 1988

Despite the unequivocal conclusions and recommendations of the Commission on Wartime Relocation and Internment of Civilians (CWRIC) and the promptness of the introduction of relevant legislation to Congress in 1983, the bill was not passed until 1987 by the House and 1988 by the Senate to ask the government to issue an official apology to Japanese Americans and to compensate each surviving detainee with $20,000. In August 1988 President Ronald Reagan signed the bill into the Civil Liberties Act, authorizing $1.25 billion to compensate about 70,000 survivors of the camps. In November 1989 President George

H. W. Bush signed the appropriations bill and the government began to make redress payments in October 1990, forty-eight years after the incarceration.

Public Law 100–383: An Act to Implement Recommendations of the Commission on Wartime Relocation and Internment of Civilians

Be it enacted by the Senate and House of Representatives of the United States of America in Congress assembled,

Section 1. Purposes

The purposes of this Act are to—

1. acknowledge the fundamental injustice of the evacuation, relocation, and internment of United States citizens and permanent resident aliens of Japanese ancestry during World War II;
2. apologize on behalf of the people of the United States for the evacuation, relocation, and internment of such citizens and permanent resident aliens;
3. provide for a public education fund to finance efforts to inform the public about the internment of such individuals so as to prevent the recurrence of any similar event;
4. make restitution to those individuals of Japanese ancestry who were interned;
5. make restitution to Aleut residents of the Pribilof Islands and the Aleutian Islands west of Unimak Island, in settlement of United States obligations in equity and at law, for—
    (A) injustices suffered and unreasonable hardships endured while those Aleut residents were under United States control during World War II;
    (B) personal property taken or destroyed by United States forces during World War II;
    (C) community property, including community church property, taken or destroyed by United States forces during World War II; and
    (D) traditional village lands on Attu Island not rehabilitated after World War II for Aleut occupation or other productive use;
6. discourage the occurrence of similar injustices and violations of civil liberties in the future; and

7. make more credible and sincere any declaration of concern by the United States over violations of human rights committed by other nations.

Section. 2. Statement of the Congress

(a) With Regard to Individuals of Japanese Ancestry.—The Congress recognizes that, as described by the Commission on Wartime Relocation and Internment of Civilians, a grave injustice was done to both citizens and permanent resident aliens of Japanese ancestry by the evacuation, relocation, and internment of civilians during World War II. As the Commission documents, these actions were carried out without adequate security reasons and without any acts of espionage or sabotage documented by the Commission, and were motivated largely by racial prejudice, wartime hysteria, and a failure of political leadership. The excluded individuals of Japanese ancestry suffered enormous damages, both material and intangible, and there were incalculable losses in education and job training, all of which resulted in significant human suffering for which appropriate compensation has not been made. For these fundamental violations of the basic civil liberties and constitutional rights of these individuals of Japanese ancestry, the Congress apologizes on behalf of the Nation.

(b) With Respect to the Aleuts.—The Congress recognizes that, as described by the Commission on Wartime Relocation and Internment of Civilians, the Aleut civilian residents of the Pribilof Islands and the Aleutian Islands west of Unimak Island were relocated during World War II to temporary camps in isolated regions of southeast Alaska where they remained, under United States control and in the care of the United States, until long after any potential danger to their home villages had passed. The United States failed to provide reasonable care for the Aleuts, and this resulted in widespread illness, disease, and death among the residents of the camps; and the United States further failed to protect Aleut personal and community property while such property was in its possession or under its control. The United States has not compensated the Aleuts adequately for the conversion or destruction of personal property, and the conversion or destruction of community property caused by the United States military occupation of Aleut villages during World War II. There is no remedy for injustices suffered by the Aleuts during World War II except an Act of Congress providing appropriate compensation for those losses which are attributable to the conduct of United States forces and other officials and employees of the United States.

Source: United States Statutes at Large, 1988, vol. 102, part 1. Washington, DC: Government Printing Office, 1990. Reprinted in Franklin Odo, ed. 2002. *The Columbia Documentary History of the Asian American Experience.* New York. Columbia University, 439–443.

Key Terms and Events

Alien land laws: These laws were passed in California and eleven other states in the 1910s and 1940s to prohibit Asian aliens, mostly Japanese, from buying or leasing agricultural lands. California's alien land laws were repealed in 1956.

Anti-Asian sentiment: Antagonism toward Asian Americans in the United States, which has been an unfortunate fact from the nineteenth century to the present. The degree of antagonism has fluctuated over time, depending on the U.S. domestic economy and foreign relations with Asian countries.

Anti-Asian violence: Violent tragedies against Asian Americans because of their ethnicity occurred throughout American history. There were three well-known cases in the 1980s, including the killing of Vincent Chin in Detroit in 1982; the murder of five Southeast Asian children in Stockton, California, in January 1989; and the murder of Jim Loo in North Carolina in July 1989.

Asian American: Term that refers to naturalized Asian immigrants and their native-born children in America. In addition to East Asian Americans (Chinese, Japanese, and Korean Americans), Asian Americans also include Filipino, Asian Indian, Vietnamese, Cambodian, Laotian, and Hmong Americans.

Asian American labor movement: A labor movement focusing on the well-being of working-class Asian Americans finally began to flourish in the 1960s, along with the larger Asian American movement. Although it gradually lost its momentum in the 1980s, after being rejected by the American labor movement for decades, Asian

Americans finally established in 1992 the first Asian Pacific American labor organization, the Asian Pacific American Labor Alliance (APALA), within the AFL-CIO.

Asian American movement: Initiated by Asian American college students during the turbulent civil rights era in the 1960s, the Asian American movement has been a social movement challenging the status quo of institutionalized powers in American society. It has consisted of pan-Asian collective actions that specifically aim to fight for racial equality and social and economic justice through racial solidarity and political empowerment.

Asymmetrical participation: This term refers to a political phenomenon that Asian Americans have been a major source of campaign contributions but a minor source of votes.

Bloc voting: A discernible voting pattern of a group of voters in favor of a particular political party is known as bloc voting. Because voting alone cannot be automatically equated with voting power, bloc voting is strategically important.

Boycott of American goods in China: This boycott in 1905 was a direct response to maltreatment of Chinese in the United States under Chinese exclusion laws. Even though it did not last long and had minimal impact on America's trade with China, it successfully brought improvement in treatment of Chinese in the United States.

Bureau of Immigration of Hawaii: Hawaii sugar plantation owners formed the Bureau in 1864 and then sent agents to recruit plantation workers by the thousands, mainly from East Asia.

Burlingame-Seward Treaty: This agreement was signed in 1868 between China and the United States to legalize the import of Chinese cheap laborers, who would be under the protection of the American government.

Campaign finance controversies: These controversies in the mid-1990s involved allegations that foreign governments and corporations in Asia and individuals of Asian background made campaign contributions to U.S. political candidates in an attempt to influence U.S. policy decisions. As a watershed event in the history of Asian American electoral participation, it has had profound impacts on the political participation of the entire community.

Chinese civil war: This intense military conflict between the Chinese nationalists and communists between 1945 and 1949 resulted in a communist victory and the establishment of the People's Republic of China. The civil war affected not only the patterns of Chinese immigration to the United States, but also the United States-

China relationship that in turn had some bearing on the treatment of Chinese Americans in the United States.

Chinese Exclusion Act: This act, which became effective in 1882, forbade Chinese immigration into the United States. As the first piece of legislation that specially excluded a particular group of immigrants, it also stipulated that those Chinese laborers already on American soil were denied the right to become naturalized citizens. The act was repealed in 1943.

"Democratic Revolution" in Hawaii: In 1954 a number of Japanese American veterans of World War II constituted a significant part of the "New Democrats" who managed to dominate both executive and legislative branches of Hawaii's territorial government. Prior to this turning point the territorial government was firmly under the control of Caucasian Republican politicians allied with the old plantation power structure. This "revolution" marked the beginning of Japanese Americans' participation in politics as elected officials in Hawaii.

Executive Order 9066: Signed by President Franklin D. Roosevelt in 1942, this order resulted in the removal of more than 40,000 Japanese from their homes on the West Coast, along with their 70,000 American-born children, and their imprisonment in internment camps. The War Department revoked the mass exclusion orders in 1944, and the executive order itself was revoked by President Gerald Ford in 1976.

Executive Order 11246: Issued by President Lyndon Johnson in 1965, this order prohibits any organizations that practice discrimination from receiving federal money. But, for nearly four decades now, it has been enforced for all Americans except for Asian Americans.

Geary Act: When the Chinese Exclusion Act expired in 1892, it was replaced with an even stricter one, the Geary Act. Under the new law, all Chinese in the United States were required to register or face immediate deportation.

Gentlemen's Agreement: This agreement was signed between the United States and Japan in 1907 to limit Japanese immigration to the United States to nonlaborers.

Huiguan: The most important community organizations in American Chinatowns, these regional associations are largely mutual aid associations created to benefit their members who are people from the same regions in China.

Immigration Act of 1965: A watershed in the American history of immigration, this act was signed by President Lyndon Johnson to abolish the discriminatory, racially based national-origin quota system, which favored European immigrants. It has profoundly changed the pattern of immigration to the United States, leading to a dramatic rise in the Asian American population in the United States in the following decades.

Interest group: An interest group is an aggregate of individuals who interact in varying degrees in pursuance of a common interest. Depending upon the type of interest being pursued, American interest groups can be roughly classified as economic interest groups (including labor, business, agricultural, and consumer groups); environmental interest groups; and equality interest groups. Most Asian American interest groups belong to the last category.

International Hotel campaign: This was one of the longest urban struggles since the end of the 1960s, as well as the first struggle that brought a large number of Asian American students into the community as political activists. The hotel was a low-cost residence mainly for retired Chinese and Filipino American workers in San Francisco. In December 1968 the hotel owner attempted to evict the tenants and build a more profitable parking lot. In response, many Asian American students organized to protest. The hotel soon became a hallmark of the Asian American resistance movement, and the campaign attracted tens of thousands of people from all nationalities in the Bay Area. However, all their efforts to save the hotel were in vain. It was finally evacuated and shut down on August 4, 1977.

Issei: This term denotes first-generation, foreign-born Japanese in America.

Japan bashing: An anti-Japanese attitude caused by trade frictions between the United States and Japan in the 1970s and 1980s, Japan bashing deepened the already existent anti-Asian American agitation.

Japan's colonization of Korea: Korea was colonized by Japan with an iron fist from 1910 to 1945. This history planted the seed of anti-Japanese sentiment among Koreans, as well as Korean immigrants in America.

Japan's invasion of China: This bitter history occurred from 1931 to 1945, leading to anti-Japanese sentiment among Chinese and Chinese immigrants in America.

Kenjinkai: This is the term for the most common and earliest community organizations created by Japanese immigrants in the United States. These prefectural (provincial) associations were to provide mutual aid and social functions to their members.

Los Angeles riots: This name was given to a four-day-long episode of urban unrest in Los Angeles that began on April 29, 1992, after four Caucasian Los Angeles police officers charged with beating an African American motorist were acquitted by a jury. More than 3,000 businesses were damaged or destroyed and property damage totaled $800 million. Korean Americans owned most of these businesses and the Los Angeles Koreatown was virtually dismantled.

Miss Saigon: This Broadway musical was seen as filled with racist misperceptions of Asian men as asexual and contemptible and Asian women as submissive and self-effacing. Asian Americans organized two demonstrations in 1991 in protest of its showing.

"Model minority": Asian Americans have been labeled the "model minority" since the mid-1960s by journalists, scholars, and politicians who have emphasized Asian Americans' virtues and accomplishments, especially in the spheres of education and economy. This "model minority" myth has proved to be harmful to Asian Americans for a variety of reasons, such as taking public attention away from social and economic problems facing many members of the Asian American community, and creating resentment of other minority groups toward Asian Americans.

Nisei: This term refers to second-generation, American-born Japanese Americans.

***Nisei* soldiers:** These military servicemen were second-generation, American-born Japanese Americans who demonstrated their loyalty by fighting for the United States on the European battlefields during World War II. Many of the more than 33,000 *Nisei* soldiers belonged to the highly recognized 100th Battalion and 442nd Regimental Combat Team.

"Not a Chinaman's chance": This was an infamous expression referring to a historical situation in the nineteenth century when Chinese were not allowed to testify in court and thus received no protection under the law. Therefore, "not a Chinaman's chance" means no chance at all.

Panethnicity of Asian Americans: Despite differences in their histories, cultures, languages, and identities, many Asian Americans of different ethnic backgrounds have united since the 1960s to protect their rights and advance their collective interests. The formation of Asian American panethnicity was conducive to the development of the Asian American movement and vice versa.

Political efficacy: A belief or perception that one's political actions are effective in making a real difference in the political world, political efficacy is one of the central determinants of political participation.

Political interest group: A political interest group is an interest group that pursues its shared interest as policy goals in the political process.

"Quiet minority": A popular image in American society of Asian Americans as being uninterested, uninformed, and thus uninvolved in politics spawned this appellation for them.

Railroad strike of 1867: This was a monumental strike organized by Chinese railroad workers in 1867. Due to inequality in wages, working hours, and other working conditions, 2,000 Chinese workers in the High Sierra went on strike. This strike was short-lived and fruitless at the end. It lasted just one week after the strikers' food ran out. Nonetheless, it was the largest, and perhaps also the earliest, strike by Chinese in the nineteenth century.

Realigning election: This term denotes an election that marks the beginning of a lasting shift in voters' support away from one political party toward another.

Redress movement: Japanese Americans began in the late 1960s to seek reparations for the ordeal they had experienced during World War II when thousands of them were removed from their West Coast homes and interned in camps. The movement was led by the Japanese American Citizens League. The Redress movement went on in the 1970s and 1980s and was concluded by the passage of the Civil Liberties Act in 1988 that authorized $1.25 billion to compensate about 70,000 survivors of the internment camps. In November 1989 President Bush signed the appropriations bill and the government began to make redress payments in October 1990.

Rotating credit associations: These are community organizations in which funds are pooled together from members and the total sum is given to just one member each month on a rotating basis until every member receives the money. This kind of association is financially important because it helps new arrivals from Asia start businesses in the United States.

San Francisco State College strike: This historic strike was a defining event for the Asian American movement. On November 6, 1968, Asian American students of the college, now San Francisco State University, joined a strike with students of other racial backgrounds under the umbrella of a multiethnic coalition, the Third World Liberation Front, calling for ethnic studies and open admissions. This five-month-long strike was the first campus uprising in which Asian American students participated as a collective force.

Swing vote: An individual vote or a group of votes that can make a difference in the result of a close race is known as a swing vote. For Asian Americans to make progress on issues important to them, it is imperative to present their voting power as a swing vote in elections.

Tiananmen democratic movement: This movement occurred in Beijing, China, in the spring of 1989. It was initiated by college students who occupied Tiananmen Square in Beijing and called for democratic reforms; they were later joined by people from other segments of Chinese society. The movement began on April 15 and ended with a massacre on June 4. After the tragedy, President George H. W. Bush decided to grant permanent resident status to about 30,000 Chinese students who were studying in U.S. colleges and universities at the time.

Tong-hoe: These "village councils" were the earliest community organizations formed as self-governing bodies by Korean laborers on Hawaii's plantations.

Resources

The East Asian American organizations and the pan–Asian American organizations listed in this section are classified into national, state, and local organizations. Information about the national organizations is primarily composed of information collected from the organizations' websites, with some information from Don T. Nakanishi and James S. Lai, eds. 2001. *National Asian Pacific American Political Almanac, 2001–2002*. 10th ed. Los Angeles: UCLA Asian American Studies Center; and Jeffrey D. Schultz, Kerry L. Haynie, Anne M. McCulloch, and Andrew L. Aoki, eds. 2000. *Encyclopedia of Minorities in American Politics. Volume I: African Americans and Asian Americans*. Phoenix, AZ: Oryx. Information about the state and local organizations is mainly based on the *National Asian Pacific American Political Almanac, 2001–2002*.

National Organizations

80–20 Political Action Committee (80–20 PAC)
P.O. Box 527340
Flushing, NY 11352
Website: http://www.80–20initiative.net

The 80–20 PAC is a national political action committee aiming to improve equal opportunity and justice for all Asian Pacific Americans through a swing bloc vote. It is basically a cyberspace political organization with an e-mail list of a large number of Asian Pacific Americans across the United States.

022

222

Asian American Government Executives Network (AAGEN)
1001 Connecticut Avenue, NW, Suite 601
Washington, DC 20036
Phone: (540) 720-8648
Fax: (540) 720-8648
Website: http://www.aagen.org

Founded in 1994, the AAGEN is a nonpartisan organization of high-ranking Asian Pacific American career and appointed executives, foreign service officers, legislative and judiciary members, and military officers in the federal, state, and local governments. It is dedicated to promoting Asian Pacific American leadership in governmental agencies at all levels.

Asian and Pacific Islander American Health Forum (APIAHF)
450 Sutter Street, Suite 600
San Francisco, CA 94108
Phone: (415) 954-9988
Fax: (415) 954-9999
Website: http://www.apiahf.org

Washington, DC, Office:
1001 Connecticut Avenue, NW, Suite 835
Washington, DC 20036
Phone: (202) 466-7772
Fax: (202) 466-6444

Founded in 1986, the APIAHF is a national organization dedicated to improving the health status of Asian Pacific American communities by promoting health policies, programs, and research efforts. It publishes *Confronting Critical Health Issues of Asian and Pacific Americans.*

Asian Pacific American Institute for Congressional Studies (APAICS)
1001 Connecticut Avenue, NW, Suite 835
Washington, DC 20036
Phone: (202) 296-9200
Fax: (202) 296-9236
Website: http://www.apaics.org

The APAICS is a nonprofit, nonpartisan, educational organization seeking to increase political participation of Asian Pacific Americans in all areas of the American political process, ranging from community service to elected office.

Asian Pacific American Labor Alliance (APALA)
815 16th Street, NW
Washington, DC 20006
Phone: (202) 842-1263
Fax: (202) 842-1462
Website: http://www.apalanet.org

Founded in 1992, the APALA is the first and only national union organization of Asian Pacific Americans. Supported by the AFL-CIO, it has become a strong voice for Asian Pacific American workers in the labor movement and in the national public policy arena.

Asian Pacific American Women's Leadership Institute (APAWLI)
P.O. Box 2330
La Mesa, CA 91943
Phone: (619) 698-3746
Fax: (619) 698-5834
Website: http://www.apawli.org

The APAWLI is a national organization working to improve leadership skills for Asian Pacific American women leaders. In addition to expanding leadership capacity, its mission includes fostering awareness of Asian Pacific American issues and creating a supportive network of Asian Pacific American women.

Asian Pacific Partners for Empowerment and Leadership (APPEAL)
300 Frank H. Ogawa Plaza, Suite 620
Oakland, CA 94612
Phone: (510) 272-9536
Fax: (510) 272-0817
Website: http://www.appealforcommunities.org

Established in 1994, the APPEAL is the only national network of organizations committed to having a tobacco-free Asian Pacific American community by providing assistance and resources on tobacco control.

Association of Asian Pacific Community Health Organizations (AAPCHO)
300 Frank H. Ogawa Plaza, Suite 620
Oakland, CA 94612
Phone: (510) 272-9536
Fax: (510) 272-0817
Website: http://www.aapcho.org

Formed in 1987, the AAPCHO is a national association of community health organizations working towards improving the health status and access of Asian Pacific Americans. More specifically, it is dedicated to establishing community-based health care that is affordable and culturally and linguistically appropriate to the Asian Pacific American community.

Chinese American Citizens Alliance (CACA)
1044 Stockton Street
San Francisco, CA 94108
Phone: (415) 434-2222
Fax: (415) 982-3728
Website: http://cacanational.org

As a nonpartisan, nonprofit organization, the CACA was founded in 1895 dedicated to promoting citizenship, civil and immigrant rights, bettering the Chinese American community, and fighting anti-Chinese American sentiment.

Chinese Consolidated Benevolent Association (CCBA)
843 Stockton Street
San Francisco, CA 94108
Phone: (415) 982-6000
Fax: (415) 982-6010

Founded in 1882, the CCBA, also known as the "Chinese Six Companies," is long recognized as the representative organization of American Chinatowns. It is a hierarchical, umbrella organization encompassing many regional, family, business, and charity organizations. It is not only a community service organization, but also a political organization that seeks to protect the civil rights of Chinese Americans.

Committee of 100
677 5th Avenue, 3rd Floor
New York, NY 10022

Phone: (212) 371-6565
Fax: (212) 371-9009
Website: http://www.committee100.org

Formed in 1990 by a number of prominent Chinese Americans, the Committee of 100 is a nonpartisan national organization committed to promoting relations between the United States and China and protecting the rights of Chinese Americans.

Congressional Asian Pacific American Caucus (CAPAC)
1023 Longworth House Office Building
Washington, DC 20515
Phone: (202) 225-0855
Fax: (202) 225-9497
Website: http://www.house.gov/wu/capacweb/

Founded in 1994, the CAPAC is dedicated to addressing issues critical to Asian Pacific Americans and ensuring that the needs of the community are met. In addition, the caucus also aims to inform other members of Congress and the public of the history and contributions of Asian Pacific Americans.

Formosan Association for Public Affairs (FAPA)
552 7th Street, SE
Washington, DC 20003
Phone: (202) 547-3686
Fax: (202) 543-7891
Website: http://www.fapa.org

Established in 1982, the FAPA is a nonprofit organization working to promote international support for the rights of the people of Taiwan and for membership of an independent Taiwan in international organizations.

Japanese American Citizens League (JACL)
1765 Sutter Street
San Francisco, CA 94115
Phone: (415) 921-5225
Fax: (415) 931-4671
Website: http://jacl.org

Washington, DC, Office:
Legislative Affairs Office
1001 Connecticut Avenue, NW, Suite 730
Washington, DC 20036

Founded in 1930, the JACL is a membership organization with its mission being to protect the civil rights of Japanese Americans and others who experience injustice, as well as to preserve the cultural heritage of Japanese Americans. It publishes a weekly, *Pacific Citizen.*

Korean American Coalition (KAC)
3727 West 6th Street, Suite 515
Los Angeles, CA 90020
Phone: (213) 365-5999
Fax: (213) 380-7990
Website: http://www.kacla.org

Washington, DC, office:
1140 Connecticut Avenue, NW, Suite 1200
Washington, DC 20036
Phone: (202) 296-6401
Fax: (202) 296-2318
Website: http://www.kacdc.org

Founded in 1983, the KAC is a national nonprofit community service and advocacy organization dedicated to promoting Korean Americans' participation in political and community activities by providing educational programs, leadership development, voter registration services, and community networking to Korean American communities throughout the nation.

Leadership Education for Asian Pacifics (LEAP)
327 East 2nd Street, Suite 226
Los Angeles, CA 90012
Phone: (213) 485-1422
Fax: (213) 485-0050
Website: http://www.leap.org

A national nonprofit organization founded in 1982, the LEAP is dedicated to promoting full participation and equality for Asian Pacific Americans and achieving a strategy of Asian Pacific American empowerment by providing leadership training, publishing policy research, and conducting community education. Its publications include *The State of Asian Pacific America: Policy Issues to the year 2020.*

National Asian American Pacific Islander Mental Health Association (NAAPIMHA)
1215 19th Street, Suite A
Denver, CO 80202
Phone: (303) 298-7910
Fax: (303) 298-8081
Website: http://www.naapimha.org

Founded in 2000, the NAAPIMHA's mission is to advocate for Asian Pacific Americans' mental health issues. It targets community-based organizations, consumers, family members, service providers, program developers, researchers, evaluators, and policymakers for networking.

National Asian Pacific American Bar Association (NAPABA)
733 15th Street, NW, Suite 315
Washington, DC 20005
Phone: (202) 421-9039
Fax: (202) 393-0995
Website: http://www.napaba.org

Los Angeles Office:
725 South Figueroa Street, Suite 1690
Los Angeles, CA 90017
Phone: (213) 955-8022
Fax: (213) 955-9250

The NAPABA was formed in 1988 as a national association of Asian Pacific American attorneys, judges, law professors, and law students seeking to advance the legal needs and interests of the community. More specifically, it focuses on advocating civil rights, fighting anti-immigrant backlash and hate crimes, increasing the diversity of the federal and state judiciaries, and promoting professional development.

National Asian Pacific American Legal Consortium (NAPALC)
1140 Connecticut Avenue, NW, Suite 1200
Washington, DC 20036
Phone: (202) 296-2300

Fax: (202) 296-2318
Website: http://www.napalc.org

Founded in 1991, the NAPALC dedicates itself to advancing the civil rights of Asian Pacific Americans through the means of advocacy, public policy research, public education, and litigation, seeking to create an inclusive society in communities at all levels. It places great emphasis on a variety of issues important to Asian Pacific Americans, such as affirmative action, anti-Asian violence prevention and race relations, census issues, immigrant rights, language access, and voting rights.

National Asian Pacific American Women's Forum (NAPAWF)

1001 Connecticut Avenue, NW, Suite 730
Washington, DC 20036
Phone: (202) 293-2688
Fax: (202) 463-2119
Website: http://www.napawf.org

Founded in 1996, the NAPAWF is committed to creating an Asian Pacific American women's movement in order to advance the social justice and rights of Asian Pacific American women.

National Asian Pacific Center for Aging (NAPCA)

1511 3rd Avenue, Suite 914
Seattle, WA 98101
Phone: (206) 624-1221
Fax: (206) 624-1023
Website: http://www.napca.org

Founded in 1979, the NAPCA is a national advocacy organization working to promote the well-being of senior Asian Pacific Americans through its employment programs, multilingual community forums, and health care education.

National Association of Korean Americans (NAKA)

3883 Plaza Drive
Fairfax, VA 22030
Phone: (703) 267-2388
Fax: (703) 267-2396
Website: http://www.naka.org

Founded in 1994, the NAKA is a civil rights organization of Korean Americans. In addition to safeguarding civil rights, it also works to promote cooperation and better understanding between Korean Americans and other groups in the United States.

National Coalition for Asian Pacific American Community Development (NCAPACD)
1001 Connecticut Avenue, NW, Suite 730
Washington, DC 20036
Phone: (202) 223-2442
Fax: (202) 223-4144
Website: http://www.nationalcapacd.org

Representing a coalition of more than forty community-based organizations that joined together in 1999, the NCAPACD is the first national advocacy organization primarily on issues of affordable housing and community development needs of Asian Pacific Americans.

National Council of Asian Pacific Americans (NCAPA)
1140 Connecticut Avenue, NW, Suite 1200
Washington, DC 20036
Phone: (202) 296-2300
Fax: (202) 296-2318
Website: http://ncapaonline.org

Founded in 1996 as a coalition of twenty-seven Asian Pacific American organizations, the NCAPA is the first national Asian Pacific American civil rights organization, providing a nationally organized voice for addressing Asian Pacific American concerns.

National Korean American Service and Education Consortium (NAKASEC)
900 South Crenshaw Boulevard
Los Angeles, CA 90019
Phone: (323) 937-3703
Fax: (323) 937-3526
Website: http://www.nakasec.org

Founded in 1994, the NAKASEC is dedicated to securing the civil rights of Korean Americans and promoting political and civic participation among Korean Americans.

Organization of Chinese Americans, Inc. (OCA)
1001 Connecticut Avenue, NW, Suite 601
Washington, DC 20036
Phone: (202) 223-5500
Fax: (202) 296-0540
Website: http://www.ocanatl.org

Founded in 1973, the OCA is a national advocacy organization with a mission to protect the rights of Chinese American and Asian American citizens and permanent residents. It seeks to achieve its mission through legislative and policy initiatives at the federal, state, and local levels.

Organization of Chinese American Women (OCAW)
4641 Montgomery Avenue, Suite 208
Bethesda, MD 20814
Phone: (301) 907-3898
Fax: (301) 907-3899
Website: http://mason.gmu.edu/~lsaavedr/ocawfinal/about.htm

Founded in 1977, the OCAW seeks to take care of the needs of Chinese American women and to educate the public about their needs by integrating Chinese American women into other women's programs, addressing unequal employment issues, and combating racial stereotypes and discrimination. It provides leadership training, access to policymaking positions, and assistance to poor immigrants in the forms of networking, job placement services, and training opportunities.

Taiwanese American Citizens League (TACL)
3001 Walnut Grove Avenue, Suite 7
Rosemead, CA 91770
Phone: (626) 571-7197
Fax: (626) 571-7197
Website: http://www.tacl.org

Founded in 1985, the TACL is a civil rights organization of Taiwanese Americans, dedicated to creating an awareness of Taiwanese American heritage and addressing concerns of Taiwanese Americans.

UCLA Asian American Studies Center
3230 Campbell Hall
Box 951546

Los Angeles, CA 90095
Phone: (310) 825-2974
Fax: (310) 206-9844
Website: http://www.sscnet.ucla.edu/aasc/

Founded in 1969, the UCLA Asian American Studies Center works to document and analyze the Asian Pacific American experiences through scholarly works and policy research. Its publications include the *National Asian Pacific American Political Almanac.*

State and Local Organizations

California

Asian American Political Alliance of Marin
P.O. Box 151401
San Rafael, CA 94915
Phone: (415) 256-9220

Asian American Political Education Foundation
1366 Manzanita Drive
Millbrae, CA 94030
Phone: (650) 589-1199
Fax: (650) 589-1720

Asian Immigrant Women Advocates (AIWA)
310 8th Street, #301
Oakland, CA 94607
Phone: (510) 268-0192
Fax: (510) 268-0194

1010 Ruff Street
San Jose, CA 95110
Phone: (408) 289-8983
Fax: (408) 289-8883
Website: http://aiwa.org

Asian Law Alliance
184 Jackson Street
San Jose, CA 95112
Phone: (408) 287-9710

Asian Law Caucus (ALC)
720 Market Street, #500
San Francisco, CA 94102
Phone: (415) 391-1655
Fax: (415) 391-0366
Website: http://asianlawcaucus.org

Asian Pacific American Coalition USA
1615 Edgewood Drive
Palo Alto, CA 94303
Phone: (650) 327-9181
Fax: (650) 327-2738

Asian Pacific American Legal Center (APALC) of Southern California
1010 South Flower Street, #302
Los Angeles, CA 90015
Phone: (213) 748-2022 ext. 43
Fax: (213) 748-0679

Asian Pacific Democratic Club of San Francisco
3145 Geary Blvd., #453
San Francisco, CA 94118
Phone: (415) 279-6877
Fax: (415) 668-5120

Asian Pacific Environmental Network
310 8th Street, #309
Oakland, CA 94607
Phone: (510) 834-8920
Fax: (510) 834-8926

Asian Pacific Islander Americans Vote
300 West Cesar Chavez Avenue, #A
Los Angeles, CA 90012
Phone: (213) 617-2665
Fax: (213) 680-2796

Center for Asian Americans United for Self Empowerment (CAUSE)
260 South Los Robles Avenue, #118
Pasadena, CA 91101
Phone: (888) 809-3888 / (626) 356-9838

Fax: (626) 356-9878
Website: http://www.causeusa.org

Chinese American Political Association
P.O. Box 4314
Walnut Creek, CA 94596
Phone: (925) 284-5533
Fax: (925) 284-5533
Website: http://www.capa-news.org

Chinese American Voters Education Committee
838 Grant Avenue, #403
San Francisco, CA 94108
Phone: (415) 397-8133
Fax: (415) 397-6617

Chinese for Affirmative Action (CAA)
The Kuo Building
17 Walter U. Lum Place
San Francisco, CA 94108
Phone: (415) 274-6750
Fax: (415) 397-8770
Website: http://www.caasf.org

Korean Immigrant Workers Advocates (KIWA)
3465 West 8th Street
Los Angeles, CA 90005
Phone: (213) 738-9050
Fax: (213) 738-9919

Silicon Valley Asian Pacific American Democratic Club (SVAPADC)
465 North Wolfe Road
Sunnyvale, CA 94086
Website: www.svapadc.org

Connecticut

National Asian American League
P.O. Box 8265
New Haven, CT 06530
Phone: (800) 922-3237
Fax: (800) 624-1248

Illinois

Asian American Institute
4753 North Broadway, Suite 904
Chicago, IL 60640
Phone: (773) 271-0899
Fax: (773) 271-1982
Website: http://www.aaichicago.org

Indiana

Asian American Network of Indiana
P.O. Box 4083
Lafayette, IN 47903
Phone: (765) 494-1259

Maryland

Coalition of APA Democrats of the State of Maryland
9600 Alta Vista Terrace
Bethesda, MD 20814
Phone: (301) 493-0377
Fax: (301) 493-0377

Republican Asian American Alliance
118 Water Street
Gaithersburg, MD 20877
Phone: (301) 330-0639
Fax: (301) 948-4493

Massachusetts

Asian Pacific Democratic Caucus
162 Plainfield Road
Concord, MA 01742
Phone: (978) 369-7001
Fax: (978) 371-0228

Chinatown Voter Education Drive
56 Beach Street
Boston, MA 02111
Phone: (617) 426-7449
Fax: (617) 482-9524

Michigan

American Citizens for Justice (ACJ)
19111 West 10 Mile Drive Road, #121
Southfield, MI 48075
Phone: (248) 352-1020
Fax: (248) 352-1020

Nevada

Asian Pacific Forum
2983 Pinehurst Drive
Las Vegas, NV 89101
Phone: (702) 739-9311
Fax: (702) 732-3313

New Jersey

Pacific Asian Coalition, N.J.
5 Stonehenge Lane
Bridgewater, NJ 08807
Phone: (908) 707-1365

New York

Asian American Affairs Republican Federation
223 Centre Street
New York, NY 10013
Phone: (212) 966-1413
Fax: (212) 343-8130

Asian American Federation of New York
120 Wall Street, 3rd Floor
New York, NY 10005
Phone: (212) 344-5878
Fax: (212) 344-5636

Asian American Legal Defense and Education Fund (AALDEF)
99 Hudson Street, 12th Floor
New York, NY 10013
Phone: (212) 966-5932
Fax: (212) 966-4303

Asian Americans for Equality
111 Division Street
New York, NY 10002
Phone: (212) 964-2288
Fax: (212) 964-6003

Chinatown Voter Education Alliance (CVEA)
39 Bowery
Box 859
New York, NY 10002
Phone: (212) 925-4325

Chinese American Voters Association of Queens (CAVA)
P.O. Box 521433
Flushing, NY 11352
Phone: (718) 461-0830

Chinese Progressive Association (CPA)
83 Canal Street, Room 304-305
New York, NY 10002
Phone: (212) 274-1891

Committee against Anti-Asian Violence (CAAAV)
191 East 3rd Street
New York, NY 10009
Phone: (212) 473-6485
Fax: (212) 473-5569
Website: http://www.caaav.org

Oregon

Asian Pacific American Network of Oregon
4424 NE Glisan
Portland, OR 97213
Phone: (503) 235-9396
Fax: (503) 235-0341

Pennsylvania

Asian Pacific Americans for Democratic Action
1700 Sanson Street, 12th Floor
Philadelphia, PA 19103
Phone: (215) 972-5100
Fax: (610) 789-1212

Texas

Asian American Democrats of Texas
5177 Richmond, #800
Houston, TX 70056
Phone: (713) 652-9200
Fax: (713) 669-9292

Virginia

Advocates for the Rights of Korean Americans
7023 Little River Turnpike, #419
Annandale, VA 22003
Phone: (703) 642-1439
Fax: (703) 642-9744

Asian Pacific American Democrats of Northern Virginia
3757 Madison Lane
Falls Church, VA 22041
Phone: (703) 998-5539

Federation of Asian Pacific American Republicans
1714 Great Falls Road
McLean, VA 22101
Phone: (703) 734-9463
Fax: (703) 790-9571

Chronology

1790	The Naturalization Act stipulates that only "a free white person" is eligible to apply for naturalization.
1820	The arrival of Chinese in America is first reported.
1830s	Several Chinese "sugar masters" work in Hawaii.
	Chinese sailors and peddlers show up in New York.
1835	The first sugar plantation is established in Hawaii.
1844	The United States and China sign their first treaty.
1848	Gold is discovered in California, and Chinese begin to arrive in large numbers.
1850	Chinese laborers are actively recruited to come to the United States.
1851	The Chinese population in California reaches 25,000.
	Chinese in San Francisco form Sanyi (Sam Yup) and Siyi (Sze Yup) Associations.
1852	The first batch of 195 Chinese contract laborers land in Hawaii.
	Over 20,000 Chinese enter California.
	Chinese first appear in court in California.
1854	Chinese in Hawaii establish a funeral society, their first community association on the islands.
	The California Supreme Court case of *People v. Hall* rules that Chinese cannot give testimony in court.
	The United States and Japan sign their first treaty.

1855   California passes a law to discourage Chinese from entering the state.

1858   California passes a law to bar entry of Chinese and "Mongolians."

1859   Chinese are excluded from attending public schools in San Francisco.

As a result of a petition by thirty Chinese parents, a separate school for Chinese children is opened in San Francisco.

1860   Japan sends a diplomatic mission to the United States, the first documented arrival of Japanese in America.

1862   Six Chinese district associations in San Francisco form a loose federation, the "Six Chinese Companies."

California imposes a "police tax" of $2.50 a month on every Chinese.

1865   The Central Pacific Railroad Co. recruits Chinese workers for the construction of the first transcontinental railroad.

1867   About 2,000 Chinese railroad workers stage a strike for a week, the largest, perhaps also the earliest, strike by Chinese in the nineteenth century.

1868   The United States and China sign the Burlingame-Seward Treaty recognizing the right of their citizens to immigrate to each other's country.

About 150 Japanese laborers are imported to work in Hawaii.

1869   The first transcontinental railroad across North America is completed.

Several dozen Japanese are imported to work in California, constituting the first group of Japanese immigrants to the mainland United States.

1870   Chinese railroad workers in Texas stop work and file suit against their company for failure to pay them wages.

Chinese in San Francisco protest against a "queue ordinance."

Colorado passes a resolution welcoming Chinese immigrants.

1871   Hundreds of Chinese railroad workers, along with workers of other racial backgrounds, seize trains to demand unpaid wages from their company.

Anti-Chinese violence breaks out in Los Angeles.

San Francisco closes its evening school for Chinese children, thus terminating the only available formal education for Chinese children.

1872   California's Civil Procedure Code drops the law barring Chinese court testimony.

1875   The U.S. Congress passes the Page Law that bars entry of Chinese, Japanese, and "Mongolian" prostitutes, felons, and contract laborers.

Chinese garment workers strike a Chinese sweatshop in San Francisco.

1876   Chinese shoemakers go on strike in San Francisco, leading to an attack on a trading company.

The "Six Chinese Companies" sends a letter to President Ulysses S. Grant, citing contributions made by Chinese immigrants to the United States, and a representative of the organization gives an address to Congress about the hardship experienced by Chinese laborers.

1877   Japanese form their first immigrant association, the Japanese Gospel Society, in San Francisco.

1878   The U.S. Ninth Circuit Court of Appeals in *In re Ah Yup* rules Chinese ineligible for naturalized citizenship.

Chinese Americans collect about 13,000 signatures to petition the California state legislature to have access to public schools.

1879   California's second constitution prevents municipalities and corporations from employing Chinese.

The California state legislature passes a law requiring all incorporated towns and cities to remove Chinese outside the city limits, but the U.S. Ninth Circuit Court of Appeals declares the law unconstitutional.

1882   The Chinese Exclusion Act (Immigration Act of 1882) is passed by Congress to bar entry of Chinese laborers for ten years.

1882 (cont.)	Chinese community leaders form the Chinese Consolidated Benevolent Association (CCBA) in San Francisco.
	The United States and Korea sign their first treaty.
1883	Chinese in New York establish a chapter of the CCBA.
1884	The U.S. Supreme Court holds that wives of Chinese laborers cannot enter the country.
	Joseph and Mary Tape sue the San Francisco school board to enroll their daughter Mamie in public school.
	The CCBA in San Francisco sets up a Chinese language school.
	The Chinese Exclusion Act is amended to require a certificate as the sole evidence for reentry.
1885	A new segregated "Oriental School" is established in San Francisco.
	Anti-Chinese violence erupts at Rock Spring, Wyoming Territory.
	The first group of Japanese contract laborers arrives in Hawaii as a result of the Japanese government's decision to lift the ban on all emigration.
1886	Chinese are expelled by residents of Tacoma, Seattle, and many other places in the American West.
	Chinese immigration to Hawaii is ended.
1888	The Scott Act renders 20,000 Chinese reentry certificates null and void.
1889	The U.S. Supreme Court in *Chae Chan Ping v. United States* upholds the constitutionality of the Chinese exclusion acts.
1891	About 300 Chinese plantation workers strike in Hawaii.
	The first Chinese-English newspaper, the *Chinese World,* begins publication in San Francisco.
1892	The Geary Law extends the exclusion of Chinese laborers for another ten years and requires all Chinese to register.
	The Chinese Equal Rights League (CERL) of New York, probably the first Asian American civil rights organization ever founded, is formed as a response to the passage of the Geary Law and successfully lobbies Congressman George W. Smith to introduce a bill to permit Chinese naturalization.

1893   The U.S. Supreme Court case of *Fong Yue Ting v. United States* upholds the constitutionality of the Geary Law.

Japanese form their first trade association, the Japanese Shoemakers' League, in San Francisco.

Attempts are made to expel Chinese from towns in Southern California.

1894   A U.S. circuit court of appeals in Massachusetts declares in *In re Saito* that Japanese are ineligible for naturalization.

1895   Japan defeats China in the first Sino-Japanese War.

The Native Sons of the Golden State (renamed the Chinese American Citizens Alliance or CACA in 1915) is founded in San Francisco.

1896   Chinatown in Honolulu is burned down during a bubonic plague scare.

1898   The U.S. Supreme Court case of *Wong Kim Ark v. United States* decides that Chinese born in the United States cannot be stripped of their citizenship.

The United States annexes Hawaii and the Philippines.

1901   The first Korean immigrant arrives in Hawaii.

1902   Chinese exclusion is extended for another ten years.

The CCBA in San Francisco collects thousands of letters protesting against the city's school segregation policy and hires a former Baptist missionary to lobby the California state legislature for changing the policy.

1902–   About 7,000 predominantly male Korean laborers immi-
1905   grate to Hawaii.

1903   Koreans in Hawaii form the New People Society and Korean Evangelical Society, and Koreans on the mainland form the Friendship Society.

Japanese and Mexican sugar beet workers jointly form a historic farm workers' union, the Japanese-Mexican Labor Association, in Oxnard, California.

About 1,200 members of the Japanese-Mexican Labor Association strike.

1904   The Chinese Exclusion Act becomes indefinite and applicable to U.S. insular possessions.

1904 *(cont.)*	Almost 1,200 Japanese plantation workers engage in a weeklong strike in Hawaii, their first organized strike on the islands.
1905	Chinese on the mainland United States and Hawaii support a boycott of American products in China, a direct response to maltreatment of Chinese in the United States.
	Korea becomes a Japanese protectorate.
	The Korean government ends emigration to Hawaii and Mexico after maltreatment of some 1,000 Koreans in Mexico.
	Koreans establish the Korean Methodist Church in Los Angeles.
	Koreans in San Francisco form the Mutual Assistance Society.
	The Asiatic Exclusion League, a group aimed at keeping Asians out of the United States, is formed in San Francisco.
	Section 60 of California's Civil Code is amended to forbid marriage between Caucasians and "Mongolians."
1906	San Francisco School Board orders Japanese and Korean students to attend a segregated public school.
1907	Under the Gentlemen's Agreement, Japan agrees to stop issuing passports to laborers who want to emigrate to the United States.
	Koreans form the United Korean Society in Hawaii.
1908	Japanese form the Japanese Association of America (JAA).
1909	Koreans form the Korean Nationalist Association (KNA) in San Francisco.
	About 7,000 Japanese sugar plantation workers strike major plantations on Oahu, Hawaii, for four months.
1910	Japan's colonization of Korea begins.
	An immigration station is established on Angel Island in San Francisco Bay.
1913	California enacts the Alien Land Law prohibiting "aliens ineligible to citizenship" from buying land or leasing it for longer than three years.
	Korean farmworkers are driven out of Hemet, California.
1915	The Japanese Chamber of Commerce is founded.
1917	Arizona passes an alien land act.

1917
(cont.)
The U.S. Congress passes the Immigration Act of 1917 to create an Asiatic barred zone, covering South Asia from Arabia to Indochina, from which immigrants are barred.

1918
Servicemen of Asian ancestry who had served in World War I receive the right of naturalization.

1919
William Heen, a Chinese, is elected the city and county attorney of Honolulu, Hawaii.

1920
About 10,000 Japanese and Filipino plantation workers organize the first major inter-Asian strike in Oahu, Hawaii (the 1920 Sugar Strike).

Japan stops issuing passports to picture brides due to anti-Japanese sentiment in the United States.

1921
Japanese farmworkers are driven out of Turlock, California.

Washington and Louisiana pass alien land laws.

1922
The U.S. Supreme Court in *Takao Ozawa v. United States* declares Japanese ineligible for naturalized citizenship.

New Mexico passes an alien land law.

The Cable Act stipulates that any American female citizen who marries an alien ineligible to citizenship loses her citizenship.

1923
Idaho, Montana, and Oregon pass alien land laws.

The ruling in the U.S. Supreme Court case of *Frick v. Webb* forbids aliens "ineligible to citizenship" from owning stock in corporations formed for farming.

1924
The Immigration Act of 1924 is passed to deny entry to virtually all Asians, including previously privileged merchants, teachers, and students.

1925
Kansas passes an alien land act.

1930
The Japanese American Citizens League (JACL) is formed.

Noboru Miyake, a Japanese, is elected a county supervisor in Hawaii.

1931
Japan's invasion of China begins.

The Cable Act is amended to allow women to retain citizenship even though they are married to aliens ineligible for U.S. citizenship.

1933
Mexican berry workers strike their Japanese owners in El Monte, California.

1935   The CACA publishes the *Chinese Digest,* the first English-language Chinese American newspaper in the United States.

1936   The Cable Act of 1922 is repealed.

A group of Chinese sailors joins the National Maritime Union, becoming part of the mainstream labor movement for the first time.

About 3,000 Chinese sailors participate in a strike organized by the National Maritime Union.

About 200 Japanese celery pickers, together with Mexicans and Filipinos, strike their Japanese growers in Venice, California.

1938   About 150 Chinese women garment workers strike for three months against Chinese-owned National Dollar Stores.

1940   The immigration station on Angel Island closes.

1941   The United States declares war on Japan following the attack on Pearl Harbor, and about 2,000 Japanese community leaders in Pacific Coast states and Hawaii are rounded up and interned in Department of Justice camps.

1942   President Franklin D. Roosevelt signs Executive Order 9066 authorizing the secretary of war to delegate a military commander to designate military areas "from which any or all persons may be excluded."

Public Law 503 imposes penal sanctions on anyone refusing to carry out Executive Order 9066.

Internment of 110,000 West Coast Japanese begins.

1943   Congress repeals all Chinese exclusion laws, granting the right of naturalization and an immigration quota of 105 per year to the Chinese.

Hawaiian *Nisei* in the 100th Battalion are sent to Africa.

1944   The draft is reinstated for *Nisei.*

The 442nd Regimental Combat Team gains fame in Europe.

The War Department revokes the mass exclusion orders (effective January 2, 1945).

1945   World War II ends.

The War Brides Act allows American servicemen to bring their brides back to the United States, but excludes those veterans of Asian ancestry.

1946   Wing F. Ong becomes the first Asian American elected to state office in the Arizona House of Representatives.

1947   The War Brides Act is amended to allow Chinese American veterans to bring brides to the United States.

1948   The Displaced Persons Act grants permanent resident status to 3,500 Chinese caught in the United States because of the Chinese civil war.

The Evacuation Claims Act is passed to provide minimal compensation to the Japanese victims of the World War II internment.

1949   About 5,000 highly educated Chinese in the United States are granted refugee status after the communist revolution in China.

Hiram Fong, a Hawaii-born Chinese, becomes the Speaker of Hawaii's territorial House of Representatives.

1950   The Korean War breaks out.

1952   The McCarran-Walter Act removes the prohibition on Asian naturalization. It abolishes the Asiatic barred zone, but creates a new restrictive zone, the Asia-Pacific triangle, covering 19 countries from India to Japan for which a total immigration quota of 2,990 is set. Under the act, Japan has a quota of 185 persons a year, while Korea has 100.

Members of the CACA appear before the Commission on Immigration and Naturalization to protest against the unfairness of the McCarran-Walter Act.

1953   The Refugee Relief Act allows Chinese political refugees and a small number of Koreans to come to the United States.

An armistice ending the Korean War is signed.

1954   The "Democratic Revolution" takes place in Hawaii when a number of Japanese World War II veterans constitute a significant part of the "New Democrats" who manage to dominate Hawaii politics.

1956   California's alien land laws are repealed after the passage of a proposition sponsored by the JACL.

Dalip Singh Saund, an Asian Indian American from Imperial Valley, California, becomes the first Asian American elected to the U.S. House of Representatives.

1959   Hawaii becomes the fiftieth state.

Representing the new state of Hawaii, Hiram Fong becomes the first Asian American elected to the U.S. Senate, and Daniel K. Inouye, a Japanese American, becomes a U.S. congressman.

1962   Daniel K. Inouye becomes a U.S. senator, and Spark Matsunaga, also a Japanese American from Hawaii, is elected to the U.S. House of Representatives.

1964   Patsy T. Mink, a Japanese American from Hawaii, becomes the first Asian American woman elected to the U.S. House of Representatives.

1965   The Immigration and Nationality Act abolishes the Asia-Pacific triangle. Under the new act, the "national origins" quota system is replaced by a preference system with a quota of 20,000 per country per year.

1968   The Asian American Political Alliance (AAPA) is first formed at the University of California, Berkeley. The AAPA is also established at San Francisco State College (now University) as the lead Asian American student organization of the San Francisco State College strike that calls for establishing ethnic studies programs.

1969   Students go on strike at the University of California, Berkeley, for the establishment of ethnic studies programs.

The International Hotel anti-eviction campaign begins in San Francisco. It is the first struggle to bring a large number of Asian American students into the Asian American community.

1970   Asian American students participate in nationwide antiwar protests.

The Japanese American Citizens League discusses a resolution on redress at its national convention in Chicago.

1971   Herbert Young Cho Choy, a Korean American, becomes the first Asian American to serve on the federal bench.

1973	The Organization of Chinese Americans (OCA) is established.
1974	The Supreme Court in *Lau v. Nichols* rules that school districts with children who speak little English must provide them bilingual education.
	March Fong Eu, a Chinese American, is elected California's secretary of state.
	Norman Mineta, a Japanese American from California, is elected to the U.S. House of Representatives.
	George Ariyoshi, a Japanese American, becomes governor of Hawaii.
1976	President Gerald Ford rescinds Executive Order 9066 and apologizes to all Japanese American internees from World War II.
	Spark Matsunaga becomes a U.S. senator, and Daniel Akaka, a Hawaiian Chinese American also from Hawaii, is elected to the U.S. House of Representatives.
	S. I. Hayakawa, a Japanese American from California, is elected to the U.S. Senate.
	The Asian/Pacific American Unit (A/PA Unit) is established within the Democratic Party.
1977	The International Hotel campaign ends with the eviction of residents from the hotel.
1978	A national convention of the Japanese American Citizens League adopts a resolution calling for redress and reparations for the internment of Japanese during World War II.
	The first "Day of Remembrance" is held in the state of Washington, commemorating the internment experience.
	Robert Matsui, a Japanese American from California, is elected to the U.S. House of Representatives.
1980	President Jimmy Carter signs Public Law 96–317 to form the Commission on Wartime Relocation and Internment of Civilians.
1981	The Commission on Wartime Relocation and Internment of Civilians holds hearings across the country.
1982	Vincent Chin, a Chinese American, is beaten to death by two Caucasian American males in Detroit, Michigan.

1982 (cont.)	The Formosan Association for Public Affairs (FAPA) is formed.
	About 20,000 Asian American garment workers march through the streets of New York's Chinatown in support of unionization.
1983	The Commission on Wartime Relocation and Internment of Civilians issues its report, *Personal Justice Denied,* to the U.S. government. The Commission concludes that the internment was a "grave injustice" and that Executive Order 9066 resulted from "race prejudice, war hysteria and a failure of political leadership."
	The Korean American Coalition (KAC) is formed.
	The American Citizens for Justice (ACJ) organizes a mass rally in downtown Detroit, Michigan, to protest the lenient sentences given to the killers of Vincent Chin.
	The Asian Pacific Caucus (APC) is founded within the Democratic Party.
1985	The Taiwanese American Citizens League (TACL) is formed.
1986	The Asian American Voters Coalition, the first major pan-Asian American political organization, is founded.
	Patricia F. Saiki, a Japanese American from Hawaii, is elected to the U.S. House of Representatives.
1987	The U.S. House of Representatives votes 243 to 141 in favor of a bill to make an official apology to Japanese Americans for the World War II internment and to pay each surviving internee $20,000 in reparations.
	The National Democratic Council of Asian and Pacific Americans (NDCAPA), the first independent national organization for Asian American Democrats, is founded.
1988	The U.S. Senate votes sixty-nine to twenty-seven to support the redress bill for Japanese Americans, and President Ronald Reagan signs it into the Civil Liberties Act.
1989	Elaine Chao, a Chinese American, is appointed deputy secretary of the Department of Transportation.
	The Tiananmen Square massacre occurs in China, resulting in President George H. W. Bush's decision to grant permanent resident status to about 30,000 Chinese students in the United States.

1989 *(cont.)*	President Bush signs into law an entitlement program to pay each surviving Japanese American internee $20,000.
	Jim Loo, a Chinese American, is killed by two Caucasian males in North Carolina.
	The Asian American Affairs Office is set up in the Republican National Committee.
1990	President George H. W. Bush proclaims the month of May Asian/Pacific American Heritage Month.
	The Committee of 100 is formed.
	Daniel Akaka becomes a U.S. senator, and Patsy Mink comes back to the U.S. House of Representatives.
1992	Riots occur in Los Angeles, causing the losses of more than 3,000 Korean American businesses.
	About 30,000 Korean Americans attend a peace rally in Los Angeles, the largest gathering of Korean Americans ever in the United States, in protest of the inability of the police to protect them during the riots.
	Jay Kim, a Korean American from California, is elected to the U.S. House of Representatives.
1993	The Chinese Americans United for Self Empowerment (CAUSE; renamed as Center for Asian Americans United for Self Empowerment in 2003) is founded in Southern California.
1994	The National Association of Korean Americans (NAKA) is formed.
1996	Gary Locke, a Chinese American, is elected governor of Washington.
	The first National Asian Pacific American Voter Registration Campaign is launched.
1996– 1997	Campaign finance controversies emerge.
1997	The National Council of Asian Pacific Americans (NCAPA), a broad coalition of twenty-one nationwide Asian Pacific American organizations, is established.
1998	The 80–20 Political Action Committee (80–20 PAC), the first national nonpartisan Asian American political action committee, is formed.

1999   The 80–20 PAC urges all presidential candidates to pledge their support for its *Declaration Concerning the 2000 Presidential Election.*

Wen Ho Lee, a Taiwanese American nuclear scientist, is accused of being a Chinese spy.

David Wu, a Chinese/Taiwanese American from Oregon, is elected to the U.S. House of Representatives.

2000   Norman Mineta is appointed secretary of commerce, becoming the first Asian American ever appointed to a cabinet level office.

Bill Lann Lee is appointed assistant attorney general in charge of civil rights at the Department of Justice.

Youth Vote 2000, a nonpartisan national coalition to promote political participation by young Asian American voters, is formed.

The Asian and Pacific Islander American Vote campaign (APIAVote 2000) for the 2000 presidential election is launched.

The 80–20 PAC endorses Democratic presidential candidate Al Gore.

Wen Ho Lee is freed after nine months in jail.

2001   Elaine Chao is appointed secretary of labor, and Norman Mineta is appointed secretary of transportation by President George W. Bush.

Mike Honda, a Japanese American from California, is elected to the U.S. House of Representatives.

2003   The 80–20 PAC sends a questionnaire to presidential candidates of major political parties to know their willingness to enforce Executive Order 11246, which prohibits granting federal money to any organizations that practice discrimination, if elected.

2004   The NCAPA releases its presidential election-year project, *Call to Action: Platform for Asian Pacific Americans National Policy Priorities 2004,* in Washington, D.C.

The Asian and Pacific Islander American vote campaign (APIAVote 2004) for the 2004 presidential election is launched.

The 80–20 PAC endorses Democratic presidential candidate John Kerry with reservation.

2005   Both Elaine Chao and Norman Mineta continue to serve in their cabinet posts under President George W. Bush's second term.

References

Chan, Sucheng. 1991. *Asian Americans: An Interpretive History.* New York: Twayne.

Ong Hing, Bill. 1993. *Making and Remaking Asian America through Immigration Policy, 1850–1990.* Stanford, CA: Stanford University.

Schultz, Jeffrey D., Kerry L. Haynie, Anne M. McCulloch, and Andrew L. Aoki, eds. 2000. *Encyclopedia of Minorities in American Politics. Volume 1: African Americans and Asian Americans.* Phoenix, AZ: Oryx.

Annotated Bibliography

Abelmann, Nancy, and John Lie. 1997. *Blue Dreams: Korean Americans and the Los Angeles Riots*. Cambridge, MA: Harvard University.

Story of Korean Americans dealing with issues of ethnic conflict, urban poverty, immigration, multiculturalism, and ideological differences after the 1992 Los Angeles riots.

Aguilar-San Juan, Karin, ed. 1994. *The State of Asian America: Activism and Resistance in the 1990s*. Boston: South End.

Collection of essays that focus on Asian American activism by analyzing issues of racism, racial identity, and empowerment.

Baron, Deborah G., and Susan B. Gall, eds. 1996. *Asian American Chronology*. New York: UXL.

Chronological compilation of significant social, political, economic, and professional milestones in Asian American history, spanning from prehistory to modern times.

Chan, Sucheng. 1991. *Asian American: An Interpretive History*. New York: Twayne.

Historical overview of Chinese, Japanese, Korean, Filipino, and Asian Indian Americans from the mid-nineteenth century to the modern time as well as an account of refugees and immigrants from Vietnam, Cambodia, and Laos since 1975. This book includes a list of films about the Asian American experience, a detailed chronology, and a bibliographic essay.

Chang, Gordon H., ed. 2001. *Asian Americans and Politics: Perspectives, Experiences, Prospects.* Washington, DC: Woodrow Wilson and Stanford, CA: Stanford University.

Anthology of articles that examine numerous aspects of Asian American politics, representing a rare example of scholarly work on the political engagement of Asian Americans in American society.

Daniels, Roger. 1993. *Prisoners without Trials: Japanese Americans in World War II.* New York: Hill and Wang.

Historical examination of Japanese American experiences from 1850 to the present. Although concentrating on the situation in the 1940s, the book also has chapters on the prewar and redress periods.

Daniels, Roger, Sandra C. Taylor, and Harry H. L. Kitano, eds. 1991. *Japanese Americans: From Relocation to Redress.* Rev. ed. Seattle: University of Washington.

Set of essays on Japanese American experiences from the internment during World War II to the Redress movement in the late 1970s and 1980s.

Edwards, George C., III, Martin P. Wattenberg, and Robert L. Lineberry. 1999. *Government in America: People, Politics, and Policy.* 8th ed. New York: Longman.

Standard text on American politics that offers the fundamentals of the American political system.

Espiritu, Yen Le. 1992. *Asian American Panethnicity: Bridging Institutions and Identities.* Philadelphia, PA: Temple University.

Pioneer study of the formation of Asian American panethnicity and how this newly formed collective identity advances the rights and interests of Asian Americans as a whole.

Fong, Timothy P. 2002. *The Contemporary Asian American Experience: Beyond the Model Minority.* 2d ed. Upper Saddle River, NJ: Prentice Hall.

Analysis of contemporary issues facing Asian Americans, including educational opportunity, the glass ceiling, anti-Asian violence, media images, family and identity, and political empowerment.

Fong, Timothy P., and Larry H. Shinagawa, eds. 2000. *Asian Americans: Experiences and Perspectives.* Upper Saddle River, NJ: Prentice Hall.

Anthology of articles that focus on a variety of Asian American issues, including race, ethnic enclaves, education, employment and occupations, popular culture and stereotypes, families, ethnic identities and culture, political empowerment, and Asian American studies.

Fugita, Stephen S., and David J. O'Brien. 1991. *Japanese American Ethnicity: The Persistence of Community.* Seattle: University of Washington.

Study of Japanese American experiences, including their social, economic, and political activities.

Gall, Susan B., and Timothy L. Gall, eds. 1993. *Statistical Record of Asian Americans.* Detroit: Gale Research.

Comprehensive statistical record of Asian Americans in a single compilation of a variety of government as well as nongovernment sources.

Hing, Bill Ong. 1993. *Making and Remaking Asian America through Immigration Policy, 1850–1990.* Stanford, CA: Stanford University.

Historical study of Asian American life through the lens of the immigration issue, including a chronology, an introduction to the post-1965 immigration system, and excerpts from selected laws and cases.

Ho, Fred, ed. 2000. *Legacy to Liberation: Politics and Culture of Revolutionary Asian Pacific America.* Brooklyn, NY: Big Red Media and San Francisco: AK Press.

Set of essays on the radical and revolutionary legacy of the Asian American movement in the United States.

Hu-DeHart, Evelyn, ed. 1999. *Across the Pacific: Asian Americans and Globalization.* Philadelphia, PA: Temple University.

Collection of essays that discuss the transnational interactions of Asian American communities in the age of globalization.

Kitano, Harry H. L., and Roger Daniels. 1988. *Asian Americans: Emerging Minorities.* Englewood Cliffs, NJ: Prentice Hall.

Detailed introduction to major Asian American groups, including Chinese, Japanese, Filipinos, Asian Indians, Koreans, Pacific Islanders, and Southeast Asians, from sociological and historical perspectives.

Koehn, Peter H., and Xiao-huang Yin, eds. 2002. *The Expanding Roles of Chinese Americans in U.S.-China Relations: Transnational Networks and Trans-Pacific Interactions.* Armonk, NY: M. E. Sharpe.

Collection of essays on the roles of Chinese Americans in shaping U.S. policy toward China and expanding networks for transnational cooperation.

Lee, John W., ed. 2002. *Asian-American Electoral Politics.* New York: Novinka.

Study of electoral politics of Asian Americans as well as an introduction to the Asian American population.

Lien, Pei-te. 2001a. *A Pilot Study of the National Asian American Political Survey (PNAAPS): Summary Statistical Report for the Entire Sample and by Ethnic Groups.* Unpublished report.

Useful statistical data on the social and political attitudes and actions of Chinese, Filipino, Japanese, Korean, South Asian, and Vietnamese Americans from Chicago, Honolulu, Los Angeles, New York, and San Francisco. It is the first survey of its kind.

———. 2001b. *The Making of Asian America through Political Participation.* Philadelphia, PA: Temple University.

One of the pioneer works on Asian American politics. It maps the political actions and strategies of Asian Americans from the early years to the present.

Lien, Pei-te, M. Margaret Conway, and Janelle Wong. 2004. *The Politics of Asian Americans: Diversity and Community.* New York: Routledge.

Presentation and analysis of the results of a large-scale political survey of Asian Americans, which is the first of its kind.

Lin, Jan. 1998. *Reconstructing Chinatown: Ethnic Enclave, Global Change.* Minneapolis: University of Minnesota.

Examination of the social, economic, and political life of New York's Chinatown in a global context.

Louie, Steve, and Glenn K. Omatsu, eds. 2001. *Asian Americans: The Movement and the Moment.* Los Angeles: UCLA Asian American Studies Center.

Collection of essays to document the Asian American movement from the perspectives of history, culture, politics, community, race/ethnicity, generation, and gender.

Min, Pyong Gap, ed. 1995. *Asian Americans: Contemporary Trends and Issues.* Thousand Oaks, CA: Sage.

Collection of essays examining the Asian American community in general, as well as issues and obstacles for Chinese, Japanese, Filipino, Asian Indian, Korean, Vietnamese, Laotian, and Cambodian Americans in particular.

Nakanishi, Don T., and James S. Lai, eds. 2001. *National Asian Pacific American Political Almanac.* 10th ed. Los Angeles: UCLA Asian American Studies Center.

Useful resource guide on Asian Pacific American politics, including a political directory of Asian Pacific American officials at the federal, state, and municipal levels.

————. 2003. *Asian American Politics: Law, Participation, and Policy.* Lanham, MD: Rowman and Littlefield.

Collection of historical documents and essays about the rights and political participation of Asian Americans.

Ng, Franklin. 1998. *The Taiwanese Americans.* Westport, CT: Greenwood.

Pioneer work on Taiwanese Americans, focusing first on the definitions of Taiwanese Americans, and then on their immigration history, social structure, culture, and identity.

O'Brien, David J., and Stephen S. Fugita. 1991. *The Japanese American Experience.* Bloomington: Indiana University.

Historical overview of Japanese Americans from the early years in the late nineteenth century to the present, mainly focusing on the discrimination facing Japanese Americans and how they organized to deal with it.

Odo, Franklin, ed. 2002. *The Columbia Documentary History of the Asian American Experience.* New York: Columbia University.

Very comprehensive collection of 155 documents from 1790 to the present, including acts, treaties, Supreme Court cases, executive orders, and many others.

Okihiro, Gary Y. 1994. *Margins and Mainstreams: Asians in American History and Culture.* Seattle: University of Washington.

Examination of Asian American experiences in mainstream American society from the perspectives of history, race, gender, class, and culture.

Ong, Paul M., ed. 2000. *The State of Asian Pacific America: Transforming Race Relations, A Public Policy Report, Volume IV.* Los Angeles: LEAP Asian Pacific American Public Policy Institute and UCLA Asian American Studies Center.

An edited volume that examines the impacts of Asian Americans on American racial identities, interactions, and policies.

Schultz, Jeffrey D., Kerry L. Haynie, Anne M. McCulloch, and Andrew L. Aoki, eds. 2000. *Encyclopedia of Minorities in American Politics. Volume 1: African Americans and Asian Americans.* Phoenix, AZ: Oryx.

Resource guide to Asian American politics, including brief introductions to notable Asian Americans, documents, organizations, Asian American members of Congress, and a timeline of Asian American history.

Takahashi, Jere. 1997. *Nisei/Sansei: Shifting Japanese American Identities and Politics.* Philadelphia, PA: Temple University.

Analysis of changing social positions and identities of Japanese Americans from the 1920s to the 1970s.

Takaki, Ronald. 1998. *Strangers from a Different Shore: A History of Asian Americans*. Updated and rev. ed. Boston: Back Bay.

Comprehensive history of Chinese, Japanese, Korean, Filipino, Asian Indian, Vietnamese, Cambodian, and Laotian Americans in forms of narrative history, personal recollection, and oral testimony.

Totten, George O., III, and H. Eric Schockman, eds. 1994. *Community in Crisis: The Korean American Community after the Los Angeles Civil Unrest of April 1992*. Los Angeles: University of Southern California, Center for Multiethnic and Transnational Studies.

Collection of papers presented at a conference held about one year after the Los Angeles riots, focusing on the state of the Korean American community before the riots and how the riots changed many aspects of the community.

Wei, William. 1993. *The Asian American Movement*. Philadelphia, PA: Temple University.

The first study of the Asian American movement, analyzing the movement's origins as well as Asian American identity, culture, portrayal in the press, organizations, and politics.

Wu, Frank H. 2002. *Yellow: Race in America beyond Black and White*. New York: Basic.

A look into Asian Americans' racial identity, social conditions, and civil rights. It also uses the case of Asian Americans to address race relations in the United States.

Zhou, Min, and James V. Gatewood, eds. 2000. *Contemporary Asian America: American Multidisciplinary Reader*. New York: New York University.

Collection of readings that address, theoretically as well as historically, a wide range of Asian American issues.

Zia, Helen. 2000. *Asian American Dreams: The Emergence of an American People*. New York: Farrar, Straus and Giroux.

Comprehensive account of Asian American experiences, covering issues of cultural assimilation, ethnic identity, and social conditions.

Index

repeal of exclusion laws, 3
New Democrats, 140–141
New Left movement, 36
Nisei, 73–75, 140, 221
Nitz, Michael, 49, 52
North Korea, 84
"Not a Chinaman's chance," 57,
 174, 221
Nye-Lea Bill (1935), 75

O'Brien, Leo, 149
Ogawa, Frank, 154
Oh, Angela E., 165–166
Oka, Tasaku, 140
Ong, Wing F., 142, 150, 251
Ooka, Carl, 154
Organization of Chinese
 Americans (OCA), 81–82, 110,
 133, 161–162, 253
Ozawa v. United States, 104, 249

Page Law (1875), 245
Pan-Asian ethnicity, 170–172, 221
Panethnic group identity, 25
Panethnic interest groups, 86–91
Party affiliation, 20–21, 122–124
Party participation, 122–126
Pearl Harbor, 250
Pei, I. M., 84
Pelosi, Nancy, 95
People v. Hall, 243
Personal Justice Denied, 54, 169, 254
Plantation economy. *See* Hawaii
Police tax, 244
Policy attitudes, 22–23
Policy issues, 95–96
Policy research organizations, 88
Political action committees, 87, 98,
 118–122, 164–165
Political efficacy, 221
Political ideology, 17, 45
Political interest group, 222. *See
 also* Interest-group politics
Political participation. *See*
 Appointed officials; Elected
 office; Electoral politics;
 Interest-group politics; Protest
 politics

Population statistics, 2–5, 7(table),
 105
Protest politics
 Asian American movement,
  35–45, 170
 Chinese immigrants, 30–32
 history of participation, 29–30
 International Hotel campaign,
  39–44, 170–171, 220
 Japanese immigrants, 32–34
 Korean Americans and the Los
  Angeles riots, 55–56, 220–221
 Redress Movement, 52–55
 response to Vincent Chin
  murder, 48–52
 San Francisco State College
  strike, 40–41
 Tiananmen democratic
  movement, 223
Public Law 96–317, 253

Quayle, Dan, 126
Queue ordinance, 31, 244
Quiet minority, Asian Americans
 as, 103, 122–123, 222
Quotas for immigrants, 2–3, 5–6

Railroad industry, 222, 244–245
Railroad strikes, 31–32, 222, 244
Reagan, Ronald, 55, 126, 213, 254
Realigning election, 222
Redress Movement, 52–55, 92,
 160, 171, 222, 253–254
Refugee Relief Act (1953), 3, 251
Regional ethnic interest groups,
 89–91
Religious organizations, 72, 77–79
Representation, political, 25, 171
Republican Party, 122–124, 126,
 128, 146
Riady family, 132
Riordan, Richard, 130–131
Rising Sun (movie), 47
Roh, Gene, 154
Rolling Stone magazine, 46
Roosevelt, Franklin D., 5, 52, 122,
 219
Rotating credit associations, 222

About the Author

Tsung Chi is associate professor of politics at Occidental College in Los Angeles. He received his B.A. in political science from National Chengchi University and his M.A. and Ph.D. in political science from Michigan State University.